Second Language Literacy Pedagogy

SECOND LANGUAGE ACQUISITION

Series Editors: **Professor David Singleton,** *University of Pannonia, Hungary* and Fellow Emeritus, *Trinity College, Dublin, Ireland* and **Professor Simone E. Pfenninger,** *University of Zurich, Switzerland*

This series brings together titles dealing with a variety of aspects of language acquisition and processing in situations where a language or languages other than the native language is involved. Second language is thus interpreted in its broadest possible sense. The volumes included in the series all offer in their different ways, on the one hand, exposition and discussion of empirical findings and, on the other, some degree of theoretical reflection. In this latter connection, no particular theoretical stance is privileged in the series; nor is any relevant perspective – sociolinguistic, psycholinguistic, neurolinguistic, etc. – deemed out of place. The intended readership of the series includes final-year undergraduates working on second language acquisition projects, postgraduate students involved in second language acquisition research, and researchers, teachers and policymakers in general whose interests include a second language acquisition component.

All books in this series are externally peer-reviewed.

Full details of all the books in this series and of all our other publications can be found on http://www.multilingual-matters.com, or by writing to Multilingual Matters, St Nicholas House, 31–34 High Street, Bristol, BS1 2AW, UK.

SECOND LANGUAGE ACQUISITION: 162

Second Language Literacy Pedagogy

A Sociocultural Theory Perspective

Kimberly Buescher Urbanski

MULTILINGUAL MATTERS
Bristol • Jackson

DOI https://doi.org/10.21832/URBANS7601
Library of Congress Cataloging in Publication Data
A catalog record for this book is available from the Library of Congress.
Names: Urbanski, Kimberly Buescher, author.
Title: Second Language Literacy Pedagogy: A Sociocultural Theory Perspective/
   Kimberly Buescher Urbanski.
Description: Bristol; Jackson: Multilingual Matters, [2023] | Series: Second Language
   Acquisition: 162 | Includes bibliographical references and index. | Summary: "This book
   provides a detailed design of a new second language literacy pedagogy and the results of
   implementing it in different contexts so as to address literacy development challenges.
   The author explains the theory behind Vygotskian Sociocultural Theory of Mind and
   Systemic Functional Linguistics and how they can inform literacy pedagogy"—
   Provided by publisher.
Identifiers: LCCN 2023002849 (print) | LCCN 2023002850 (ebook) |
   ISBN 9781800417601 (hardback) | ISBN 9781800417632 (paperback) |
   ISBN 9781800417625 (epub) | ISBN 9781800417618 (pdf)
Subjects: LCSH: Language and languages—Study and teaching. | Literacy—Study and
   teaching. | Second language acquisition.
Classification: LCC P53.475 .U73 2023 (print) | LCC P53.475 (ebook) |
   DDC 407.1—dc23/eng/20230314 LC record available at https://lccn.loc.gov/2023002849
LC ebook record available at https://lccn.loc.gov/2023002850

British Library Cataloguing in Publication Data
A catalogue entry for this book is available from the British Library.

ISBN-13: 978-1-80041-760-1 (hbk)
ISBN-13: 978-1-80041-763-2 (pbk)

Multilingual Matters
UK: St Nicholas House, 31–34 High Street, Bristol, BS1 2AW, UK.
USA: Ingram, Jackson, TN, USA.

Website: www.multilingual-matters.com
Twitter: Multi_Ling_Mat
Facebook: https://www.facebook.com/multilingualmatters
Blog: www.channelviewpublications.wordpress.com

Copyright © 2023 Kimberly Buescher Urbanski.

All rights reserved. No part of this work may be reproduced in any form or by any means without permission in writing from the publisher.

The policy of Multilingual Matters/Channel View Publications is to use papers that are natural, renewable and recyclable products, made from wood grown in sustainable forests. In the manufacturing process of our books, and to further support our policy, preference is given to printers that have FSC and PEFC Chain of Custody certification. The FSC and/or PEFC logos will appear on those books where full certification has been granted to the printer concerned.

Typeset by Nova Techset Private Limited, Bengaluru and Chennai, India.

This book is dedicated to Jeff, Maya, Jack, Pat, and Kathy. Thank you for all of your support and love.

Contents

Figures		ix
Tables		xi
Acknowledgements		xiii
1	Introduction – Current State of Second Language Reading Pedagogy and Pedagogical Concerns	1
	Purpose, Aim and Scope of the Book	1
	Current Pedagogical Practices	2
2	Second Language Reading/Literacy and Pedagogy	7
	Introduction	7
	Reading – Ontology and Epistemology	8
	Literacy – Ontology and Epistemology	12
	Specific Reading and Literacy Components	19
	Common Tools and Strategies	25
	Use of the L1 in Pedagogy	27
	Conclusion	28
3	Vygotskian Second Language Literacy Pedagogy	29
	Introduction	29
	Concept-Based Language Instruction	29
	Division-of-Labor Pedagogy	34
	Details from the Research-Teaching Studies	36
	Research Design	53
	Conclusion	58
4	Developing Second Language Narrative Literacy	59
	Introduction	59
	Survey Data	59
	Scores on Pre- and Post-Test Summaries for both Mid- and High-Level Texts	62
	Change in Mid-Level Text Summary Scores from Pre- to Post-test	65
	Change in High-Level Text Summary Scores from Pre- to Post-Test	69
	Learners' Overall Change in Score and Percent Change from Pre- to Post-Test	71

	Learning Potential Scores	73
	Scores on Pre- and Post-Test Summaries for both Mid- and High-Level Texts by Summary Category	75
	Overall Results RS1 and RS2	84
	Conclusion	86
5	Developing Awareness in Literacy Concepts	88
	Introduction	88
	Verbalizations	88
	Conclusion	106
6	Tracing Literacy Development	108
	Introduction	108
	Claire's Perspective on the C-BLI/DOLP Process	110
	Claire's Understanding of the Concepts and Roles	117
	Change in Mediation	141
	Conclusion	146
7	Future Developments in Vygotskian Second Language Literacy Pedagogy	147
	Introduction	147
	Discussion	148
	Implications	151
	Limitations	153
	Future Directions	155
	Conclusion	156
	Appendix	158
	References	159
	Index	168

Figures

Figure 2.1	Indirect mediated activity (adapted from Cole, 1996, adapted from Vygotsky, 1978)	15
Figure 3.1	Materialization of the L2 Narrative Literacy concept	36
Figure 3.2	Materialization of the Foundation Concept	39
Figure 3.3	Materialization of the new Foundation concept (base of image from: https://clipartstation.com/wp-content/uploads/2017/11/building-foundation-clipart-9-300x200.jpg)	40
Figure 3.4	Materialization 1 of the Organization concept (adapted from Hudson, 2007: 180 as adapted from Mandler, 1987; Graesser et al., 1996)	42
Figure 3.5	Materialized representation of the Organization concept	43
Figure 3.6	Materialization of the Genre concept (created from Byrnes et al., 2010; Halliday & Hasan, 1989)	46
Figure 4.1	Graph of mid-level pre- and post-test text summary scores for RS1 and RS2	67
Figure 4.2	Graph of mid-level pre- and post-test text summary scores for RS3	69
Figure 4.3	Graph of high-level pre- and post-test text summary scores for RS1 and RS2	70
Figure 4.4	Graph of high-level pre- and post-test text summary scores for RS3	71
Figure 4.5	Graph of mid-level pre- and post-test summary scores for the main idea category for RS1 and RS2	77
Figure 4.6	Graph of high-level pre- and post-test summary scores for the main idea category for RS1 and RS2	78
Figure 4.7	Graph of mid-level pre- and post-test summary scores for the supporting details category for RS1 and RS2	79
Figure 4.8	Graph of high-level pre- and post-test summary scores for the supporting details category for RS1 and RS2	80
Figure 4.9	Graph of mid-level pre- and post-test summary scores for the synthesis category for RS1 and RS2	80
Figure 4.10	Graph of high-level pre- and post-test summary scores for the synthesis category for RS1 and RS2	81

Figure 4.11	Graph of mid-level pre- and post-test summary scores for the generalizations category for RS1 and RS2	82
Figure 4.12	Graph of high-level pre- and post-test summary scores for the generalizations category for RS1 and RS2	82
Figure 4.13	Graph of mid-level pre- and post-test summary scores for the accuracy category for RS1 and RS2	83
Figure 4.14	Graph of high-level pre- and post-test summary scores for the accuracy category for RS1 and RS2	84
Figure 4.15	Graph of all summary scores including instructional texts for RS1 and RS2	85
Figure 4.16	Graph of mid-level text summary scores including instruction for RS1 and RS2	86
Figure 4.17	Graph of instructional text summary scores for RS1 and RS2	86

Tables

Table 3.1	Materialization 2 of the Organization concept	42
Table 3.2	First distribution of roles in the Division-of-Labor Pedagogy	49
Table 3.3	Second distribution of roles in the Division-of-Labor Pedagogy	50
Table 3.4	Third distribution of roles in the Division-of-Labor Pedagogy	50
Table 3.5	Fourth distribution of roles in the Division-of-Labor Pedagogy	50
Table 3.6	Goal of the Division-of-Labor Pedagogy	51
Table 3.7	Level of difficulty rank ordering and word count totals for French texts	55
Table 4.1	Pre-test summary scores for mid- and high-level texts for RS1 and RS2	62
Table 4.2	Pre-test summary scores for mid- and high-level texts for RS3	64
Table 4.3	Post-test summary scores on mid- and high-level text for RS1 and RS2	65
Table 4.4	Post-test summary scores on mid- and high-level text for RS3	66
Table 4.5	Mid-level text summary scores for pre- and post-test for RS1 and RS2	67
Table 4.6	Mid-level text summary scores for pre- and post-test for RS3	68
Table 4.7	High-level text summary scores for pre- and post-test for RS1 and RS2	70
Table 4.8	High-level text summary scores for pre- and post-test for RS3	72
Table 4.9	Rank order of overall gain score and percentage of change for learners from RS1 and RS2	72
Table 4.10	Rank order of overall gain score and percentage of change for learners from RS3	73
Table 4.11	Learning Potential Score for mid- and high-level text summaries for RS1 and RS2	74

Table 4.12	Learning Potential Score for mid- and high-level text summaries for RS3	76
Table 4.13	Mid- and high-level text summary scores for pre- and post-test by summary category for RS1 and RS2	77
Table 6.1	Transcription conventions	110

Acknowledgements

I would like to express my gratitude to the French students who agreed to participate in my research. I am grateful to the members of the dissertation and Sociocultural Theory reading groups as well as attendees of the Sociocultural Theory and Second Language Learning Working Group meetings over the years for the thought-provoking discussions and for pushing my development forward. I am thankful for Eduardo Negueruela-Azarola, Celeste Kinginger, Matt Poehner, Karen Johnson, Merrill Swain, Adam van Compernolle and especially Jim Lantolf who have mediated my thinking on this research. Their *obuchenie* prolepted me into my current research-teaching abilities. I am grateful to Heather McCoy and to my independent raters for all of their help with my research. Thanks are also due to Jeremy Gevara and Xian Zhang for their guidance on the statistics. I am also thankful for the research funding that I received as a Gil Watz Dissertation Fellow granted by the Center for Language Acquisition and the College of the Liberal Arts and through the RGSO Dissertation Support Competition granted by the College of the Liberal Arts at Penn State University. I would also like to thank Mariana Lima Becker, Marina Lepekhova, Juan David Gutierrez Hincapie, Vannessa Quintana Sarria, Tianxuan (Rachel) Wang, Meizi Piao, Aram Ahmed, Yuge Duan and especially Minh Nghia-Nguyen. A thank you is also due to my editor, Laura Jordan, and to an anonymous reviewer whose comments, questions and recommendations have helped to strengthen this book.

I am especially grateful for the support of my family and in particular my husband, Jeff, and my parents, Pat and Kathy. I am also appreciative of the support of my friends and colleagues around the world. Finally, special thanks are due to Joan Linneman, Eduardo Negueruela-Azarola and Julius Lester for their crucial support at critical junctures in my life.

1 Introduction – Current State of Second Language Reading Pedagogy and Pedagogical Concerns

Purpose, Aim and Scope of the Book

The purpose of this book is to present a comprehensive design of a new second language literacy pedagogy and the results of implementing this pedagogy in different contexts in order to demonstrate that it is possible to address some long-standing second language (L2) curriculum and literacy development challenges. To be clear, the use of 'L2' in this context refers to any language beyond a person's first language. To develop L2 literacy, learners must come to understand basic and advanced literacy concepts and develop control over their application during literacy activities. Because the use of these concepts while reading texts involves a complex interplay of processes, it often leads teachers to believe that learners are not able to read authentic texts until they have acquired or developed 'enough' of the L2. Once this is achieved, it is believed that learners can combine their L2 language knowledge with their first language (L1) reading knowledge to successfully read L2 texts. Current L2 reading pedagogy and practices (described in more detail below) therefore result in learners with minimal experience reading authentic texts in their early coursework. An oft-cited curricular gap has resulted, making it difficult for students to traverse between introductory (language-focused) and advanced (literary or content-focused) L2 courses (e.g. Bourns *et al.*, 2020; Byrnes *et al.*, 2010; MLA, 2007; Paesani, 2016; Paesani *et al.*, 2016; Swaffar & Arens, 2005). As this stubborn gap persisted, bridge courses were designed to address it; however, many of these courses are lacking a pedagogy designed for literacy development. The Georgetown University German Department (GUGD), a notable exception, revamped its entire curriculum to create a coherent, holistic and integrated program from the introductory through the advanced classes (Byrnes *et al.*, 2010).

The pedagogy offered in this book was designed to help learners understand and develop control over the concepts and processes involved in reading, comprehending, interpreting and analyzing texts and therefore render the current bifurcated system in many L2 classrooms unnecessary. A pedagogy informed by a theory of mind – Sociocultural Theory of Mind – and a meaning-based theory of language – Systemic Functional Linguistics – allows learners to develop L2 literacy as intermediate-level learners. This book aims to explain the theory behind Vygotskian Sociocultural Theory of Mind (V-SCT) (see Lantolf & Poehner, 2014; Lantolf & Thorne, 2006) and Systemic Functional Linguistics (SFL) (see Halliday & Hasan, 1989) and how they can inform literacy pedagogy in the form of Concept-Based Language Instruction (C-BLI) and a Division-of-Labor Pedagogy (DOLP). Detailed qualitative and quantitative analyses of multiple forms of data from multiple contexts will be provided to demonstrate the effectiveness of the L2 literacy C-BLI and DOLP. First though, the current state of L2 reading pedagogy will be further explained in order to contextualize how the L2 literacy C-BLI and DOLP can better address the intricate and interdependent nature of the concepts and processes needed for L2 literacy development. The background and theory explanation will provide all of the details necessary for teachers, researchers and graduate students to appreciate both the theory and its application to practice.

The intended audience for this book is teachers, researchers and graduate students who are interested in developing their students' L2 literacy, in helping to eliminate the L2 curricular gap, in researching L2 literacy development, in understanding Vygotskian praxis, in pursuing other concepts to teach from a Vygotskian perspective, in understanding the power of highly attuned mediation for individuals, small groups and whole classes, and in seeing the power of a collective and its impact on learner development. This book also aims to help the reader appreciate the interdependent nature of the concepts in L2 literacy development and the power in the two guiding theories, Vygotskian Sociocultural Theory (V- SCT) and Systemic Functional Linguistics (SFL), to offer a comprehensive way of reconceptualizing literacy and literacy development for L2 learners. Hopefully it will become clear how necessary it is to help learners develop their understanding and control of these interdependent concepts with the use of collectives through a DOLP.

Current Pedagogical Practices

Alderson's (1984) question and subsequent research investigating the Language Threshold Hypothesis aimed to identify how much L2 learners rely on their L1 reading knowledge and how much they rely on their L2 proficiency to help them read in an L2. By investigating this question, researchers aimed to determine when learners would have a 'sufficient' amount of L2 proficiency to use in conjunction with their L1 reading knowledge to read L2 texts. In this way, L2 pedagogy could focus on teaching the language until they achieved the determined level, after which the pedagogy could shift to focus on using the language to read content (i.e. literature, history, culture). Additionally, as reading L2 texts involves many concurrent processes which may strain learners' working memory (Koda, 2005), this separation of pedagogical foci was seen as a way for learners to gain 'sufficient' L2 proficiency so that the strain on their working memory would be adequately reduced. An unintended effect, or perhaps seen as an unavoidable consequence, is the now well-documented curricular gap mentioned above that exists in L2 pedagogy between the introductory and advanced courses – between the language-focused courses and the content-focused courses. Although this curricular gap is most evident at the university level, the outcome of reading research concerning the Language Threshold Hypothesis in the 1980s and 1990s still affects the pedagogical focus of many L2 classrooms.

As a result of the dichotomous pedagogical foci in language classrooms, in beginner/early intermediate language courses, students typically have little opportunity to read L2 texts. If learners do read L2 texts, they are often short or shortened, adapted, contain simplified language or are created to introduce pertinent vocabulary or grammatical elements for a particular textbook chapter (e.g. Allen & Paesani, 2010; Bourns *et al.*, 2020; Paesani *et al.*, 2016). Therefore, these texts generally do not include authentic language or the natural redundancy that is typical of authentic texts, do not allow learners sufficient text to become familiar with a genre and its normal organization, and do not provide an opportunity to develop meaning-making resources in the activity of reading a text.

Reading is used minimally and in ways that generally support the vocabulary or grammatical focus on the textbook chapters. In some textbooks, the texts are relegated to the supplementary section at the end of the chapter and as such, they are often bypassed due to time constraints, given a cursory glance, or assigned as homework with little in-class discussion (e.g. Paesani *et al.*, 2016). In fact, reading in L2 classes, whether at the elementary, intermediate or advanced level, is rarely an in-class activity. If reading is a part of an L2 course, it is most often assigned for homework and is often accompanied with the following tasks: answering pre-reading questions, completing vocabulary or grammatical exercises pertaining to the text or answering post-reading multiple choice or short answer comprehension questions.

Texts that students have access to are generally glossed, whereby the appropriate equivalent in the learners' L1 is provided either on the side or at the bottom of the text. If the texts are not glossed, students often have access to a dictionary in the back of the book with difficult words from the text and L1 equivalents that fit the particular context of the text. Students are sometimes asked to infer an unknown word's meaning from the context, or they may use online translators to find an L1 equivalent. Less commonly, students use a bilingual dictionary (paper or online) to find the meaning of unknown words. Students' reading homework is then either collected for credit or discussed in class. Often students who have understood the reading readily volunteer their responses to the questions. In most classrooms, there is little focus on literacy development, or how learners should develop the ability to comprehend, analyze and interact with texts.

Unfortunately, as I have witnessed first-hand, there are often intermediate-level students who have not understood a reading even at the most basic level. In a class that I observed, I overheard a student whisper to a classmate, 'wait, did he die?' to which the classmate replied 'no idea' with a shrug. In the text, the untimely event had in fact happened and was a crucial element in the story; the teacher was unaware that at least some of the students who were not responding to the assigned comprehension questions had not understood one of the most basic or important elements in the text. Soon the class moved on to the next text and I can imagine that this scene may have repeated itself for much of the semester. These students had achieved 'sufficient' L2 proficiency and had L1 reading knowledge but were unable to use these to successfully read texts. For most students, waiting to achieve 'sufficient' L2 proficiency in order to read successfully in an L2 is not the only ability that they need.

In many foreign language L2 courses in the United States, learners are generally capable readers in their L1 (Byrnes *et al.*, 2010) and the ways in which they understand or make meaning from a text in their L1 have become implicit. In other words, students are generally not sure what it is that they do or had to do to make meaning from the words in a text when they read in their L1. Therefore, they struggle with applying similar techniques in their L2. Reading in their L1 has become second nature to them and because of this they are often unable to adequately draw on the range of their resources when they encounter a difficulty while reading an L2 text. As an avid reader in my L1 and a serious learner of my L2, I too found it difficult to use my first language reading knowledge and my second language proficiency to read authentic French texts.

As mentioned already, texts in introductory and intermediate classes often contain glosses or text-based dictionaries to help students quickly access an L1 equivalent for an unknown word in the particular context. In other words, these practices aim to supplement any lack of L2 proficiency or reduce any strain on working memory students may have so that they can better comprehend the text. While they do help students to understand what a particular word means in this context so that they can continue reading, one drawback is that these practices often leave students with the understanding that each word in a language contains one exact equivalent in another language. Online translators can be even more problematic as they often do not even provide a correct L1 equivalent for a particular context, instead offering the most common equivalent for the word. For example, once a student wanted to tell me that she was a 'fan' of Chinese food. When I read the sentence that she had submitted using an online translator, because of the 'fan' equivalent in French that she had used, I instead had the impression of Chinese food flying out of a device that moves air. Although glosses and text-based dictionaries provide access to texts for learners, they do not promote learners' literacy development as students are not able to learn how to go about finding out what words mean in a non-glossed text. From glosses and text-based dictionaries, students do not learn the nature of languages, that people make choices about the language that they use instead of filling in a slot with the one right answer, and that words in each language have their own particular usages, connotations and collocations.

In contrast, bilingual dictionaries provide these usages, connotations and collocations for each word which can enrich students' understanding of languages. To develop literacy, learners must learn how to use dictionaries as a meaning-making tool to support their reading. They must learn how to find the appropriate lexicogrammatical element in question, in the right form and select the appropriate usage for the context using the grammatical and collocational information included in the dictionary. This tool provides them with an understanding of unknown words, practice selecting an L1 equivalent for the context and determining if their previous understanding of the context is still appropriate, gives them insight into authors' word choices and helps them understand lexicogrammatical intricacies in context. Because authentic texts do not contain glosses or text-based dictionaries and are not accompanied by pre- and post-reading questions or lexicogrammatical exercises, we need to promote students' literacy development with meaning-making tools that they can use to read texts of their own choosing.

In introductory language courses, instructors generally expect their students to be able to decode and comprehend texts. However, in more advanced courses, especially those focused on reading literature, teachers require their students to be able to interpret and analyze texts (e.g. Paesani et al., 2016). If learners are not provided with a pedagogy aimed at literacy development or even how to use their L1 reading knowledge and L2 proficiency to read texts, it is unclear how beginner and intermediate-level students develop the ability to traverse the gap from decoding and comprehending to interpreting and analyzing. In places where intermediate-level bridge courses have been created to 'bridge the gap' between the introductory and advanced courses, learners are given more access to texts, but the pedagogy is generally not sufficient for literacy development as learners are not given the tools to be able to interpret and analyze texts and they are 'charged with the nearly impossible task of crossing this language-content divide in one semester' (Bourns *et al.*, 2020: 24).

The most common recommendations in classrooms for intermediate-level students when they are having difficulty understanding a text are to read the text again, make educated guesses about unfamiliar vocabulary and skim for the main idea. While these are not poor ideas, they are not ones that promote literacy development. As a student, I also tried similar recommendations, but progress was slow. If students are not given the tools to read, interpret and analyze L2 texts, they will not be able to understand texts, discuss their ideas or access texts of their own choosing. If learners are not able to shift from decoding and comprehending to interpreting and analyzing texts, they are less able to successfully participate in upper-level literature classes and therefore less likely to continue enrolling in L2 courses. However, if students are equipped with meaning-making tools and mediated to develop their L2 literacy abilities, they would be better able to read texts that they choose and make the choice about whether to continue with advanced L2 coursework.

The larger goal of my research is to help eliminate the gap between the introductory and advanced courses altogether, by promoting learners' L2 literacy development so they can read, interpret and analyze texts for meaning. This book presents a pedagogy designed to promote intermediate-level L2 learners' literacy development.

2 Second Language Reading/Literacy and Pedagogy

Introduction

In this chapter, I will outline a cognitivist perspective on second language reading including bottom-up, top-down and interactive approaches to reading, reading research and implications from this perspective. I will contrast a cognitivist perspective with an L2 literacy perspective and then specifically from a Vygotskian Sociocultural Theory approach. Finally, I will provide background on the research on each of the elements involved in the process of reading and literacy such as lexical and grammatical challenges, texts, textual organization, genre, working memory, learners' use of their L1 and second language (L2), and common reading tools and strategies.

In social science research, it is necessary to first determine the ontology of the object or process under investigation. Once it has been defined, researchers can make choices about how to best investigate, document and analyze the object or process. It is, therefore, the ontology that determines the epistemology. How we define reading or literacy and the process by which people acquire or develop reading or literacy will determine how we study it. Because the ontology of the process of reading acquisition and literacy development differ drastically, the epistemologies are also qualitatively different. The most prolific decades of research on all aspects of reading were the 1980s and 1990s; however, the majority of the research was from a cognitivist perspective. In order to highlight the differences in ontologies and epistemologies between cognitivist perspectives and a V-SCT perspective, I will use 'reading' to refer to the former and 'literacy' to refer to the latter as well as to social approaches in general. I will outline how 'reading' has been defined and therefore how it has been studied and will then contrast it with how 'literacy' has been defined and studied. Rounding out the chapter will be a discussion on more specific components of reading and literacy.

Reading – Ontology and Epistemology

Reading from a cognitivist perspective

The ontology of reading has generally been understood as a process of extracting meaning from a text. For Bernhardt (2010), 'the act of reading...refer[s] to how written text is processed in the brain by a reader and how that processing brings about a conceptualization of what is written' (2010: 7, 8). By considering the brain as a 'processor' (Bernhardt, 2010: 8) and written text as 'the nature of the *input* language' (2010: 8, my emphasis), it leads to understanding the activity of reading through an input processing perspective and using the commonly employed computer metaphor. From this perspective, there is a one-way relationship between the text and the reader (Bernhardt, 2010) and texts can be interpreted in only one possible way – the way intended by the author or the 'right' way.

From this way of understanding reading, L1 readers are considered to have a 'complete' version of the software needed to read or process texts in the L1, whereas L2 readers would necessarily have an 'incomplete' version, and without the possibility to ever have a complete version because their L1 differs (Bernhardt, 2010). For L2 readers, 'the input text and the software are only partially compatible' due to 'an incomplete or degraded set of second-language rules' (Bernhardt, 2010: 9). One of the pedagogical implications of this perspective is that L2 learners, until they have a sufficiently high level of language proficiency followed by extensive L2 reading experience, would be unlikely to be able to extract the correct and full meaning from a text, if they are ever able to. Of course, L1 readers may also form different interpretations of a text, even with a 'complete' version of the software, which a cognitivist or input processing perspective does acknowledge; however, L2 readers are still considered to have a 'deficiency' and studied using a deficit model. In addition, although my L1 is English, I am not sure that I will ever have a 'complete' version as I learn new words in English on a regular basis. From this perspective, L2 reading pedagogy thus requires learners to have an 'enhanced...input processor' (Bernhardt, 2010: 12–13) before they are able to read texts in the target language successfully. One way that this is achieved from this perspective is by learning a 'sufficient' amount of the L2 language before reading texts.

Bottom-up approach to L2 reading

Following from this understanding, a cognitivist perspective on reading has focused on three main approaches: bottom-up, top-down and interactive models. The bottom-up orientation generally focuses on word recognition, decoding skills and pronunciation (Paesani *et al.*, 2016). Sufficient lexical and morphosyntactic proficiency (i.e. vocabulary and grammar) are seen as essential elements for successful reading and lead to text comprehension. In early bottom-up research both miscue analysis

(Goodman, 1973) – where readers read aloud and researchers note any mistakes – and eye tracking (Cattell, 1885, as cited in Bernhardt, 2010) – where focus is on eye movements including the location of eye gaze, duration and direction of movement – were common research methods. Researchers who relied on eye tracking believed that movement would reveal the reader's comprehension needs (Carpenter & Just, 1977). In other words, the longer a reader gazed at a particular element of the text, the more difficult this element was for them to comprehend. Bernhardt (2010) noted that although eye movement showed what readers' eyes were physically doing while reading a text, it did not reveal how they were reading or comprehending the text. In bottom-up pedagogy, L2 learners tend to focus on reading word-for-word and tend to translate the text to aid their comprehension (Auerbach & Paxton, 1997).

Top-down approach to L2 reading

Researchers adopting a top-down approach to L2 reading generally focus on readers' use of background knowledge of the world, texts and domain content knowledge to comprehend the main idea of a text and to make predictions while reading (Bernhardt, 2010; Paesani *et al.*, 2016). In other words, reading is considered to be 'conceptually-driven' (Bernhardt, 2010: 36) and tends to have a comprehension focus, thus encouraging overall comprehension at the expense of a detailed, linguistic-based understanding of a text (Han & D'Angelo, 2009). Researchers investigate readers' use of schemas or scripts, which were created and shaped by the reader's knowledge and experience in the world and with texts. These schemas or scripts act as a 'frame which enables humans to interpret their experiences and one another' (Cole, 1996: 128). A script may include, for example, 'the people who appropriately participate in an event, the social roles they play, the objects they use, and the sequence of actions and causal relations that applies' (Cole, 1996: 126). For example, we may all have scripts about how going to a restaurant works.

These schemas and scripts guide both L1 and L2 reading, but given the cultural nature of schemas and scripts, L1 and L2 schemas and scripts do not share a one-to-one correspondence. According to Bernhardt (2010),

> comprehension is far more layered in a second language than in a first. And because layers are inconsistent with the expectations or the 'layers' that a first-language group possesses, the interaction between and among the layers of knowledge is not necessarily supportive and may actually impede comprehension. (2010: 14)

In other words, a reader's L1 script of going to a restaurant may be different than the going-to-a-restaurant script in their L2, which may cause readers to fill in the gaps of their understanding of an L2 text with their L1 scripts and these may not necessarily fit in the context. This is common in L2 classrooms when reading texts. Although L1 readers are considered native speakers of a language, and therefore are considered to have a 'complete' version of the software from this perspective, there are still cultural layers to reading even in one's L1. Nevertheless, access to different cultural understandings within an L1 may be more easily attainable.

Interactive approaches to L2 reading

The focus of reading research from a cognitivist perspective shifted from bottom-up and top-down approaches to interactive models. Coady (1979) argued for reading to include the interaction between background knowledge, conceptual abilities and strategies for processing and Hall (2001) later called for an expanded view of reading which included both bottom-up and top-down approaches. Bernhardt's (2010) compensatory processing model serves as a noteworthy example of how an interactive model works.

Bernhardt's (1986, 2010) compensatory processing model includes phonemic/graphemic abilities, syntactic feature recognition, word recognition, prior knowledge, metacognition and intratextual perceptions. These bottom-up and top-down components not only interact, but also can compensate for each other in order to help a reader comprehend a text. Her model is dynamic and flexible in order to account for the effect of readers' level of L2 proficiency, the nature of their L1 and L2, as well as the effect different text types exert on readers' comprehension of texts. It is the reader that selects which language to focus on for processing and which resource may be helpful in that particular moment (Bernhardt, 2010). The aim of her research on the compensatory processing model as an interactive approach is to develop a 'coherent, theoretically consistent and research-based portrait of how literate adolescents and adults comprehend [texts]' (2010: ix).

Bernhardt (2010) has called for more research using a compensatory processing model to not only investigate how readers comprehend a text but also how readers '*learn* to comprehend at greater levels of sophistication, and whether that ability can be enhanced by instruction' (2010: ix, italics in original). For Bernhardt,

> [a]nalyzing how readers understand and reconstruct text makes for efficient instruction. Isolating learners' efforts at understanding, and searching within those efforts for features that cause comprehension breakdown, are the keys to enhanced, effective instruction, and, ultimately, to better and more sophisticated theory development. (2010: 39)

Although her goal is to develop a coherent understanding of L2 reading which includes L2 reading pedagogy, her model has been critiqued for its purely descriptive account of reading that offers little in the way of instrumental advice. She has acknowledged the critiques, indicating that thus far her work on a compensatory processing model has been 'unsatisfactory speculation given that there is little empirical evidence that the suggestions evolved from compensatory theory translate easily into effective pedagogical practice' (2010: 115). There have been two noteworthy follow-up studies: McNeil (2012) worked to extend Bernhardt's (2010) compensatory processing model and Ismail *et al.* (2015) investigated how classroom readers may be using compensatory reading.

Research from a cognitivist perspective

Research from a cognitivist approach, including Bernhardt's compensatory processing model, generally focuses on isolating, manipulating and studying the effect of particular variables on L2 reading. The studies involve participants with a range of L1s, L2s and L2 proficiency levels. Generalizations are then made from the accumulation of the noted effects of the variables on L2 reading across different groups of readers. Some research has also continued to focus on investigating the Language Threshold Hypothesis, in an attempt to answer Alderson's (1984) question concerning the extent of the effects of L1 reading abilities and L2 proficiency level on L2 reading ability. Bernhardt (2010) has pointed out that reading comprehension, in comparison to speaking and writing, is difficult to study as it 'is relatively invisible and can only be inferred, never directly accountable for processes in the way that one can hear or see that a particular linguistic form has been integrated or not' (2010: viii). Researchers from this perspective therefore generally focus on already-formed abilities and external manifestations of these abilities (e.g. responses to multiple choice comprehension questions or text recall).

Implications of a cognitivist perspective on L2 reading

The cognitivist approach to L2 reading as an extraction process, the study of already formed abilities, and the belief, from research investigating the effect of L2 proficiency on L2 reading, that L2 readers cannot successfully read until they have a 'more complete version of the software', have all likely contributed to the gap in most L2 instructional programs between the lower-level language and upper-level literature courses. From this perspective, reading is used to practice language forms, usually to demonstrate how the chapter's vocabulary and grammar is used in a text. The intention is for learners to be able to replicate the vocabulary and grammar that they see in the texts. Additionally, from this perspective, 'the de facto goal of reading is uncovering *the* meaning, *the* theme, *the* point of the text' (Kern, 2003: 44). In other words, language becomes about getting the right answer and not about meaning making.

The influence of Piaget's view that 'learning to read was seen as an exercise in the use of existing cognitive resources rather than the creation of new resources for thinking' (Olson, 1995: 97) on L2 pedagogy may have contributed to the gap as well. Implications of cognitivist research include the assumptions that only when L2 learners have developed sufficient proficiency in the lower-level language courses are they then capable of successfully reading the canon in upper-level literature courses (c.f. Maxim, 2006; Paesani *et al.*, 2016; Swaffar & Arens, 2005). From this perspective, L2 reading pedagogy therefore may not be necessary because students will be able to bridge the gap on their own, by relying on L1 reading ability and L2 lexical and morphosyntactic proficiency, or by somehow developing reading ability in the new language.

Literacy – Ontology and Epistemology

The ontology of literacy contrasts sharply in key ways with a cognitivist perspective of L2 reading outlined above. Whereas reading is traditionally limited to decoding and comprehension, literacy additionally involves interpretation and analysis. Literacy involves a multidimensional relationship not only between the writer and reader, but also between the text, world, background knowledge and L1/L2s (Kern, 2000; Roebuck, 1998). Literacy is a meaning-making process (Olson, 1995) as texts do not have meaning *per se*, but 'meaning potentialities', which are brought out through the activity of reading a text (Roebuck, 1998; Rommetveit, 1991, 1992, as cited in Appel & Lantolf, 1994). The meaning potentialities of a text that develop are influenced by these different relationships between a writer, reader, text, world, background knowledge, L1 and L2. Different interpretations are therefore possible, although this is not to suggest that any interpretation is possible as meaning potentials are still constrained by the language of the text.

In contrast to reading, a literacy perspective is not only about using existing cognitive resources, but, additionally, and crucially, about using literacy as a tool for thinking. Kern (2000) suggested 'becoming literate … [is] a matter of engaging in the ever-developing process of using reading and writing as tools for thinking and learning, in order to expand one's understanding of oneself and the world' (2000: 39). We learn tools that can help us to understand, interpret, critique and analyze texts and we can then use these texts to think more deeply about the world. In addition, from this understanding of literacy, a deficit model is eschewed as it is acknowledged that learners bring a variety of resources to literacy activities. While these may be different from the resources that they may bring to a text in their L1, they should be seen as assets and the focus should not be on what the learners have not yet developed.

Some researchers within the literacy perspective use the term *multiliteracies*, coined by the New London Group (1996), to capture the 'multiplicity of communications channels and media, and the increasing saliency of cultural and linguistic diversity' (Cope & Kalantzis, 2009; Kern, 2000; New London Group, 1996: 63). This term is used to highlight multiple perspectives and ways to communicate and the diversity of language

(Paesani *et al.*, 2016). The term is also used to make clear that there is not one 'right' form of language nor one 'right' way to use language (Cope & Kalantzis, 2015). While the research in this book is in line with a multiliteracies perspective, I will continue to use the umbrella term of *literacy* to maintain the contrast between reading and literacy. The interested reader should read for example, New London Group (1996), Cope and Kalantzis (2009, 2015), Kern (2000, 2003), Paesani (2016) and Paesani *et al.* (2016) for more details on multiliteracies and multiliteracy pedagogy.

Social approach to L2 literacy

One of the epistemologies for literacy is found within the larger umbrella of social approaches to research. From this perspective, research is not concerned with isolating variables or accumulating their individual effects because variables are not considered as interactive or even compensatory. Instead, they are seen as interrelated and interdependent in a dialectic manner. Developing literacy, from a social approach, 'commonly lead[s] to modifications or transformation of certain Available Designs' (Kern, 2000: 63). These Available Designs include the 'linguistic, schematic, visual, gestural, audio and spatial features of texts a learner attends to when engaging in the act of meaning design' (Paesani, 2016: 271). They include one's L1 and L2 knowledge and how language can be used to achieve particular purposes (New London Group, 1996). People bring their Available Designs to the activity of reading a text and in the process of reading or designing, their Available Designs are expanded and transformed, or redesigned, thereby providing new Available Designs when reading future texts (New London Group, 1996). In addition, Hasan (1996: 410) argued that:

> If literacy is what education is about … and if the aim of education is to enable participation in the production of knowledge – and not just reproduction – then it follows that we would need to develop in all pupils the ability to reflect, to enquire, to analyse and to challenge.

A Freirian perspective aligns with this as his goal was for students to read the world and the word (Freire, 1985). Expanding and transforming Available Designs, helping students to develop the ability to analyze texts and read the word and world are all possible from a social approach to literacy.

Instead of isolating variables, Kern (2000) called for researchers to instead investigate the particulars; in other words, 'how particular readers use particular strategies in particular ways in particular contexts' (2000: 318) if they want to better understand and investigate literacy. Researchers from social approaches use 'ethnographic approaches, thick descriptions, interviews and think-aloud procedures' (Kern, 2000: 318) to study L2 literacy. It is not generalizing across different contexts that is important, but rather what is helpful in a particular context.

V-SCT approach to L2 literacy

Because the ontology is different between reading and literacy, the research, or epistemology, from a V-SCT standpoint must be different. Vygotsky (2012) argued that the type of methodology proposed by cognitivists was in fact based on faulty premises. I will first present some background on Vygotsky's approach to psychology before I return to address literacy specifically.

In Vygotsky's approach to psychology, humans are simultaneously animals and not animals. In other words, our biology (animal) and culture (not animal) become dialectically interconnected as we develop. In adult, fossilized or fully formed thinking, we are unable to investigate the role that our biology has played and the role our culture has played because they are already dialectically interconnected and therefore difficult to disentangle and identify in research. Vygotsky (1997) pointed out that traditional experimental methods used in the study of natural sciences would not be able to disambiguate the roles of biology and culture in the formation of human consciousness. This is because experimental methods using reaction time responses are more appropriate for the study of reflexes consisting of externalized physical behavior of some sort. In order to study the role that culture plays, a new epistemology is needed – one that will allow for understanding and explaining the dialectical nature of human thinking.

From a V-SCT standpoint, 'the task of psychology … is to understand how human social and mental activity is organized through culturally constructed artifacts' (Lantolf, 2000: 1). In order to accomplish this, we need to trace, reconstruct or create the process, i.e. study its history, in order to understand it. In this way, we can see the role that biology and culture have each played in our development in a particular process. According to Vygotsky (1997),

> to study something historically means to study it in motion. Precisely this is the basic requirement of the dialectical method. To encompass in research the process of development of some thing in all its phases and changes – from the moment of its appearance to its death – means to reveal its nature, to know its essence, for only in movement does the body exhibit that it is. Thus, historical study of behavior is not supplementary or auxiliary to theoretical study, but it is the basis of the latter. (https://www.marxists.org/archive/vygotsky/works/1931/research-method.htm)

To capture the orienting powers of culturally constructed mediating artifacts, consciousness must be studied 'in flight' (Vygotsky, 1978: 68), meaning in activity, in the process of its genesis (Vygotsky, 1994). According to Rubenstein (1940), 'consciousness is both formed and manifested in activity'; therefore, in activity, the mind 'becomes cognizable for others' (as cited in Petrovsky, 1985: 23, 24). What all this means is that if we want to study how culture and cultural artifacts shape our thinking and activity, we have to investigate it in the process of development and in the process of development, researcher-teachers can see the process.

A new methodology is needed to study something that is ontologically different. The introduction of an auxiliary stimulus to a process that is not yet fossilized, or fully formed, allows researcher-teachers not only to see the contribution of both biology and culture, but also to promote the development of higher psychological functions. Becoming fully human means that we learn to control nature (biology) through social means (culture) such as mediating artifacts. The research and teaching from this viewpoint involve the creation and development of symbolic tools, which allow learners to control the task at hand through external means and to internalize the symbolic tools to guide their thinking in future activities. The creation, development and shaping of both the tools and the use of the tools for our own needs is both the tool and the result of the research (Negueruela, 2008).

Figure 2.1 – adapted from Cole (1996), who represented Vygotsky's idea of indirect mediated activity with a triangle – represents both biology, in the line connecting stimulus and response, and culture, in the addition of auxiliary stimuli, mediating artifacts, symbolic tools or culturally constructed artifacts. These different terms all represent the role that culture plays and allow humans to form an indirect, or mediated relationship, with the world.

According to Bruner, 'learning and thinking are always *situated* in a cultural setting and always dependent upon the utilization of cultural resources' (1996: 4, italics in original), but that does not mean that we lose the ability of our biologically based functioning. Humans, once they develop higher psychological functions or use culturally constructed mediating artifacts as tools for thinking, can voluntarily or intentionally control their biological mental processes. For example, if a teacher acted as if they were going to throw a whiteboard eraser at their students, some

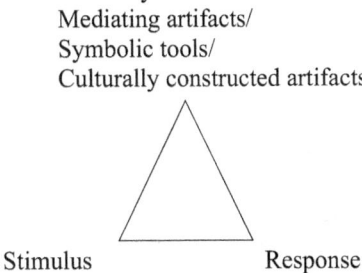

Figure 2.1 Indirect mediated activity (adapted from Cole, 1996, adapted from Vygotsky, 1978)

students may flinch, but others would not. From the biological side, if we perceive that someone is going to throw something at us (stimulus), we may duck or flinch or react in some way (response). Because we have learned from culture that teachers do not typically throw things at students or that a whiteboard eraser would not hurt us even if it was thrown at us, our cultural side tells our biological side that there is in fact no reason to respond. Our response has therefore been mediated by culture. Likewise, even though we may feel hunger while we are working, studying or playing, we can culturally know that now is not an appropriate time to eat or that we will be eating soon and can ignore our biological impulses.

Higher psychological functions allow humans to prepare and plan concrete objective activity on the mental plane before acting in and on the world. For example, we can think about possible outlines or storylines for a book that we want to write or how we would like our furniture to be rearranged in our minds before we have to act in the world by actually writing the book or moving our furniture. Likewise, if we were to renovate a house, we are able to plan in our minds with internalized cultural tools or through the use of external cultural tools how we will accomplish these tasks. An internalized cultural tool might be the experience that one gained from doing a previous project or from watching videos of experts doing the task. An external cultural tool might be the use of graph paper to draw to scale or an expert to guide you through the process. According to Lantolf (2000: 13), 'the convergence of thinking with culturally created mediational artifacts...occurs in the process of internalization, or the reconstruction on the inner, psychological plane of socially mediated external forms of goal-directed activity'. Therefore, it is through the process of developing higher psychological functions through internalization that our thinking can be mediated by social/cultural artifacts, which allow us to change the way in which we can act upon the world.

The investigation into the process of internalizing cultural mediation instead of the product of internalized mediation requires a new epistemology, as Vygotsky (1997) called for. Sakharov (1930), one of Vygotsky's colleagues, developed the instrumental or 'functional method of double stimulation' (as cited in Vygotsky, 2012: 110). The method of double stimulation involves several steps: (1) present learners with an activity that they cannot yet accomplish along with forms of mediation, or auxiliary stimuli, that they can use to carry out the activity; (2) investigate and intervene in the process of the learners' development of higher psychological functions by using appropriate forms of mediation; and (3) document the changes that take place (Vygotsky, 2012). The method of double stimulation allows researchers-teachers access to the internal processes that Bernhardt (2010) pointed out were 'invisible' and could only be 'inferred'. Because higher mental functions are not ready-made, access to the internal processes is possible by studying the process of their formation in activity.

Higher mental functions are formed in the external, or social, activity of individuals with culturally constructed mediating artifacts or symbolic tools and other individuals who attune mediation to learners' developmental needs (Vygotsky & Luria, 1994; Vygotsky, 1997). The artifacts, tools and individuals who serve mediating roles in activity are all part of the social context that is essential from this perspective. In activity, higher mental functions are understood, used, taken control of and internalized by the learners. It is important to note that internalization entails a change from inter- to intra-mental or, in other words, what was once social has become psychological and therefore allows the person to regulate their actions and their thinking through culturally constructed artifacts. The outcome of internalization is not the acceptance of the artifact as it is but what it allows the person to do with it in other contexts, for their own needs. Humans, who have internalized previous forms of mediation then continue to remake them for others (Vygotsky, 1997).

With this methodology, it is not necessary to wait until learners have a high level of L2 proficiency to allow them access to reading L2 texts, nor is it useful to study L2 learners who are already capable of reading L2 texts. From a V-SCT standpoint, development is not only possible in the activity of reading L2 texts, for example, but it is the point of what Vygotsky (1978) called experimental–developmental research as well as developmental education (see Lantolf & Poehner, 2014).

To form higher mental functions in developmental education requires recognition of the dialectical unity of teaching–learning that Vygotsky captured in the Russian term *obuchenie* (Cole, 2009). Teaching and learning are in dialectical unity because, although they are different activities, they need each other. In other words, without teaching, there is not learning and without learning, it is not considered teaching. If we take a pencil as an example of a dialectic, there is lead and there is an eraser. One creates writing and the other removes it. Both are needed though to make meaning.

For *obuchenie* to be effective, it must be attuned to the learners' zone of proximal development-in-activity (ZPD-in-activity) (Poehner, 2008; Vygotsky, 2012). The ZPD-in-activity is the metaphorical space between what learners are able to do independently and what they are able to do with mediation (Vygotsky, 2012). In addition, we use the metaphor of a ZPD to 'observe … and understand … how mediational means are appropriated and internalized' (Lantolf, 2000: 17). If our *obuchenie* is attuned to learners' ZPD-in-activity, it will lead the development of their ripening abilities. By our teaching–learning 'leading development' we mean that it is the quality of our teaching/mediation that promotes learners' development. This is in contrast to perspectives, based on Piagetian principles, that rely on waiting for learners' abilities to ripen on their own to indicate that they are ready for teaching (see Egan, 2002). From this perspective,

> [w]hen we investigate the highest functions of behaviour which are composed of complicated internal processes, we find that this method [double stimulation] tends in the course of the experiment to call into being the very process of formation of the highest forms of behaviour, instead of investigating the function already formed in its developed stage. (http://www.marxists.org/archive/vygotsky/index.htm; Vygotsky, 1994)

From a V-SCT standpoint, the focus of researchers-teachers should be on creating the developmental process to help learners understand, use and internalize the relevant concepts (and mediating artifacts) in practical goal-directed activity. This allows the developmental process to not only occur, but for researchers-teachers to study it in its process of formation. A V-SCT approach takes Marx's eleventh thesis on Feuerbach seriously, 'Philosophers have hitherto only *interpreted* the world in various ways; the point is to *change* it' (https://www.marxists.org/archive/marx/works/1845/theses/, italics in original). Creating or intervening in the developmental process, in this case in L2 literacy development, is necessary in order to provide learners with full access to textual content and help them develop their ability to interpret and analyze this content in a new language.

The process of internalization involves learners 'gain[ing] control over natural mental functions by bringing externally (socioculturally) formed mediating artifacts into thinking activity' allowing learners to begin to 'voluntarily organize and control memory, attention, planning, learning and development' (Lantolf & Thorne, 2006: 153). In the process, the intra-mental is reconstructed and results in learners developing a new relationship with the world, one that entails voluntary control of the higher mental functions in order for learners to use them as needed and as they want in practical goal-directed activities (Lantolf, 2000; Lantolf & Thorne, 2006; Vygotsky, 2012; Vygotsky & Luria, 1994). As learners are able to internalize mediational means, they are then able to imitate, which is a creative endeavor and not verbatim copying. Imitation allows the learners to begin trying out their new conceptual understanding in new contexts (Lantolf, 2000; Vygotsky, 2012). In developmental education, imitation is part of the developmental process initiated through effective *obuchenie*.

In L2 literacy instruction from a V-SCT approach, the researcher-teacher is able to understand both what L2 learners can do on their own and what they are able to do with access to culturally constructed artifacts. The researcher-teacher is able to study the learners' developmental process, but crucially at the same time is able to and must promote learners' L2 literacy development. Mediating artifacts, whether they are language, dictionaries, a division-of-labor pedagogy, or a researcher-teacher, may help learners complete the reading activity but more importantly they will help learners to develop the abilities needed to become independent readers in the L2. From this perspective, the goal is psychological development, not task completion. What began as cooperation during an L2 literacy activity between a person, text, mediational means, world, researcher-teacher and an L2 reading collective, can become a psychological form of cooperation as the mediating artifacts become internalized. The internalized tools help to restructure the learners' mind, allowing the learners to take control of these artifacts, use them to self-regulate – in this case, read independently in an L2 – and therefore create different understandings and relationships with the word and world. They can use these literacy tools in the ways that they wish.

Specific Reading and Literacy Components

In this section, research findings on reading/literacy components that impact literacy development will be outlined to give the reader a sense of this wide body of literature. The interested reader should read further to gain a full sense of the nuances in each of these areas. These components include: (1) the roles and interaction of learners' L1 and L2 on reading; (2) lexical issues; (3) grammar/discourse/morphosyntactic issues; (4) the effect of working memory; (5) texts, text structure, and genre; (6) common tools and strategies; and (7) use of L1 in pedagogy.

Roles and interaction of learners' L1 and L2

Many reading researchers have extensively investigated the effect of L1 reading knowledge and L2 proficiency on L2 reading ability. In these studies, L2 proficiency generally includes both lexical and morphosyntactic knowledge (Brisbois, 1995; Koda, 2005). L1 reading ability and L2 proficiency have both been found to have an effect on L2 reading ability, with the combined effect ranging from approximately 30–55% of the variance depending on the study (e.g. Bernhardt, 2010; Bernhardt & Kamil, 1995; Bossers, 1991; Brisbois, 1995; Carrell, 1991; Lee & Schallert, 1997; Koda, 2005; Yamashita, 2002a, 2002b; Yamashita & Shiotsu, 2017). The extent of the effect of L1 reading ability and L2 proficiency differed depending on the proficiency level of the L2 learners at the outset of the study. L2 proficiency had a more significant impact on lower-level learners' L2 reading ability, while L1 reading abilities had a more significant impact on upper-level learners' L2 reading ability (e.g. Brisbois, 1995). From McNeil's (2012) study, the contribution of strategic knowledge played a larger role than L2 language knowledge and the L1 reading ability for higher-proficiency L2 readers, whereas for lower-proficiency readers, the L2 language knowledge played a much larger role than either strategic knowledge or L1 reading ability. In Jeon and Yamashita's (2014) meta-analysis, they found that L2 vocabulary knowledge and L2 grammar knowledge correlated very strongly with L2 reading, as well as L2 decoding and L1 reading ability, although to a lesser extent. They also found that vocabulary learned in a context versus in a decontextualized list had a greater effect on reading. In addition, the nature of the L1 and L2 and how similar they were had an impact on L2 reading.

One implication from these findings, which has greatly influenced L2 reading/literacy pedagogy, is that 'some sort of threshold or language competence ceiling has to be attained before existing abilities in the first language can begin to transfer' (Alderson, 1984: 20). Perhaps one of the outcomes of this implication is that 'language students opting to continue their L2 studies seem to comprise a select group of highly literate individuals' (Brisbois, 1995: 574). Other students might opt to continue their L2 studies if they were provided access to effective L2 literacy *obuchenie* though. In addition, Koda (2005) cautioned against assumptions related to the research on the effect of these two components on both theoretical and empirical bases. For instance, she indicated that there is 'no real support for the presumption that word-recognition skills are the automatic outcome of increased linguistic knowledge' (2005: 38) nor that 'processing skills improve automatically as a by-product of increased linguistic knowledge' (2005: 10). For Bernhardt (2010), the following two questions 'remain absolutely key': 'How does the existence of language knowledge and literacy knowledge operate in second-language text processing? and How can learners be encouraged to draw on their knowledge sources to function and comprehend in second languages?' (2010: 52). She has called for additional research on how these two important components interact and compensate for each other; however, the call is for studies with a larger number of participants so that more generalizations can be made about these effects (Bernhardt, 2010). From an L2 literacy development standpoint, it is important to know that both L1 reading knowledge and L2 language knowledge have an effect on L2 reading, but the nature of the effect of these for particular learners and therefore of the pedagogy needed has not yet been investigated.

Lexical issues

In terms of research on vocabulary/lexical issues in L2 reading, Koda (2005: 31) noted that 'visual sampling skills are required' and that 'local (word-level) and global (context-level) processing are highly interactive, and … mutually enhancing'. In addition, L2 learners, according to Bernhardt (2010), 'often have a concept for a particular word as well as that word in their L1 oral/aural vocabulary' and therefore, 'the process for many second-language readers … [involves] attach[ing] a new oral/aural representation to a concept that already exists' (2010: 14). However, L1 and L2 concepts do not necessarily overlap and the difference between two concepts may cause difficulties in L2 reading if learners use their L1 concepts to interpret L2 texts. In addition, 'although L2 learners may recognize words', they frequently 'do not know how extended their reference may or may not be' because they 'lack a culturally appropriate memory schema' in the L2 (Brisbois, 1995: 569, 570). Reed *et al.* (2016) found that both vocabulary and spelling knowledge were important predictors of reading comprehension. Finally, Bernhardt (2010) listed several areas where future research on vocabulary in L2 reading is needed: word acquisition, cognates versus non-cognates, the effect of word frequency on acquisition, the use of technology in vocabulary acquisition and, finally, the acquisition of metaphorical uses of lexical items.

Researchers have also investigated how students learn vocabulary in instructional contexts, which Bernhardt (2010: 14) called 'critical to learning to read'. L2 learners acquire vocabulary by inferring meaning from the context (Bengeleil & Paribakht, 2004; de Bot *et al.*, 1997), from extensive reading (Anderson, 2009; Horst, 2005; Pigada & Schmitt, 2006; Webb & Chang, 2015), and through the use of a dictionary (Hayati & Pour-Mohammadi, 2005). Anderson (2009: 124) remarked that 'extensive reading plays an essential role in providing the multiple contexts that readers must have to learn new words and make them their own'. Alessi and Dwyer (2008) found that having students investigate vocabulary during reading as opposed to pre-reading was better for L2 reading comprehension. However, learners often need instruction on how to best use bilingual dictionaries (Prichard, 2008).

Grammar/discourse/morphosyntactic issues

The research in this section focuses on the grammar, discourse and morphosyntactic issues in L2 reading. Much less is known on the role of L2 grammatical knowledge in L2 reading and how L2 learners approach grammatical difficulties in texts compared to the role of L2 vocabulary in L2 reading. Kieffer and Lesaux (2012) found that morphological awareness had an impact on reading comprehension. Koda's (2005) research has found that structural complexity can, in fact, enhance L2 reading comprehension but may increase demands on L2 learners' working memory. Stevenson *et al.* (2007) found that despite learners' increased focus on grammatical difficulties during L2 reading, they were able to maintain their focus on comprehension. Lee (2007) reported that by manipulating texts to highlight grammatical features, L2 learners could learn these grammatical forms while reading; however, Leow (2001) and Leow *et al.* (2003) found no effect on the manipulation of grammatical forms on comprehension.

There is more research needed which investigates L2 readers' use of grammatical elements and the nature of compensation used for grammatical difficulties when reading L2 texts in order to 'understand the nature of morphosyntactic patterns that predict second-language reading comprehension and whether generalizations about morphosyntax hold consistently across languages with different morphosyntactic realizations' (Bernhardt, 2010: 131). Research of this nature only makes sense from a cognitivist perspective on reading because it does not focus on the particulars, as Kern (2000) called for, nor does a V-SCT approach find generalizations across languages necessary or insightful for how particular L2 learners develop higher mental functioning through the development of L2 literacy.

The effect of working memory

Given that people have a limited amount of working memory (Baddeley, 2010) and that L2 reading/literacy involves a complex set of interactive and interdependent processes (e.g. decoding, understanding vocabulary, morphosyntax, cohesive devices, story structure and genre, incorporating background knowledge, inferencing, developing meaning potentials, planning, monitoring, synthesizing, interpreting, making predictions and revising), the working memory of L2 readers, especially beginner or intermediate learners, is quickly taxed (Jeon & Yamashita, 2014; Koda, 2005). Shin *et al.* (2019) found that the more working memory an L2 reader had, the more they could use their background knowledge than those with lower working memories. Much more research is needed on this important topic.

One solution that many researchers/teachers have employed is to delay L2 reading until some of the processes become automated in order to reduce the demand on learners' working memory (Abu-Rabia, 2003; Kern, 2000; Koda, 2005). For her part, Adams (1994) suggested improving vocabulary recognition before engaging learners with texts. Koda (2005: 31) agreed because as 'word recognition involves the extraction, rather than the construction, of information, automaticity can be relatively easily achieved'. Some researchers believe that, for students to comprehend a text, they need to be able to recognize 98% of the words in a text (Laufer & Ravenhorst-Kalovski, 2010; Nation, 2006; Schmitt *et al.*, 2011). This does not take into account the role that pedagogy may play in this process. Another common solution is to have L2 learners with a lower level of proficiency read short, simplified or adapted L2 texts or wait to read more extensive or authentic texts until they have 'sufficient' L2 proficiency. More research is needed on other solutions to accommodate strains on working memory besides waiting for learners to have 'sufficient' L2 proficiency.

Texts, text structure and genre

Texts

The types of texts commonly assigned to lower-level L2 learners differ dramatically from those assigned to upper-level learners. In the former, L2 textbooks often have short texts that were created to teach the vocabulary and grammatical elements of the chapter, texts that have been altered for pedagogical purposes or written primarily for L2 students and abridged or simplified excerpts of authentic texts that are usually found in the supplementary portion at the end of the chapter (Allen & Paesani, 2010; Bernhardt, 2010; Bourns *et al.*, 2020; Graden, 1996; Maxim, 2002; Paesani *et al.*, 2016). In the upper-level courses, the texts are authentic, which means that they were 'written for, viewed by, or spoken to native speakers of that language' (Swaffar & Arens, 2005: 18). Authentic texts are often not used in lower-level L2 courses because they may seem to be too difficult given that the lexicon, morphosyntax and cultural references have not been edited or simplified, but this may not be the case. Authentic materials, by their very nature, tend to provide a natural redundancy that edited texts may not (Gascoigne, 2002; Maxim, 2002; Swaffar *et al.*, 1991; Swaffar & Arens, 2005). In fact, research has shown that the simplification of a text does not in fact help L2 learners comprehend the text better (Keshavarz *et al.*, 2007; Oh, 2001). Furthermore, in her research, Graden (1996: 391) reported on two teachers who had stopped teaching reading in their L2 classes because their students 'didn't understand, they got bored, [and] they got tired' reading materials found in textbooks. Fortunately, researchers are more consistently using authentic texts in their L2 reading research (Bernhardt, 2010) and hopefully authentic texts will become the norm in L2 classrooms as well.

Authentic texts importantly 'lead learners not only to new language but also to new textual messages...new ideas...new discourse situations...to language learning in the context of a culture's ideas, values and practices' (Swaffar & Arens, 2005: 18). From a literacy viewpoint, authentic texts are preferred because they provide L2 learners access to learning about another languaculture (Agar, 1994) during the activity of reading. Understanding another culture through their texts, learning new/expanding cultural perspectives and schemas, changing one's way of thinking about the world are all more likely when reading authentic L2 texts (Kern, 2000; Paesani *et al.*, 2016). From a V-SCT standpoint and a general sociocultural perspective, the source of learners' development is the social world (Vygotsky, 2012); therefore, the kinds of texts that L2 learners read fundamentally change the quality of their development. Finally, the use of created texts for lower-level courses and authentic texts for upper-level courses contributes to the curriculum gap, making it difficult for L2 learners to successfully cross the divide. Paesani *et al.* (2016: 137) report that students feel frustrated with 'the expectation that once they have completed lower-level courses, they are considered ready to interpret and analyze intellectually and linguistically challenging texts'.

Text structure

Although L2 learners may have developed 'a knowledge of story structure' quite early in life in their L1, Hudson (2007: 179) argued that other genres, such as expository ones, 'require explicit instruction and training'. Mandler (1984: 33), however, distinguishes between explicit and implicit knowledge about story structure, arguing that what people use when reading stories 'is procedural knowledge that works beyond awareness'. Although L2 learners may have an implicit understanding of the structure of narratives in their L1, many have not developed an explicit conceptual understanding of the concept of narrative or narrative literacy in any language. According to Riley (1993), even within the narrative genre, as the text structure difficulty increased, it impeded the comprehension of lower-level learners more than upper-level learners. Knowledge of both text structure and its instruction has been shown to aid in text comprehension (Carrell, 1985; Koda, 2005). More research is needed on the effect of instruction on narrative text structure and the concept of narrative literacy with L2 learners.

Genre

Genres involve more than a similar text structure, however. They are 'typical ways of engaging rhetorically with situations that recur' (Hudson, 2007: 205) whether the rhetorical engagement is in oral or written form. They are 'typical' because texts within a genre have a 'shared set of communicative purposes' (Bhatia, 1993; Swales, 1990: 46) and the shared purposes lead to particular, recognizable and similar text structures (Hudson, 2007). For example, editorials, because of their shared purpose, are organized in similar ways and these are different to how sonnets are organized which fit their shared purpose. In addition, people engage as social and cultural beings in the creation of texts within genres and others within this cultural community are able to understand the texts because of their shared social context (Bhatia, 1993; Bourns *et al.*, 2020; DeFina & Georgakopoulou, 2012; Hudson, 2007; Martin, 1984). Furthermore, as 'texts are patterned in reasonably predictable ways according to patterns of social interaction in a particular culture' (Cope & Kalantzis, 1993: 7), different cultures may have different genres or variations in the rhetorical structure within a particular genre than another culture. Each text is situated both within a particular genre and 'in [a] particular sociocultural context' (Byrnes *et al.*, 2010: 108).

The GUGD's (Georgetown University German Department) L2 literacy pedagogy, based on SFL, includes activities which help students analyze the field, tenor and mode (ideational, interpersonal and textual metafunctions) of particular texts (Byrnes *et al.*, 2010). In SFL, 'the aim is to be able to state consciously, and to interpret, processes that go on unconsciously all the time, in the course of daily life – in other words, to represent the system that lies behind these processes' (Halliday & Hasan, 1989: 14). From the GUGD students' analysis and development of these concepts, they were also able to develop their writing abilities in the particular genre (Byrnes *et al.*, 2010). The concepts of field, tenor and mode, constructs used in the studies outlined in this book, will be explained in more detail in Chapter 3. Byrnes *et al.* (2010: 198) found that 'genre provided the crucial nexus for language learning and cultural content simultaneously', which allowed them to close the gap for their writing pedagogy between their language and literature courses. Pedagogy using SFL 'afford[s] students access to the full range of societal practices as these are manifested in a society's textual practices' (Byrnes *et al.*, 2010: 2). The concept of genre must be defined for L2 learners, made explicit through instruction and learners must have opportunities for practice, with mediation in the ZPD by instructors. Ferreira's (2005) research, on writing instruction using the concept of genre for L2 learners, and the GUGD curriculum are examples of compatible links that have been made between SFL, a functional theory of language and V-SCT, a theory of mind, in order to develop effective L2 literacy pedagogy.

Common Tools and Strategies

Some of the more common tools and strategies used in L2 reading/literacy activities include using dictionaries, incorporating background knowledge, identifying the main idea, making predictions while reading and collaborating on L2 reading tasks. Prichard (2008) investigated learners' use of bilingual dictionaries and found that it improved reading comprehension and vocabulary acquisition in general. However, as mentioned earlier, he pointed out that learners may need instruction on how to best use a bilingual dictionary. If the pedagogy relies on texts that contain glossing for the potentially problematic lexical items or does not teach students how to use a bilingual dictionary as a tool to make meaning with a text, they are often limited to glossed texts or have to wait until they have a sufficiently extensive L2 vocabulary.

Researchers who study the use of background knowledge in L2 reading/literacy activities focus on readers' knowledge of the content of the text, the culture and/or text knowledge (i.e. formal schema) and the extent to which readers use this knowledge to understand a text. Although several studies have identified an effect of background knowledge on L2 reading comprehension (e.g. Abu-Rabia, 1996, 1998a, 1998b; Clapham, 2013; Leeser, 2007) and that learners are able to compensate for a lack of background knowledge with proficiency (Chan, 2003), Bernhardt (2010) claimed that overall there was no clear link between background knowledge and proficiency. Clapham (2013) found that the higher proficiency the student had the more they used background knowledge and that perhaps there may even be a threshold below which learners are not able to make use of their background knowledge. Even with the improved Hare scale, measuring the depth of readers' background knowledge (Hare, 1982), this factor has not been found to correlate with 'proficient performance' (as cited in Bernhardt, 2010: 31). As Bernhardt noted with regard to one of her own studies, 'some readers used background knowledge effectively; others did not. Some had knowledge and used it; some had knowledge and did not use it' (2010: 31). The inconclusive research on the effect of background knowledge 'led to the logical conclusion that some texts were either going to be comprehended or not and that comprehension depended upon a reader's internally determined knowledge base' (Bernhardt, 2010: 32). Although L2 readers' background knowledge is highly individualized as they each bring different knowledge about the world and texts to L2 reading activities, the difficulty in finding conclusive results may come from generalizing effects on the basis of a large number of participants. As for instruction, Anderson (2009) argued that activating learners' background knowledge during pre-reading activities may help improve their text comprehension.

Summaries can be used in L2 literacy activities as both a learning and assessment tool (see Poehner, 2008, on dynamic assessment). They can serve as an aid for readers to create meaning from a text (Oded & Walters, 2001; Shih, 1992) besides being used to assess learners' comprehension of a text. Oded and Walters (2001) compared L2 readers' text comprehension when they were asked to summarize during reading or to list the main ideas of the text. They found that summary creation correlated with higher comprehension scores because it helped learners to create a 'mental model of the text' (2001: 360). The effect of summary creation on L2 reading comprehension for lower-level readers and for more difficult texts was larger than for higher-level readers or less difficult texts. Higher-level L2 readers may already create 'mental models' and therefore, even if they were asked to list the main ideas in the text, their mental model creation may have sufficiently helped them with text comprehension. A second reason may be that the level of processing that lower-level learners needed to read the difficult texts allowed them to better remember the text (Kintsch, 1994). Lower-level learners may also have benefitted from an explicit task that maintained their focus on meta-level understanding such as selecting main ideas, creating a 'mental model' and incorporating new information into the model. The ability to complete an appropriate summary due to the creation of a coherent 'mental model' necessarily indicates a high level of text comprehension.

Once L2 readers have a coherent 'mental model' for a text, they will be better able to make predictions about future events in the text (Oded & Walters, 2001). Asking students to make predictions while reading is commonly used in L1 and L2 reading/literacy research and pedagogy (e.g. Anderson, 2009; Cole, 1996; Dixon-Krauss, 1996; Palincsar & Brown, 1984). It is essential to provide L2 readers with other resources to make predictions besides their background knowledge and L1 schemas and scripts, for example, through the creation of a mental model, requiring text-based justification for their predictions.

Swain's (2000) research highlighted that student collaboration on making predictions, for example, was more effective in mediating their learning than instruction alone. From a cognitivist perspective on reading, rarely are L2 learners allowed to collaborate on a reading task and almost never on an assessment of L2 reading. Individual work allows for the isolation of variables whereas collaboration does not. Only individualized efforts are accepted so that generalizations can be made about the impact of particular variables on L2 reading comprehension. If a group were to collaborate, the researcher would no longer be able to solely attribute the effects to particular variables. There has been some work on collaboration since Swain (2000), but more is needed. Ghaith (2003) found a positive effect of cooperative learning on reading comprehension and Kern (2000) reported that reading while working in collaboration with other L2 readers was not as difficult as it was when working alone. From a V-SCT perspective, cooperation or better yet, working as a collective, may serve a more profound mediating role in the development of learners' L2 literacy. More discussion on collectives and the use of collaboration in L2 literacy activities will be outlined in Chapter 3.

Use of the L1 in Pedagogy

The role of the L1 in L2 reading/literacy activities, and in L2 courses, is still quite limited, as the belief that L2 learners/readers should predominantly or exclusively use the L2 in all aspects of L2 reading or L2 activities in general still persists (Graden, 1996) despite there being a lack of evidence. From an L2 literacy viewpoint, however, Swaffar et al. (1991) pointed to the need for learners to use the L1 when their conceptual understanding would not be apparent through the use of the L2. For example, if you are assessing comprehension in the L2 and students use the language of the text because they know that this general area is where the answer is found, we may not know if they truly understand what the text means. Furthermore, the use of the L1 is important and necessary when learners need to use it as a tool for thinking, in other words, as a 'mediator between the world of objects and the new language' (Vygotsky, 2012: 170–171). L2 learners are generally quite competent in thinking about difficult concepts in their L1 but may not yet be able to think about these concepts if they are forced to rely exclusively on their L2. We could wait until they have enough L2 proficiency, or we can use their L1 to talk about, for example, field, tenor and mode from an SFL perspective and how that impacts texts. Then learners could use these concepts to investigate an L2 text. In L2 literacy pedagogy, it is important for L2 learners to be able to understand and use literacy concepts to guide their thinking in literacy activities, therefore using their L1 as a tool for thinking is acceptable and encouraged.

Conclusion

The studies presented in this book, from a V-SCT perspective on L2 literacy, will argue that effective *obuchenie* can help L2 learners to develop L2 narrative literacy abilities which will allow them to become independent, successful readers thereby contributing to the closing of the curriculum gap between lower-level language and upper-level literature courses. The nature in which the studies presented in this book have addressed and incorporated the research on each of the reading/literacy components presented above will be addressed in Chapter 3.

Note

(1) In SCT, terms that are inseparable or in dialectical unity, that cannot be written in English in a way that represents this inseparability, such as researcher-teacher, are written with a hyphen (-) or a slash (/).

3 Vygotskian Second Language Literacy Pedagogy

Introduction

In this chapter, I will present the design of a Vygotskian approach to L2 literacy pedagogy and research including Concept-Based Language Instruction and a Division-of-Labor Pedagogy. I will also discuss specific details that pertain to the research-teaching design of the three focus studies such as scientific concepts, roles, texts, mediating artifacts, mediation, literacy activities and data.

Concept-Based Language Instruction

In developmental education from a V-SCT perspective, *obuchenie*, or teaching-learning, must lead development (Lantolf & Poehner, 2014). By 'lead development', I mean that it is the quality of the teaching-learning activity that is what promotes development. We do not have to wait for biology or maturity to indicate that a student is developmentally ready, and our teaching is then possible, but instead it is our teaching-learning activity that creates the development. Gal'perin (1989b, 1992) was the first to create and develop a theory of developmental education from Vygotsky's theory of mind, which he called Systemic-Theoretical Instruction. Gal'perin essentially applied Vygotsky's theory of how people develop to how to best accomplish teaching-learning (see Gal'perin, 1989b, 1992; Haenen, 1996, 2000, 2001; Lantolf & Poehner, 2014). Those applying Vygotsky's and Gal'perin's work specifically to L2 development have referred to it as Concept-Based Instruction (CBI) or now Concept-Based Language Instruction (C-BLI) to distinguish it from Content-Based Instruction (Lantolf *et al.*, 2021).

In C-BLI, there are five essential components: (1) scientific concepts, (2) materializations, (3) practical goal-directed activities and (4) verbalizations which lead to (5) internalization. C-BLI, 'begins with high-quality systematic knowledge (i.e. scientific concepts) and seeks to help learners not merely to understand the concepts, but to appropriate them for use in concrete practical activity' (Lantolf & Poehner, 2014: 80). Scientific concepts, needed in C-BLI, differ from everyday concepts. It is in the everyday world that people have access to, and are able to develop, everyday concepts. But for Vygotsky, education was the place where learners had access to, and could develop, scientific concepts (Lantolf & Poehner, 2014; Lantolf & Thorne, 2006; Vygotsky, 2012). In our everyday understanding of the world, it is perfectly acceptable to talk about the sun rising in the east and setting in the west. In school, and from a scientific perspective, however, it is not the sun that moves, but instead the Earth that revolves around the sun. If students were to use their everyday understanding of the sun's movements, it would be difficult to understand the solar system. It is our understanding and use of scientific concepts that allow us to understand the solar system and solve complex problems regarding it.

Scientific concepts are often developed by specialists 'through the systematic analysis of a particular domain' (Lantolf & Poehner, 2014: 64). For example, if we want to understand how French prepositions work and how they contrast with English prepositions, we must systematically collect uses of French prepositions and analyze the use of each French preposition and the degree to which it overlaps in use with different English equivalents (Buescher & Strauss, 2015, 2018). In teaching-research focused on L2 development, theories of language that foreground meaning (instead of structure) such as Systemic Functional Linguistics or Cognitive Linguistics, are particularly well suited to guide researchers in their development of systematic knowledge about language. The systematic knowledge that is developed then becomes the scientific concepts required by C-BLI.

Scientific concepts, to be maximally effective in L2 development, must be systematic, complete, explicit, abstract and recontextualizable (Karpov, 2003; Lantolf, 2011; Lantolf & Poehner, 2014; Lee, 2012; Negueruela, 2003; Toomela, 2010). They must be systematic and complete so that the entire concept is accounted for and in a clear and organized manner. They must be able to be explained explicitly and directly. They are also abstract as opposed to concrete. If we think about the concept of a circle, it must include something to the effect that it is a round figure whose points are all equally distant from the center. This would allow for circles of all sizes. If we used concrete examples of circles such as wheels or pancakes, students would have difficulty understanding fully what a circle is and what other objects could be appropriately classified as such. With the abstract, systematic, explicit concept of circle, it is essentially recontextualizable in the sense that students could identify or create circles of varying sizes and for varying purposes. Owing to these characteristics, scientific concepts allow learners to fully develop their understanding of them so that they can use these concepts in goal-directed activity to function in new ways, in this case, in the L2. Everyday concepts, as they lack these characteristics, do not allow for the same kind of development. This is not to say that everyday concepts are not important as they are perfectly fine in the everyday world. The aim of C-BLI is to help learners develop their understanding and use of scientific concepts as tools-and-results, meaning that the concepts are 'both the content and the tool for thinking' (Negueruela, 2008: 192). In other words, students will not only be able to understand the concept itself, but also how to use the concept to create the meanings that they wish to express in the L2.

Since Negueruela's (2003) study using C-BLI to teach tense/aspect and mood in Spanish (see also Negueruela, 2008; Negueruela & Lantolf, 2006), researchers have begun to incorporate Vygotsky and Gal'perin's insights into their research on L2 development: (1) Ferreira (2005) and Ferreira and Lantolf (2008) on writing instruction through genre analysis; (2) Lapkin et al. (2008) on the grammatical concept of voice; (3) Serrano-Lopez and Poehner (2008) on Spanish locative prepositions; (4) Yàñez-Prieto (2008) on aspect and metaphor in Spanish; (5) Gánem-Gutiérrez and Harun (2011) on English tense/aspect; (6) García (2012, 2015, 2017) on Spanish aspect; (7) Lai (2012) on tense and aspect in Chinese; (8) van Compernolle (2011, 2012, 2014), van Compernolle and Henery (2014) and van Compernolle et al. (2016) on pragmatic features in French; (9) Lee (2012) on English phrasal verbs; (10) White (2012) on English phrasal verbs; (11) Lai (2012) on the Chinese temporal system; (12) Polizzi (2013) on aspect in Spanish; (13) Kim (2013) on the concept of sarcasm; (14) Harun (2013) on English tense/aspect; (15) Kao (2014) on Chinese rhetoric; (16) Zhang (2014) on Chinese word order using the Topic Hypothesis; (17) Harun et al. (2014) on English tense/aspect; (18) Buescher (2015) on L2 literacy development; (19) Buescher and Strauss (2015, 2018) on French prepositions; (20) Fogal (2015) on English voice construction; (21) Infante (2016) on L2 English writing; (22) Poehner and Infante (2017) on English tense and aspect; (23) Bakhoda et al. (2016) on English reading comprehension; (24) Kurtz (2017) on L2 legal reasoning; (25) Walter and van Compernolle (2017) on German declension; (26) Ohta (2017) on Japanese honorifics; (27) Fazilatfar et al. (2017) on English tense/aspect; (28) Fogal (2017) on developing CBI pedagogical content knowledge; (29) Esteve Ruesca (2018) and Lantolf and Esteve (2019) on language teacher education; (30) Harun et al. (2019) on grammatical competence; and (31) Tsai (2020) on verb–noun collocations. Thus far, the majority of L2 studies using C-BLI for L2 development have focused on grammatical development, although it has started to expand to other foci in recent years as shown previously.

The second key component of C-BLI, materializations, are visual and holistic depictions of the scientific concept, meaning that an image attempts to capture the complete concept. In addition, they must be 'understandable for learners ... [and] allow them to deploy the concept in ... concrete goal-directed activities' (Lantolf & Poehner, 2014: 65). Once the scientific concepts have been developed and are abstract, explicit, recontextualizable, systematic and complete, a visual depiction is developed which includes minimal verbal language. In this way, learners do not simply memorize a verbal explanation of the concept but develop their own understanding of the concept. They can then use that understanding in goal-directed activities (Lantolf & Thorne, 2006; Lantolf & Poehner, 2014). Materializations for C-BLI are often in the form of a SCOBA, or Schema of a Complete Orienting Basis of an Action (Gal'perin, 1989a, 1992; Lantolf & Poehner, 2014). SCOBAs 'serve as materialized reminders of the knowledge required to engage in a particular action' (Lantolf & Poehner, 2014: 64). In addition to visual SCOBAs, concepts can also be represented in a materialized form. Physical objects, such as Cuisenaire rods, can be used to capture concepts that learners can manipulate in order to understand and use the concept to make meaning (e.g. Buescher, 2015; Zhang, 2014). Using your body, or specifically your hands, in the form of kinesthetic learning and memory can be powerful mediating tools. Both materializations and materialized forms of the concept 'aim to support the internalization of relevant concepts' (van Compernolle, 2014: 21).

Once the scientific concepts and materializations/materialized forms of them have been developed, learners need a way to use these concepts to make meaning in the L2. Practical goal-directed activities require learners to use their understanding of scientific concepts to make meaning. In the process, they rely on the materializations or materialized forms to develop their understanding of the concept and use it to make the meanings that they want to make. The goal-directed activities must be purposeful and meaningful in the sense that they are focused on making meaning and not focused on creating accurate structures. These activities will differ depending on the concepts being developed. Gal'perin's work on Systemic-Theoretical Instruction 'demonstrated... that mental activity was not a mysterious internal process occurring solely within the brain of the individual. Instead mental activity arose in and through practical, material activity' (van Compernolle, 2014: 20). As outlined in Chapter 2, 'consciousness is both formed and manifested in activity' (Rubenstein, 1940, as cited in Petrovsky, 1985: 24), meaning that it is through the purposeful use of concepts in activity that learners develop higher psychological functions. In the process of developing their understanding and use of the concept, they begin internalizing the concept. Therefore, how they use the materializations or materialized forms may change and become abbreviated. Finally, not only is learners' development possible through activity, but also researcher-teachers' ability to study learner development.

Throughout the process of learners developing their understanding of the scientific concepts and using the materializations and materialized forms in practical goal-directed activities, from this perspective, researcher-teachers must also ask students to verbalize their understanding and use of the concepts to guide their thinking and meaning-making performance in the goal-directed activities. The activity of learners verbalizing their thinking, in oral or written form, helps them to not only think through how to use the concepts but also how they understand the concepts themselves. In other words, 'language (understood as a communicative activity) not only mediates social activity but also mediates mental behavior' (Lantolf, 2011: 310). Verbalizations promote learner development and in the process allow researcher-teachers to better understand learners' developmental process and what type and amount of mediation might further their development.

Verbalizations are based on Gal'perin's idea of *communicated thinking* (see Haenen, 2001), which is 'overt or social speech' that learners use to 'communicate about the action and to think aloud as they perform it' (2001: 163). Although Swain's research on collaborative verbalizations, mentioned in Chapter 2, shares some similarities with Gal'perin's communicated thinking, the two processes differ in terms of their function. For Swain (2000: 113), the function was 'problem-solving' and 'knowledge building'. For Gal'perin, verbalizations serve as a transitional phase between the materialized and mental action, leading to internalization of the concept (Haenen, 2001). When communicated thinking turns inward and becomes 'external speech to oneself' (Haenen, 2001: 164), it changes from 'communicated thinking' to 'dialogical thinking' or 'covert speech'. According to Korthagen (1999), dialogical thinking can then be used when carrying out the action, reflecting on the action, or planning for future actions (Haenen, 2001).

Verbalizations allow the 'learners ... to externalize and therefore confront their own thinking and potentially modify it as necessary' as well as shift from I-You (communicated thinking) to I-Me (dialogical thinking) dialogues (Lantolf, 2011: 311). As development leads to internalization, 'the action becomes more and more routine and abbreviated' (Haenen, 2001: 164). Verbalizations can, and should, lead to abstractions, which 'enable learners to free themselves from concrete empirical contexts of concept use and empower them to deploy a concept in a wide array of contexts linked to a broad scope of goals' (Lantolf & Poehner, 2014: 66). These shifts in verbalizations and dialogue types as well as abstractions lead to the learners' internalization of the relevant concepts.

Finally, as outlined in Chapter 2, the goal in C-BLI is for the learners to internalize the concept(s), which means that the mediating artifacts have become tools for thinking and allow learners to achieve voluntary control of these higher mental functions and use them for their own purposes in a wide variety of practical goal-directed activities (Lantolf, 2000; Lantolf & Thorne, 2006; Vygotsky, 2012; Vygotsky & Luria, 1994). These tools for thinking will 'change both the circumstances of [learners'] language development and who they are as learners' (Negueruela, 2008: 190) and will allow them to be able to function in new ways in the L2. It should be noted as well that the conceptual development of learners is not a smooth linear process; instead, it is uneven, and as described by Vygotsky (1987), a 'revolutionary' process consisting of leaps, twists, backtracking, and pauses that nevertheless continually moves forward. The details of the C-BLI as they relate to the present studies will be outlined below.

Education or schooling, from this standpoint, is the unique place for learners to have access to scientific concepts, to have opportunities to use these concepts in purposeful language activities and to develop these concepts as tools for thinking in the L2, and therefore to achieve voluntary control of new higher psychological functions. C-BLI is a form of praxis, the dialectical unity of theory and practice, as scientific or conceptual knowledge, drawn from theories of language and epistemology from V-SCT, is united in practice with the use of conceptual knowledge in practical goal-directed activities. Theory and practice, from this approach, are necessarily mutually informing.

Division-of-Labor Pedagogy

A division of labor is when the labor, or the work that needs to be accomplished, is divided and assigned to different people. It is a term commonly used in business and economic ventures. In classrooms, teachers often assign group work, using various arrangements for differing purposes. Some reasons that group work is implemented include community building, social purposes, pooling and sharing resources, sharing ideas to refine them and considering diverse perspectives. While all of these may be important and productive, a DOLP (Division-of-Labor Pedagogy) should also be considered. A division of labor requires collaboration but is based more specifically on the need for collectivity. Petrovsky (1985) explained the nature of how collectivity is created:

> Owing to group work conducted in an atmosphere of the joint coordinated interaction of pupils, envisaging the exchange of the products of activity and thus the emergence of relations of interdependence and mutual control, the process of *learning* can acquire traits of genuine collectivity. (1985: 183, italics in original)

Let's break down each part of what collectivity is. It is group work but one that requires 'joint coordinated interactions' by students. This means that there is a distinct process of how students work together and interact. The students must also 'envisag[e] the exchange of the products of activity', meaning that they understand what the process entails and what the end result should be. In this collective activity, 'relations of interdependence and mutual control [emerge]'. Built into the activity and the collectivity is the need to depend on each other and for each person to have a stake in the process. Learners must be interdependent, share the effort required to accomplish the task by pooling their independent efforts in particular ways, to be able to accomplish more than they would be able to independently, all while envisioning what they hope to accomplish. Through their 'joint intellectual activity', learners are able to participate in the whole activity, achieving beyond their individual capabilities, even though they are responsible for only a portion of the total effort (Lantolf, 2000; Petrovsky, 1985). As a collective, learners are able to perform beyond their individual abilities. In other words, this collective process prolepts learners into their future abilities, as they develop their understanding and abilities in the internalization process from the various forms of mediation available in the collective activity, or DOLP (Cole, 1996). What once required the collective can, in the future, be done independently and it is the nature of collective action in combination with the teacher's expertise and mediation that leads learners' development.

In a DOLP, based on collectivity, each student is responsible for a particular portion of the activity. Their efforts are then pooled together and the product of their collective work is created. In this way, learners are able to participate in the product of the entire activity even when they bear only a portion of the responsibility at the beginning of the process (Cole, 1996). As each learner develops, the nature of the DOLP, and collectivity, must also change. The full and final future result is when learners are able to accomplish the full 'product of activity' independently. The size of each group, the nature of the joint coordinated interaction in each group and the exchange of the products of activity can differ between groups depending on the learners' needs.

Owing to the nature of a DOLP, researcher-teachers have opportunities to provide attuned mediation for individuals and groups. During the time when each student is preparing their portion of the activity, one-on-one mediation can take place to help the student develop their understanding of the part of the concept that they are responsible for and how to use the concept to guide their preparation. It allows the researcher-teacher to discover what the student does and does not understand in order to best attune the mediation. In addition, it is during this time that I-You (communicated thinking) and I-Me communication (dialogical thinking) occurs. I-You communication (communicated thinking) also occurs when learners share the product of their own preparation for the benefit of the group. During this time, there is ample opportunity for researcher-teachers, as well as fellow group members, to mediate the group's understanding. '[I]n joint intellectual activity ... [where] the pooling of mental efforts ... [is used] to overcome difficulties, ... communication of a higher type takes shape' (Cole, 1996: 183). The particular types of communication possible in a DOLP, which allow each participant to confront their own and others' perspectives, serve an important mediating role in the movement towards internalization.

Mediation, in the DOLP, is also present in the forms of Miller's (2011) first and second orders of mediation. The first order is through the use of culturally constructed mediating artifacts, which can be found in both the concepts and their SCOBAs. The second order of mediation can be in the form of a researcher-teacher who employs verbal, gestural and material mediation that is attuned to the individual and group's particular ZPD-in-activity in order to promote their development.

Details from the Research-Teaching Studies

In this section, I will outline the specific details that pertain to the literacy studies in particular, for the small group studies and for the classroom-based study. These include the scientific concepts and SCOBAs, division of labor, literacy activities, mediation and data collected. My focus for these studies was to determine (1) the extent to which a C-BLI approach to L2 literacy helps learners to develop their understanding of the scientific concepts (Foundation, Organization and Genre) and therefore their L2 reading abilities; (2) the extent to which a DOLP results in learners' appropriation and internalization of the roles created for each concept; and (3) the nature of the changes in mediation over time as the learners' L2 reading ability developed.

Scientific concepts and SCOBAs

As was outlined above, second language learners must use their L1 reading knowledge, their L2 language knowledge, their background knowledge, their knowledge of genres and how texts are organized to read L2 texts (Hudson, 2007). For the present studies, the overarching concept of L2 narrative literacy, comprising three interrelated and interdependent concepts of Foundation, Organization and Genre, as depicted in Figure 3.1, was developed.

The materialization of L2 narrative literacy is that of a triangle with the concepts of Foundation, Organization and Genre comprising roughly

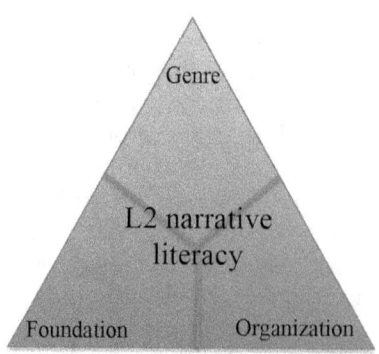

Figure 3.1 Materialization of the L2 Narrative Literacy concept

three equivalent portions of the triangle. The faint the lines separating the interrelated and interdependent concepts is done for pedagogical purposes. Although successful L2 literacy requires all three, in the development process students may need to focus on them separately at the start. Each concept builds on the next from Foundation, to Organization, to Genre. Once learners are able to take on the responsibility for each of the full concepts, the separation between the concepts would no longer be necessary. The basis for each concept will be outlined below along with its related materialization or materialized forms.

Foundation concept

The Foundation concept aptly serves as the foundational level for understanding the language of a text. It was created and adapted from Cole's (1996) research on Question-Asking-Reading (QAR) with young at-risk L1 readers. For Cole (1996: 272), 'reading instruction must emphasize both decoding and comprehension in a single, integrated activity'. For learners to comprehend a text, they need to understand the vocabulary and grammar/discourse. With their new understanding, they are then able to summarize the main idea of the text and predict what might happen next in the text.

In terms of vocabulary, beginner and intermediate L2 learners often consider reading a text in the L2 to be equivalent to creating a word-for-word translation. Some learners try look up every unknown word in a dictionary, while others try to guess mostly from context. When trying to contextually infer word meanings, L2 learners often end up inventing possible English equivalents because they fit with surrounding known lexical items and make sense from the perspective of their L1 schemas and scripts. As technology has changed, lately learners have been found to type large swaths of text into Google translate and even more so if it is an electronic text where they can simply copy and paste. One solution that has been proposed is to delay asking students to read until they have 'enough' language to know at least 98% of the words in the text (Laufer & Ravenhorst-Kalovski, 2010; Nation, 2006; Schmitt *et al.*, 2011). Other variations on this include altering texts or creating texts based on the vocabulary of the chapter in a textbook. All of the above can be problematic for different reasons and are not necessary from this perspective.

Learners first need to be taught how to deal with unknown words in a text. For the studies outlined in this book, as the researcher-teacher read a section of the text aloud, learners would follow along on their text, marking words that they did not know. From these, they need to determine if they can resolve any lexical difficulties easily and confidently through the use of context. Students may become overwhelmed with the number of potentially unknown lexical items, regardless of how often they may have seen the words in question before or in another form. Of the words that they are not able to resolve through use of the context, learners should first select the ones that they feel will be most beneficial for understanding the text to look up in a dictionary. Other unknown words may be able to be resolved later through their growing understanding of the context. These steps are important if learners are to avoid looking up every unknown word in a dictionary, as this is not developmentally helpful, nor is it an efficient use of time.

Next learners need to understand how to use bilingual dictionaries to help them develop their understanding of the particular lexical difficulties they have chosen. They often do not know how to use the grammatical and/or collocational information included in a dictionary entry to help them choose an appropriate English equivalent. They also generally do not investigate all of the possible meanings in order to choose the one that best fits the context. Researcher-teacher mediation will likely be necessary, depending on learners' particular needs, in order to help them develop an understanding of how to use the grammatical and collocational information, sort through the possible meanings, select the most appropriate English equivalent and put it into the context to verify. In this way, they are also building up their understanding of the context as they proceed, which may lead to solving other lexical difficulties through their growing understanding.

In terms of grammatical/discourse level difficulties, learners often do not pay adequate attention to resolving these, likely because they do not understand their impact on comprehension and are not sure how to resolve them. Difficulties that arise may include such morphosyntactic features of the text as prepositions, verbal tense and aspect, discourse markers and cohesive devices, for example. In addition, learners may identify repeated uses of a particular grammatical or discourse feature and need to understand the author's use of the feature in the narrative. As with resolving lexical difficulties, learners should consider if they are able to resolve any difficulties through thinking about verb stems and endings, for example. A second glance may be sufficient to remind them of what they already know. Researcher-teacher mediation will likely be necessary to guide learners' use of L2 grammatical resources. Both the immediate grammatical issue that will need to be resolved (i.e. determining the meaning and nature of the use of particular features within the context), and understanding the particular feature more in depth for future usages that they may encounter in the text are equally as important. Otherwise, each time they come across a similar usage, which is likely to occur in the context of a particular text, they would need to investigate the difficulty anew instead of understanding that it is a variation of what they had already investigated. Researcher-teacher mediation will also likely be necessary to help learners disambiguate lexical from grammatical/discourse difficulties, for the purpose of pedagogy. For example, if a learner comes across '*il lisait*', on the lexical side, they would need to know that '*il*' means 'he' and '*lisait*' comes from '*lire*', which means to read. On the grammatical side, they would need to know that *'lire'* is in the *imparfait* or imperfect form and to know how that form affects the meaning of the verb. As the *imparfait* does not have a direct English equivalent, this form often needs to be investigated by learners so that they fully understand the context.

To be able to summarize the main idea of a text, learners must have investigated a sufficient amount of lexical and grammatical/discourse elements to comprehend the language of the text. Learners must also be able to sift through extraneous details in order to create a mental model and a written or oral summary. Once the main idea has been established, predictions about future events in the text can be determined based on the mental model or summary. It is essential that predictions be based on events in the text, especially for L2 literacy, rather than on learners' L1 schemas and scripts of similar events, as they may be different in the L2. In the process of preparing a summary and making predictions, learners may become aware of misunderstandings or gaps in their mental model, which may be able to be resolved through further investigation of vocabulary and grammar/discourse difficulties.

The materialization, used in the studies, for Foundation, in Figure 3.2, unites the four tasks of investigating vocabulary and grammar/discourse and preparing a main idea and prediction. The nature in which the tasks build upon each other is also represented in their ordering, with Vocabulary as 1, Grammar/Discourse as 2, Main Idea as 3 and Prediction as 4. A black background behind the four elements of Foundation serves as a reminder that all are needed and that they are interdependent.

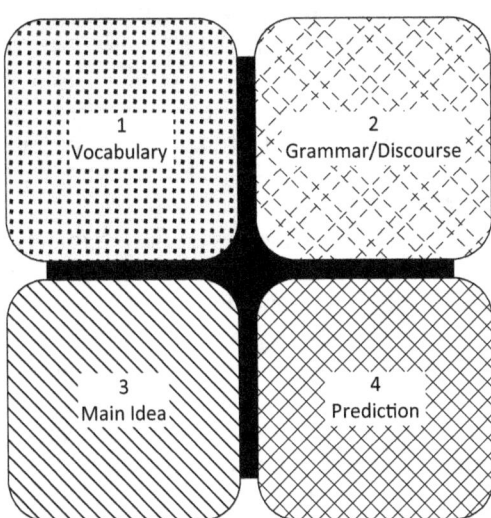

Figure 3.2 Materialization of the Foundation Concept

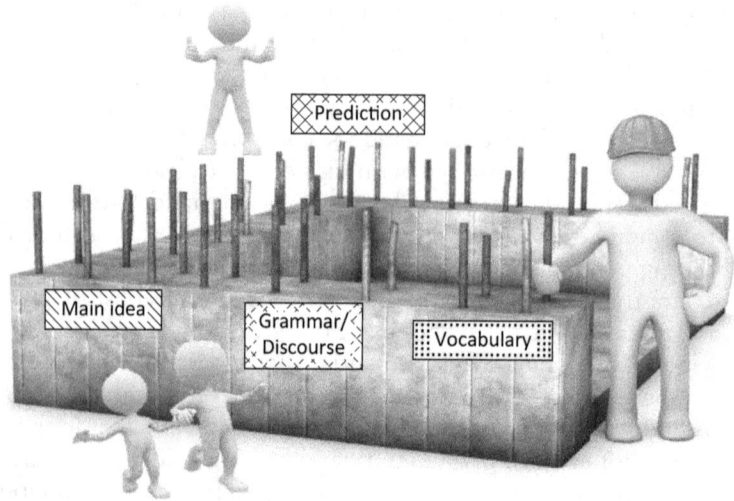

Figure 3.3 Materialization of the new Foundation concept (base of image from: https://clipartstation.com/wp-content/uploads/2017/11/building-foundation-clipart-9-300x200.jpg)

Even though the materialization in Figure 3.2, used in the studies described here, was productive and helpful for learners, I have since developed a new SCOBA for future use, see Figure 3.3. The visual aspect of the SCOBA has been enhanced to add in a representation that the Foundation concept serves as the foundation of what we are working on, in this case our understanding of the text, but typically represented as the foundation of a building. In addition, there are four 'people' present, which was implied before and explained to learners in the DOLP, but not explicitly represented. Finally, the location of the tasks with Vocabulary being the closest in the foreground, followed by Grammar/Discourse, which then lead to Main Idea and then to Prediction. The nature of the DOLP for each concept will be explained in detail later in the chapter.

Organization concept

The Organization concept aptly focuses on the organization of a text and it builds on learners' understanding of Foundation. Each genre of texts has their own organization and may be different in different languacultures (Agar, 1994). For these studies, we are concerned with the organization of French narrative texts. According to Hudson (2007: 179), '[t]he conceptual basis for narratives lies in sequences of experiences and events that are based in a culture'. In fact, '[n]arratives represent experiences based on events that are organized into knowledge structures' (2007: 179). How people experience an event may be different even though the event was the same. Take for example, an event such as a commencement ceremony at a university. Whether you are one of the graduates, professors, parents, ushers, president/chancellor, or security officer, you are likely experiencing the same event in different ways. Even within a group, such as graduates, each person may be experiencing it differently and therefore talk about their experience of the event in different ways. Furthermore, the way a person retells their experience of an event to one interlocutor may differ from how they retell it to another interlocutor depending on the nature of the relationship between the interlocutors. For example, if a graduate were to tell their child versus their grandparent versus their colleague versus someone on public transit on their way home from the commencement about it, the story would likely be different. It may include different details, a different ordering of events to create a particular effect, or different registers or lexical choices etc. Even with all of these differences, narratives in general are organized in recognizable ways within a particular languaculture.

The basis of the Organization concept, used in the present studies, is Mandler's (1984) *story grammar*, which is a part of schema theory. Story grammar is a framework for understanding how narratives can be organized and the nature of the hierarchical relationships present. Although we all have internalized L1 story schemas, or 'expectations about the way in which stories proceed' (Mandler, 1984: 18), they are generally implicit. This means therefore that they are unlikely to be open to conscious inspection without explicitly directed attention, as occurs in educational settings. For example, when students read a text in their L1, they may generally have a feeling about how stories unfold but if asked to talk about text organization or hierarchical relationships, they would have difficulty if they have not had explicit instruction about text organization. In addition, because events take place within particular languacultures and the people who experience the events are cultural beings, both the story schemas and the organization of texts from different languacultures may differ, at least to some degree. The goal of Organization is to help learners develop a conceptual understanding of the nature of the hierarchical relationships in texts and how these affect the organization of narrative French texts, so that this concept can become a tool for thinking and participating in literacy activities.

In *story grammar* (see Figure 3.4 below), a narrative, or story, is made up of a setting and at least one episode. Each episode has a beginning, development and ending. The development of each episode is made up of a complex reaction and goal path. Each complex reaction is comprised of a simple reaction and a goal and each goal path of an attempt and outcome (see Hudson, 2007; Mandler, 1984). Figure 3.4 is one of the materializations for the Organization concept that depicts the organization of stories, using *story grammar*.

In Figure 3.4, some components such as Story comprise other components – in this case, Setting and Episode. Others do not comprise other components (i.e. they have nothing below them in the figure), such as

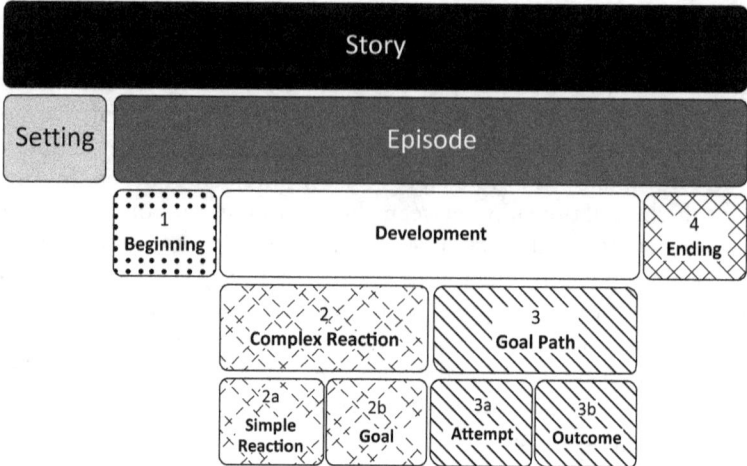

Figure 3.4 Materialization 1 of the Organization concept (adapted from Hudson, 2007: 180 as adapted from Mandler, 1987; Graesser et al., 1996)

Setting or Simple Reaction. For these latter components, definitions were provided to learners so that they could have a reference for understanding what each component entails. The Setting is the description of the characters, time and location. The Beginning is an event that initiates the Complex Reaction, whereas the simple reaction is an emotional or cognitive response. The Goal is a state that a character wants to achieve, and the Attempt is an intentional action or plan of a character to achieve that goal. The Outcome is a consequence of the Attempt, specifying whether or not the goal is achieved, and the Ending is a reaction to the achievement of the Attempt, or lack thereof. These definitions as they were provided to participants can be found in Table 3.1.

Because narratives, or stories, can have more than one episode, we also need a way for students to represent how episodes can be connected.

Table 3.1 Materialization 2 of the Organization concept

Setting	description of the characters, time, location
Beginning	an event that initiates the Complex Reaction
Simple Reaction	an emotional or cognitive response
Goal	a state that a character wants to achieve
Attempt	an intentional action or plan of character
Outcome	a consequence of the Attempt, specifying whether or not the goal is achieved
Ending	a reaction

Note: Adapted from Hudson, 2007: 180, as adapted from Mandler, 1987; Graesser et al., 1996

Episodes can be either causally or temporally connected. Temporally connected means that the episodes are told in the order they unfolded in time – first one event happened and then the next – and they are only connected through time. Causally connected, on the other hand, means that one event causes the next. For example, dropping a glass on the floor causes a person to sweep up the mess. In addition, the embedding of episodes can 'occur at the outcome or the ending' (Mandler, 1984: 23). For example, some stories may include an overall goal but have sub-goals that need to be accomplished first. The telling of a sub-goal would be an episode which is embedded within the episode of the overall goal. For example, one person may need to buy some yarn but in order to do that they may need to earn some money so that they can pay for the yarn. Finally, particular components can be deleted or can be inferred from the surrounding components. Depending on the types of connections, locations of embeddings, deletions and inferred elements, different hierarchical relationships and therefore different effects are created. Because of this, the materialization in Figure 3.4 would need to be expandable, rearrangeable, or manipulatable in order to capture that. With a materialized form of a concept, however, which allows students to manipulate objects, students are able to represent the organization of each particular narrative, with its unique connections, embeddings, deletions and inferred elements.

The concept of Organization was materialized through the use of Cuisenaire rods to represent the elements of a narrative/story. Cuisenaire rods are multi-colored and range in length from one to ten units, each unit with their own color, as they were originally used for learning basic math concepts. The Cuisenaire rods in Figure 3.5 have been constructed to match Figure 3.4 in order to demonstrate what each rod length and pattern/color represent. Story is represented by a light gray, Episode by a dark gray and the Development of an Episode with a longer white rod.

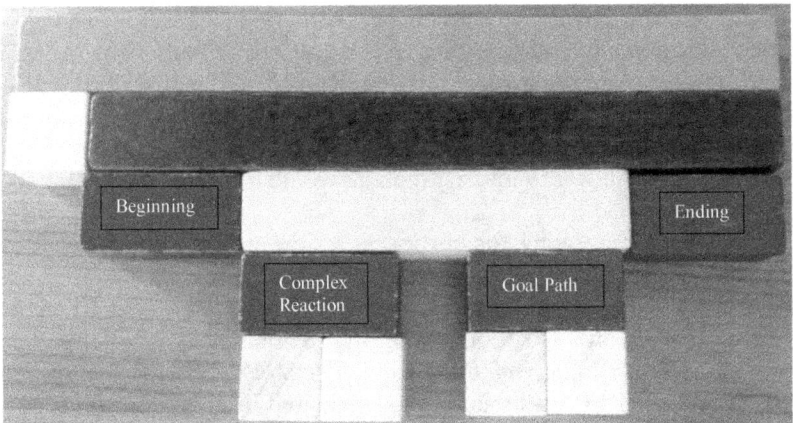

Figure 3.5 Materialized representation of the Organization concept

Beginning, Complex Reaction, Goal Path and Ending are all labeled on smaller dark rods. Finally, Setting, Simple reaction, Goal, Attempt and Outcome are the small white cubes. Importantly the materialized form allows learners to manipulate the rods to create the particular representation of the story grammar for each text. In other words, as different texts have different hierarchical relationships, the organization of each text, represented visually by the rods, will have different shapes. Manipulating the rods allows learners to represent the elements visually for each text, see the hierarchical relationships present in the organization of the text, compare the hierarchical relationships in different texts, and connect the different shapes/hierarchical relationships with the effects that they create on the reader. In Mandler's (1984) story grammar, graphic, but static, tree structures were used to represent the story grammar for different texts. Cuisenaire rods have the pedagogical advantage, over static representations, of allowing students to physically manipulate each rod representing a component in a story and in this way enhance their internalization of the concept and mediating artifact.

Genre concept

The Genre concept continues to build on the preparation and results of the Foundation and Organization concepts and aptly focuses on investigating the genre of the text. The Genre concept for these studies is based on the theoretical underpinnings of SFL in particular Halliday and Hasan's (1989) foundational work and Byrnes *et al.*'s (2010) overview of the GUGD's genre-based L2 curriculum. SFL, as mentioned in Chapter 2, is a meaning-based theory of language, and therefore focuses on the functional aspect of language; in other words, how language is used to convey meaning in a particular social context for a particular purpose (Halliday & Hasan, 1989). On this view, genres are 'purposeful, situated, and "repeated" (Miller, C., 1984) social responses...to demands of a social context' (Johns, 2002: 3). Let us take two different genres; for example, a grocery list and an autobiography. In a grocery list, to best convey meaning, that is to remind you what you need to purchase, language is best used in abbreviated bulleted form. No verbs are needed for the purpose of reminding you that each item needs to be bought. The abbreviations are sufficient for the buyer to understand and would be potentially changed if the buyer changes.

For an autobiography, the purpose is for the author to render a telling of their life, or portions of it and in the process to explain who they are, why they are the way they are, or to make sense of their life. For this reason, they are often written temporally, meaning from when they were young and advancing through their life. The author provides details and facts about their life and who else participated in it. The differences in how language is used in these two genres come from their different purposes and different social contexts.

Within a genre, each text has unique qualities due to the different particularities in the social context. It is 'an object in its own right... an instance of the process and product of social meaning in a particular context of situation' (Halliday & Hasan, 1989: 11). To continue with the example genres earlier, although we all may make grocery lists to remind us of what to buy, there might be variations in how we do it. We might use different abbreviations, and some might use paper while others might use their phone for the list. For an autobiography, a defining moment in my life might be when I was in high school and I will therefore highlight that, while for you it may have been in middle school or when you were in your first job. Yet the purpose for creating each of these texts, despite the nuances, will still be the same for each of them.

In order to investigate the 'social meaning in a particular context of situation' for a text, Halliday and Hasan (1989) developed a conceptual framework which includes the components of field, tenor and mode. The field refers to 'what is being talked about, or more broadly, what is going on in terms of the social activity of a situation' (1989: 49). The text might be about dinosaurs, about food items, or about meaningful life events and we would know that through looking at the language of the text. Tenor investigates 'how social roles and relations are being enacted' (1989: 49). The social roles and relations between the author and reader(s) for example can be found in how the writer addresses the reader, whether the writer uses academic language or language meant for young children. To continue the grocery list example, I might use quite abbreviated language for myself but would include many more details or even text pictures of the items needed if someone else in my household will be responsible for the shopping. The focus of the mode is on the role that language plays in the text as well as the channel, whether written or spoken, of the text (Halliday & Hasan, 1989). For example, does the language in the text give it a more spoken or written feel, despite the fact of whether it is a spoken or written text. For example, a speech is often written but performed orally and therefore, depending on the purpose or context, it may have a more spoken or written feel. For example, a presidential address is delivered orally but is prepared in a written form and has a written feel to it, even when delivered orally. The three components of field, tenor and mode are interrelated and are all affected by the purpose of the text.

Using the concept of Genre, which 'treat[s] both text and context as semiotic phenomena, as "modes of meaning"' (Halliday & Hasan, 1989: 11, 12), and the conceptual framework of field, tenor and mode, 'we can go from one to the other in a revealing way' (1989: 12). In fact, the context of situation is 'encapsulated in the text... through a systematic relationship between the social environment... and the functional organization of language' (Halliday & Hasan, 1989: 11). The difficulty in reading texts is that 'there is not a situation except the external situation of ourselves as readers... [therefore] we have to construct the inner situation entirely from

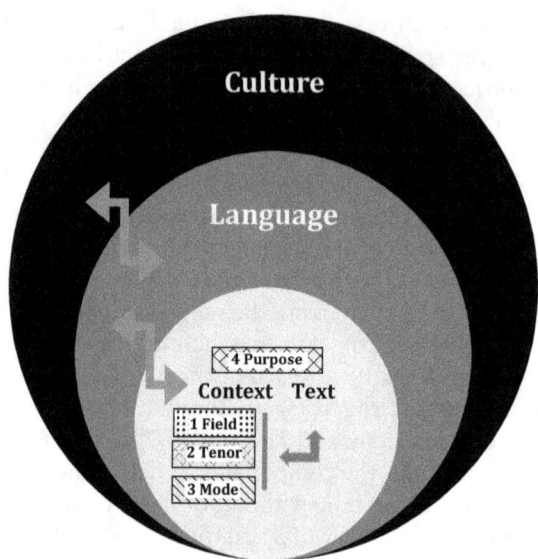

Figure 3.6 Materialization of the Genre concept (created from Byrnes et al., 2010; Halliday & Hasan, 1989)

our reading of the text' (Halliday & Hasan, 1989: 36). Through a detailed analysis of the language and purpose of the text, learners can understand the context of situation in which the text was created. The materialization in Figure 3.6 is used to conceptualize the key elements of genre as well as how to investigate and construct the context of situation and purpose of a text from the functional use of language in terms of field, tenor and mode. In the Genre materialization, the inner circle represents a particular text and context of situation, which is situated within a particular language and a particular culture. The arrow in the inner circle indicates the movement between a text and the context of situation and how that is done through field, tenor and mode. The arrows between the three circles or between a particular text/context of situation, language and context indicate how they are interrelated, interdependent and influence each other.

One challenge for learners is that they often have only an implicit and general pre-understanding of genre, which includes text types, but they rarely have an explicit or conceptual understanding of Genre, which they could use to investigate and analyze the language of a text. In other words, they rarely understand Genre as a tool for thinking that they can use in literacy activities. Genre builds on the learners' developing understanding as well as the results of the Foundation and Organization concepts. In order to appreciate the functional use of language in terms of Genre, it is necessary to understand the lexical and morphosyntactic features of the text as well as how the language differs in distinct elements in the organization of a narrative or story. Although the terms field, tenor and mode were used with the students in the study for convenience, these terms were also discussed in a way that was easier to understand. For example, Field was discussed as the subject matter or topic of the text, tenor as the relationship between participants and mode as the role of language in the interaction. Learners examined the text for how language was used to convey meaning in each of the three areas through, for example, vocabulary, pronoun usage (i.e. *tu/vous*), verbal elements (i.e. use of commands or modals) and what is foregrounded or thematized in each sentence (Byrnes *et al.*, 2010).

GUGD's genre-based curriculum included the use of scaffolding by instructors in the learners' ZPD; therefore, helping to establish a link and compatibility between SFL and V-SCT. The studies outlined in this book incorporated C-BLI, along with the concepts of Foundation and Organization in addition to Genre, as well as a DOLP. The goal was to maximally promote the learners' L2 narrative literacy development so that the concepts could become tools for thinking. The three concepts used in the C-BLI are interrelated, interdependent and necessary. For beginner or intermediate-level learners, none of the three concepts alone would likely be sufficient to maximally promote development in L2 narrative literacy.

Division-of-Labor Pedagogy

From L2 literacy and V-SCT viewpoints, learning to read is a 'joint, mediated, meaning-making activity between teachers and students in which the distribution of cognitive work must be systematically transformed' (Cole & Engeström, 1993: 22). This view is in line with Petrovsky's (1985) idea of a collective, outlined above, as it involves 'joint coordinated interaction', 'pooling of mental efforts to overcome difficulties', the 'exchange of the products of activity' and 'interdependence' (1985: 183). Importantly, in a collective, using a division of labor, learners with different abilities and different roles (in these studies) are all focused on achieving the same goal, which is to learn how to read, understand, interpret and analyze texts. A collective, using a division of labor, is in direct contrast to cognitivist approaches to L2 reading and differs from other group or collaborative activities as outlined above. Cole's (1996) QAR work, which served as the inspiration for this study, used a division of labor and roles in order to prolept students into their future abilities to independently read texts for meaning. Cole's QAR research was an adaptation of Brown and Palincsar's (1982) reciprocal teaching.

Prolepsis, according to the Merriam-Webster dictionary means, 'the representation or assumption of a future act or development as if presently existing'. In other words, it is a way of projecting the future in the present, or from Marx's perspective, studying history forward (Ollman, 2003). In this case, the future, complete act of reading, interpreting and analyzing texts presently exists in the form of the DOLP. What once needed to be shared will be able to be done independently in the future; what was once interdependent will become independent. Vygotsky's ZPD is another example of prolepsis as there are seeds of the ideal in the present; what a person can do with help today, they may be able to do on their own tomorrow. A division of labor is a way to collectively create the future. In the division of labor in Cole's research,[1] the L1 readers were able to participate in the entire activity of reading as a group before they each internalized the mediation and were able to independently read for meaning. The cultural artifacts and other forms of mediation helped students to participate successfully in the activity of reading for the first time and to take on more responsibility throughout the process. The students internalized the components in the activity of reading as psychological tools to enable them to read for meaning. As the students' ZPD-in-activity changed, so too did the mediation because it must be continually attuned to learners' individual and collective needs.

For the DOLP implemented in these studies, the concepts of Foundation, Organization and Genre were divided into their component parts and each component became a role. For Foundation the roles were: Vocabulary, Grammar/Discourse, Main Idea and Prediction. The roles for Organization were composed of the elements in an episode; in other words, the Beginning, Complex Reaction (including both Simple reaction and Goal), Goal Path (including both Attempt and Outcome) and Ending. In Figure 3.5, the roles are labeled on the dark two-block long Cuisenaire rods with the sub roles in white cubes below them. For Genre the roles were: Field, Tenor, Mode and Purpose. These roles were present in each of the materializations in Figures 3.2, 3.4 and 3.6 in polka dots, double broken cross hatch lines, diagonal lines, and single plain cross hatch lines. Laminated role cards were used to identify each role using a particular color (represented as patterns here) of paper with the role name written on each and to divide up the roles among the group members so that it was clear who was doing each role.

Small group studies DOLP

At the beginning of the C-BLI and DOLP for the small group studies, each learner was responsible for one role at a time for a particular concept. This division of labor was based on the learners' pre-test results and, as will be explained more later, the eight lowest scoring learners on the pre-test were chosen to participate in the study. So, for example, during the reading of the first text, for the first section of that text, each learner was responsible for one of the roles of Foundation. One learner was responsible for Vocabulary, another for Grammar/Discourse, another for Main Idea and the fourth for Prediction. The researcher-teacher read the portion of the first text aloud and then learners had time to prepare their roles. During the role preparation time the researcher-teacher would provide mediation one-on-one with each learner as needed to make sure that they understood how to prepare for their role and to help them develop the abilities they needed to prepare their role. Once all of the learners had prepared their roles, they shared with the group the results of their preparation, in the order of the roles, so first Vocabulary and lastly Prediction, as the roles build upon one another. Then each role would rotate to the next person so that each person had the opportunity to be responsible for each role over the course of the literacy activities. The pattern would continue until the text had been read in its entirety. The length of the section read, throughout the literacy activities, was based on the complexity of the text and on the learners' developing performance. Once the Foundation work had been completed for the first text, each learner was responsible for one role in Organization for each episode until the entire organization of the text had been determined. Roles rotated among the four learners after each episode. Finally, each learner was then responsible for one of the roles associated with Genre for the text as a whole.

For the DOLP, the roles for each concept were distributed among the learners and the results of their role preparation were shared collectively so that each learner could participate fully in the literacy activity even though at the outset they only bore a portion of the responsibility. As learners develop, they take on the responsibility for more roles at one time becoming more independent until they are able to participate fully and independently in the entire activity.

Table 3.2 represents the first possible distribution of roles in the Division-of-Labor Pedagogy.

In Table 3.2, Foundation is represented by the letter F, Organization by the letter O and Genre by the letter G. Each quadrant represents one learner, and each line of text represents one pass through of the text. The number in front of the symbol F, O or G represents the number of role(s) being focused on at one time for each learner. In the first distribution, the learners were responsible for one Foundation role for each section of the text until the text was complete, then one Organization concept role for each episode of the text, and lastly, one Genre concept role for the text.

All future distributions of roles were dependent on the performance of the learners in the literacy activities. The second distribution for the small group studies involved learners being responsible for two roles at a time, first with Foundation, then Organization and finally Genre, with the roles rotating after each section for Foundation and after each episode for Organization

Table 3.2 First distribution of roles in the Division-of-Labor Pedagogy

1 F	1 F
1 O	1 O
1 G	1 G
1 F	1 F
1 O	1 O
1 G	1 G

Table 3.3 Second distribution of roles in the Division-of-Labor Pedagogy

2 F 2 O 2 G	2 F 2 O 2 G
2 F 2 O 2 G	2 F 2 O 2 G

(see Table 3.3). There were still three passes through the text, with the focus first on Foundation, then Organization and finally Genre. In the case where two people were each responsible for roles such as Vocabulary and Grammar/Discourse, they first prepared their roles individually and then they shared them with the group. This way they were all continuing to develop their understanding of the roles and concepts and how to prepare their roles and taking on additional roles to be responsible for in the process.

Once learners were ready for the third distribution, they were each responsible for all four roles for each concept at the same time; again, with three passes through the text, first for Foundation, then Organization, and finally Genre (see Table 3.4).

The fourth distribution entailed the learners having responsibility for all four roles for each concept during a single pass through the text instead of in iterations, but still as a group of four (see Table 3.5). The fourth distribution could also have been done in pairs, again depending on what was appropriate for particular learners. Although the pair distribution was in the plan for the small group studies, it could not be implemented, due to time constraints.

Table 3.4 Third distribution of roles in the Division-of-Labor Pedagogy

4 F 4 O 4 G	4 F 4 O 4 G
4 F 4 O 4 G	4 F 4 O 4 G

Table 3.5 Fourth distribution of roles in the Division-of-Labor Pedagogy

4 F + 4 O + 4 G	4 F + 4 O + 4 G
4 F + 4 O + 4 G	4 F + 4 O + 4 G

Table 3.6 Goal of the Division-of-Labor Pedagogy

4 F + 4 O + 4 G
4 F + 4 O + 4 G
4 F + 4 O + 4 G
4 F + 4 O + 4 G

The goal of the DOLP is to develop independent readers, who are able to read a text, by appropriating and controlling the three relevant concepts: Foundation, Organization and Genre. The separate boxes in Table 3.6 represent the goal: four independent readers.

The researcher-teacher does not necessarily need to follow each distribution if the learners' development indicates that they are ready to go on to a later distribution. In the small group studies outlined in this book, learners did need to go through the distributions one by one and this was likely due to the fact that the process of developing an understanding of the L2 literacy concepts as well as how to participate, integrate and coordinate the many elements that reading and literacy in a second language entail takes time.

Full classroom study DOLP

For the full classroom DOLP, as there were 21 students with a range of literacy ability levels, the grouping for the DOLP was different. After analyzing the pre-test results, 12 students started with the first distribution of roles (as seen in Table 3.2) in three groups of four, six started with the second distribution (as seen in Table 3.3) but as three sets of pairs. Three students started with the third distribution of roles (as seen in Table 3.4) but as a group of three.

The concepts and roles were explained in a full class format. During the literacy activities, we had three groups of four students, three pairs and three individuals that checked in at the end scattered around the room. The researcher-teacher worked one-on-one and with groups as needed.

Participants

The learners in the two small group studies (now: research study 1 – RS1 and research study 2 – RS2) were all students enrolled in (an) intermediate course(s) in French that focused on either oral communication and reading comprehension and/or on grammar and composition. Both courses are considered fourth semester bridge courses (between the language and literature courses) and the first courses beyond the three required basic-level courses. Many students who enroll in these courses plan to continue studying French. Learners were either registered for one of the courses or both as the two courses can be taken in either order or concurrently. Participants were recruited from the bridge courses because they had completed the three basic-level French courses either at the university or taken their equivalent during middle and/or high school or at a combination of all three levels. Additionally, they were interested in continuing to study French and may have needed assistance to be prepared for interpreting and analyzing texts in the advanced literature courses. In the full classroom study (now research study 3 – RS3), all students were enrolled in a regularly scheduled fourth semester French oral communication and reading comprehension course. Some were additionally enrolled in the other bridge course focused on grammar and composition. There were four students in RS1, four in RS2 and 21 in RS3. Of those students, one student in RS1 was L1 Mandarin and two students in RS3 were L1 Ecuadorian Spanish and L1 Russian.

For RS1 and RS2, students interested in participating in the study took the pre-test and the lowest eight scores, as determined by independent raters, were selected for the study. Through happenstance, the four lowest scoring participants were available for one time slot (RS1) and the four students with the second lowest set of scores were available for the other time slot (RS2). The lowest scoring students were chosen because (a) they could benefit the most from participating in a study focused on L2 literacy development, (b) they were not likely to have access to other assistance, (c) they were the least likely to continue with their French studies, if they did not receive assistance and (d) it would provide the greatest challenge for the DOLP implemented in the study. All learners in both RS1 and RS2 remained in the study for the full 12-week course of instruction and assessments. In RS3, there was a total of 21 students enrolled in the section. All students took the pre-test, and it was rated using the same rubric as for RS1 and RS2, this time only by the researcher-teacher. Groupings for the DOLP were made based on the pre-test results.

The students in all three research studies had various backgrounds in French, some having started in middle school, some in high school and some at the university level. However, they all had been placed into their university level coursework through the use of a placement test. Three students were non-native English speakers across the three studies, but all were proficient English speakers, enrolled at the university level of an American university. Some of the learners wanted to major in French, others to minor in French, and some wanted to continue their French studies but did not mention majoring or minoring in it. Many indicated that they planned to study, travel, or work abroad in the future.

Research Design

Research questions

The three main research questions addressed in these studies relate to the development of L2 narrative literacy in intermediate learners of French:

(1) To what extent does a C-BLI approach to L2 narrative literacy give rise to learners' conceptual understanding of the Foundation, Organization and Genre concepts, and through these concepts promote the development of L2 literacy abilities?
   (a) To what extent does L2 learners' ability to read a text improve, as measured by the difference in scores on written summaries from pre-test to post-test?
   (b) To what extent does L2 learners' conceptual understanding of narrative literacy concepts – Foundation, Organization and Genre – improve as determined by changes in the quality of their verbalizations?
(2) Does a Division-of-Labor Pedagogy result in learners' appropriation and internalization of the four roles that comprise each of the three concepts: (a) Foundation – vocabulary, grammar/discourse, main idea and prediction; (b) Organization – beginning, complex reaction, goal path and ending; and (c) Genre – field, tenor, mode and purpose?
(3) How does mediation change over time as learners' L2 reading ability develops?

French texts

Texts chosen for the study were authentic French narratives with a range of lengths and difficulty levels. Narrative texts were chosen as opposed to other genres in order to help prepare learners for their upper-level literature courses. The texts did not have English translations readily available, which was important because the groups did not finish texts within the bounds of a particular instructional session, and I did not want them to be able to find English translations to read outside of the instructional sessions. It was also essential that none of the learners had previously read any of the proposed texts; therefore, texts with a limited likelihood of having been previously read by the learners were selected. Finally, each text was typed so that they could be double-spaced and additionally, no pictures were included for any text. No pictures were included so that I could determine that the meaning they gained from the text was from the words and not from the images. Finally, every reasonable effort was made to have each page end in a place that would be ideal for making predictions about what would happen next in the text.

The list of possible texts for the program included: *Archimémé* (Friot, 2007a); *Enquête* (Friot, 2007b); *Le Tableau* (Friot, 2007c); *Poubelle* (Friot,

2007d); *Papa Long Nez* (Delye, 2006); *La Belle au Doigt Bruyant* (Dumas & Moissard, 1980); *Le Champ du Lièvre* (Mbodj, 2005a); *La Pierre Qui Parle* (Mbodj, 2005b); *Le Roi et le Génie du Lac* (Mbodj, 2009); *L'Enfant et L'Allumeur de Rêves* (Piatek, 2006); *Le Prince Blub et la Sirène* (Gripari, 1997a); *Le Roman D'Amour d'une Patate* (Gripari, 1997b); *Celui Qui N'Avait Jamais Vu la Mer* (Le Clézio, 1978a); *Voyage au Pays des Arbres* (Le Clézio, 1978b); and *Le Gardien de L'Oubli* (Gisbert, 2006). The texts range in length from 700 to 6722 words.

Both L1 and L2 French instructors were recruited to rank order the fifteen French texts named above.[2] Four raters, who had agreed to participate, and the researcher-teacher read all fifteen French texts and rank ordered the texts in terms of expected level of difficulty for intermediate L2 French students. Any number of texts could be ranked at the same level of difficulty if a rater determined that they could be considered equally difficult. Raters were also asked to comment on the reason for their rating. A text was given a score of 1 if it was ranked as the lowest level of difficulty or easiest text to read and a score of 15 if it was ranked as the highest level of difficulty or most difficult of the fifteen texts to read. If texts were ranked at the same level of difficulty, each text was given the average of the score slots that they would have occupied if listed individually. For example, if three texts were tied as second easiest, they would have occupied slots two, three and four, and therefore each would receive the average score of three. The score for each text was then averaged across the independent raters and rank ordered. This ordering was used throughout the three studies to determine mid- and high-level texts for the pre- and post-test texts and to determine the order in which to read the texts for the instruction portion of the study. Table 3.7 shows the rank ordering of the difficulty level for the fifteen texts along with the number of words contained in each text. Asterisks in the table indicate where there was more variation in the rank ordering of the texts and with the exception of *Le Tableau* on the pre-test, these texts were not used.

For RS1 and RS2, *Le Tableau* and *Le Roi et le Génie du Lac* were chosen for the mid-level pre- and post-test texts respectively as their ratings were the closest (with the post-test given the text with the higher, more difficult rating) with ratings of 6.3 and 7.7, respectively. They differed in length by 555 words, with the post-test text being longer. *La Belle au Doigt Bruyant* and *Le Gardien de L'Oubli* were chosen for the high-level pre- and post-test texts respectively as their ratings were equivalent. They also differed in length by 1486 words, making both post-test texts almost double in length from the pre-test texts. This is important to note given that the learners had to complete the pre- and post-tests within a two-hour time limit.

For RS3, *Le Tableau* and *Le Roi et le Génie du Lac* were also used for the mid-level pre- and post-test texts respectively. *Le Gardien de L'Oubli* and *Le Prince Blub et la Sirène* were chosen for the high-level pre- and

Table 3.7 Level of difficulty rank ordering and word count totals for French texts

Text	Rater mean	Word count
Le Champ du Lièvre	1.9	1110
La Pierre qui Parle	2.7	1090
*Poubelle	5.3	791
Archimémé	5.4	608
Enquête	5.4	740
*Le Tableau	6.3	700
*Roman D'Amour d'une Patate	6.7	1998
Le Roi et le Génie du Lac	7.7	1255
L'Enfant et L'Allumeur de Rêves	8.8	1257
Papa Long Nez	9.6	2328
La Belle au Doigt Bruyant	11.3	1855
Le Gardien de L'Oubli	11.3	3341
Le Prince Blub et la Sirène	11.3	4000
Voyage au Pays des Arbres	11.9	2497
Celui Qui N'Avait Jamais Vu la Mer	14.4	6722

post-test texts respectively as their ratings were equivalent. Both post-tests were longer than both pre-tests, by a total of 1214 words. *La Belle au Doigt Bruyant* was no longer used after realizing that it could skew results because of its similarity to an English text. In RS1 and RS2, if its similarity helped learners to better understand the text, it only served to lessen the difference between pre- and post-test scores and render the results less significant.

Outline of the research design

In all three studies, learners first completed the mid-level and high-level pre-tests and verbalizations of Foundation, Organization and Genre of texts to determine their pre-understanding of these concepts and to determine their actual level of development, or what they were able to do independently. The scores from the summaries of the mid- and high-level texts served not only to make the final selection of participants in the first two research studies and to determine the appropriate distribution of roles for the DOLP, but it was also used to select the appropriate level of difficulty for the French text that would be used at the start of the literacy instruction.

At the start of the instruction phase, the researcher-teacher explained the concepts of Foundation, Organization and Genre and used an English text for learners to begin applying their understanding of the concepts to a text that they could easily read. For RS1 and RS2, learners then wrote verbalizations of their current understanding of the concepts and how they planned to use the concepts in their reading of French texts.

Our literacy activities included reading gradually more difficult French texts using the DOLP. The researcher-teacher read a portion of the text aloud, learners would prepare their role(s), and the group would come back together to share their role work. Then the roles would rotate, and the cycle continued. Mediation was provided according to the needs of the learners and the group through the use of cultural artifacts, the DOLP, and through the use of language/gesture by the researcher-teacher and group members. One of the researcher-teacher's goals was for the learners to continually take on as much responsibility for working through a role as they were ready for. Learners could use French or English at any time during the literacy activities. As instructional texts were completed, learners independently wrote a summary of the text, which was evaluated by the researcher-teacher using the rubric (see Appendix).

Data collected

For RS1 and RS2, data were collected over the course of twelve weekly sessions in Spring 2014 for each group of four learners, with each session lasting two hours. All sessions were audio- and video-recorded. Other data sources include: (1) survey data on learners' L2 background, (2) written verbalization data, (3) written summary for each text for each learner, (4) scores from independent raters on pre- and post-instruction assessments and from the researcher-teacher for all assessments, (5) notes made by the learners and (6) scores from the independent raters on the level of text difficulty ranking. The survey data on learners' L2 background included questions about their L1 and L2 experience (e.g. studying, traveling, living), the nature of their perceived use of the L2 in the future (e.g. major, minor, travel), and the nature of their past L2 reading experience (e.g. texts, interests, difficulties, goals, strategies and resources used, purpose of reading L2 texts, and any past L2 reading instruction). For RS3, everything was the same except, they met during their regularly scheduled class time each week during Spring 2016 and the score rating for the pre- and post-instruction assessments was done only by the researcher-teacher.

Verbalization data

As mentioned earlier, learners wrote verbalizations to document their understanding of the concepts and the nature of second language reading and how they planned to use, are using, or did use the concepts to guide their reading of texts. These verbalizations were completed before the concepts were explained, after they were explained (for RS1 and RS2), during the instructional phase and at the end of the instructional phase.

At the end of RS3, learners also created their own version of the SCOBAs for each concept according to their own understanding.

Summaries of French texts

Learners wrote summaries for each text read, which were anonymized and coded for scoring purposes. For the pre- and post-tests, the summaries were evaluated by independent raters and the researcher-teacher for RS1 and RS2 and solely by the researcher-teacher in study 3. For all instructional texts, the researcher-teacher scored the learners' written summaries. Summaries were evaluated in terms of learners' ability to employ 'conceptual generalizations based on discrete textual details' (Kern, 2000: 157) in a succinct, coherent synthesis of the main ideas without any unnecessary detail or inaccurate portrayals/details (Cordero-Ponce, 2000; Hedgcock & Ferris, 2009; Hudson, 2007; Kintsch & van Dijk, 1978; Riley & Lee, 1996; van Dijk & Kintsch, 1983). The scoring rubric (see Appendix) included five categories: (1) Main Ideas, (2) (lack of) Supporting Details, (3) Synthesis, (4) Generalizations and (5) Accuracy. For each of these five categories, there were five possible scores ranging from one to five with descriptors included for scores of one, three and five. Any scores from the independent raters that differed by two or more points per summary category between at least two raters were re-evaluated at the end of the study. The raters reviewed the French texts, the summaries, and their notes on the scoring, discussed their understanding of the rubric, and resolved any discrepancies.

Mediating artifacts and researcher-teacher mediation

The mediating or cultural artifacts included French-English dictionaries, French grammar reference books, notebooks, writing utensils (including pencils, pens, colored pencils, highlighters and markers), role cards, Cuisenaire rods, SCOBAs for each concept, and computers for writing and emailing the written summary for each text. Other bilingual dictionaries were used as needed by learners whose L1 was not English. In addition, language-based mediation was available from the researcher-teacher and from other learners/members of the collective during the instruction sessions. The researcher-teacher was available to mediate individual learners while they prepared their roles and the collective during the sharing of their role work. During the pre- and post-tests, learners did not have access to researcher-teacher or group mediation. Although the learners' role work served to mediate their peers' understanding through the DOLP, for this book, the analysis of mediation will focus on the researcher-teacher's mediation as she had developed the ability to provide highly attuned mediation, and this was her aim during the research-teaching process.

Conclusion

This chapter provides the link between the theoretical and the practical. In other words, how an understanding of literacy, Vygotskian Sociocultural Theory and Systemic Functional Linguistics can be applied to contexts with second language students who need to develop their literacy abilities. In Chapter 4, I will present the quantitative data and analysis from the three research studies. Chapter 5 will include an analysis of the learners' verbalizations about their understanding and use of the concepts in this study: Literacy, Foundation, Organization and Genre. In Chapter 6, I will focus on tracing the development of a student from the beginning of the research to the end including her changing understanding of the concepts and the change in her need for mediation over time.

Notes

(1) Cole's (1996) research was an application of Rommetveit's (1974 : 183) discussion of human discourse as a form of prolepsis 'in the sense that the temporarily shared social world is in part based upon premises tacitly induced by the speaker'.
(2) The texts were first scored using the Kandel and Moles French readability index (based on the Flesch Kincaid readability index used for English texts; http://www.standards-schmandards.com/2005/measuring-text-readability/). However, R. Kern (personal communication, 11 November 2013) and E. Bernhardt (personal communication, 3 December 2013) both L2 reading researchers, suggested that readability measures not be used as they are not very helpful, reliable, or valid and recommended instead that a group of French teachers be asked to rank order the texts.

4 Developing Second Language Narrative Literacy

Introduction

This chapter presents the analysis of the product of the learners' development of L2 narrative literacy from the three studies and answers the first part of the first research question: (1a) To what extent does L2 learners' ability to read a text improve, as measured by the difference in scores on written summaries from pre-test to post-test as assessed by independent raters? First, the results of the survey data are presented for RS1 and RS2 and for some questions for RS3 in order to provide more context and a deeper understanding of the learners and their past L2 reading experience. Next, the pre- and post-test scores for both mid-level and high-level texts will be compared and analyzed, including their Learning Potential Score (see Kozulin & Garb, 2002). The change in the scores of the learners' pre- and post-test text summaries for mid- and high-level texts will then be analyzed by summary category: main idea, supporting details, synthesis, generalizations and accuracy for RS1 and RS2. Finally, the overall results, including the scores of the instructional text summaries, will be presented.

Survey Data

The survey that the learners completed at the outset of the RS1 and RS2 studies included questions about texts that they had read in French, goals for reading in French, the reading strategies that they use, the resources that they use, their purpose for reading French texts, their past reading instruction and any difficulties that they have with reading. Some of these questions were also asked of the learners in RS3 and their results will be shared as well. The learners' background information provides some context in which to frame who the participants are as learners and readers, along with being able to understand not only their L2 reading history, but also the nature of any past reading instruction.

In terms of texts that learners had read in French prior to RS1 and RS2, only three learners indicated that they had read texts in their French textbooks. It is quite likely that they all had read created/adapted texts or excerpts of texts in their textbooks as this is very common in beginner and intermediate French courses. As a result of their response to this question, we may be left with the impression that learners do not actually consider their textbook reading as reading given that most did not mention it. Besides texts in their textbooks, the participants reported reading short fables, short stories, fairy tales and online current event articles. They also listed well-known French texts including *Candide*, *Le Petit Prince*, *Jean de Florette* and *Manon de Source* in addition to the French translation of a well-known text in English, *Harry Potter à L'École des Sorciers* (*Harry Potter and the Philosopher's/Sorcerer's Stone*). Both *Candide* and *Le Petit Prince* are commonly read in fourth-year high school French courses. These elements are not known, however: the nature of the text (i.e. whether abridged, glossed or if the language of the text was simplified), whether the texts were read in class or at home or if they were accompanied by overt reading instruction or activities. In RS3, some learners mentioned reading 'small passages/excerpts in French textbooks', 'assisted reading of a couple French novels', *Le Petit Prince*, 'an abridged version of Phantom of the Opera' and some guided readings. These are not only in line with the learners in RS1 and RS2, but also in terms of what students commonly read in lower-level courses.

In terms of learners' goals for reading in French in RS1 and RS2, their responses include wanting to be able to understand the main ideas and plot, or what the text mainly describes and expresses, to being able to read French texts more easily or without using resources (dictionaries or Google Translate), to read more complex texts, to improve French in general and to participate in the business world. While some responses focused on achieving basic comprehension, others focused on changes in the process of reading French texts – whether that be through relying less on online translators or for L2 reading to become more fluent like L1 reading so that regular use of a dictionary would not be needed. In RS3, the learners' goals included gaining confidence, learning 'how to effectively use a second language in reading', 'improving comprehension when reading', and even 'read[ing] a text and fully understand[ing] the ideas presented in it'. Learners' goals are generally to better understand texts, which is an important goal, though the goals of the studies aimed to help them develop well beyond simply comprehending what they are reading.

The learners' reading strategies are very closely linked, not surprisingly, with their French reading goals. Their reading strategies include participating in the study, studying in general, reading, practicing, reading shorter amounts, making inferences from contextual clues, learning French morphosyntax and vocabulary, using bilingual dictionaries and immersing oneself in the language through movies and music. The first four strategies as well as the final one listed above would generally not be considered reading strategies *per se*. Using contextual clues or dictionaries or learning in general more 'vocab/grammar' will be helpful, but these should not be the only strategies. While more reading or practicing do help, and reading shorter amounts may lighten the cognitive load, there are better tools that they can use to improve their literacy.

The resources that participants used when reading in French include texts, instructors, bilingual dictionaries, online resources such as Google Translate and wordreference.com, conjugation books and movies made of the text. Often when learners are not able to read a required text and do not feel that they have any other recourse, they will type into Google Translate any portion or all of a French text that they do not understand or watch the movie to get a general understanding of the text.

Their purpose for reading French texts includes the completion of coursework as the most common response. The learners also read French texts to improve their reading comprehension, to improve their general ability in the language, to increase their French knowledge, or improve their writing, speaking and reading ability, as well as for their personal interest.

In terms for L2 reading instruction, learners reported either that they had no prior L2 reading instruction or that instruction consisted of reading a text on their own followed by a quiz, or a discussion of the text, or by a series of comprehension questions. These are all quite common L2 reading activities, formative or summative assessments, or ways to clear up any confusion learners had. One learner mentioned that their teacher had them complete organizational charts which is likely the only one that had any type of instruction on how texts are organized.

The learners reported the following difficulties when they read French texts including understanding complex sentences, translating sentences completely, new vocabulary and grammar, and reading in general. The majority of their responses represent challenges stemming from L2 lexical and morphosyntactic proficiency and in the studies were addressed in the Foundation concept of the C-BLI. The learners in RS3 reported the following difficulties: finding the main theme, 'lack of knowledge of understanding how to effectively read in a second language', being slow at reading, understanding the key or smaller details, knowing enough vocabulary, knowing the tenses and being able to distinguish them, and difficulty with 'read[ing] and comprehend[ing] at the same time'. These are in line with the learners from RS1 and RS2 and are not surprising given the literature reviewed in Chapter 2 on learners' difficulties. While they completed their lower-level language courses and are in the bridge courses, they are cognizant of what their needs are given their future upper-level coursework.

The final question on the survey asked learners if there was anything else that they would like the researcher-teacher to know about their experiences with French or with reading in French. Two learners from RS2 responded, and both indicated that while they do not generally have difficulty with French vocabulary in texts, they do have difficulties with comprehension, especially as sentences become increasingly complex.

Scores on Pre- and Post-Test Summaries for both Mid- and High-Level Texts

Pre-test scores

RS1 and RS2

As outlined in Chapter 3, after learners in RS1 and RS2 read two texts for the pre-test, they wrote a summary of each in English. The two texts were: at a mid-level *Le Tableau*, and at a high-level *La Belle au Doigt Bruyant*. The summaries were rated by independent raters using a rubric (see Appendix) with the following five categories: main idea, (lack of) supporting details, synthesis, generalizations and accuracy. Each category received a score from one to five points, with five points as the minimum total score and twenty-five points as the maximum total score. Table 4.1 includes the scores on the summaries of both texts for both RS1 and RS2. The names are listed in order of mid-level scores from lowest to highest.

If learners were unable to finish reading the high-level text in the given time on both the pre- and post-test, they indicated the point in the text they had reached and wrote a summary for this portion of the text. Summaries were rated for the portion that the learner had read. Using both a Mann–Whitney U test (0.029, < 0.05) and Kolmogorov–Smirnov test (0.037, < 0.05) for two independent samples, there was only a significant difference between groups one and two for the mid-level pre-test summary scores. It is important to note that the high-level pre-test text,

Table 4.1 Pre-test summary scores for mid- and high-level texts for RS1 and RS2

Pseudonym	Group	Mid-level score	High-level score
Gisele	RS1	9.67	13.33
Daisy	RS1	11	15
Ella	RS1	12	10.33
Claire	RS1	12.67	5.33
Marie-Claire	RS2	13.67	11.33
Sean	RS2	15	9.67
Madeline	RS2	15.33	17
Elizabeth	RS2	17.67	7

La Belle au Doigt Bruyant, was an adaption of Sleeping Beauty, *La Belle au Bois Dormant*, with which participants may have been familiar and therefore the pre-test scores for the high-level text may be higher than if an adaptation had not been used. This potentially skewed the high-level pre-test scores higher, which may serve to reduce the significance of the difference between pre- and post-test. Most learners' scores decreased from the mid- to the high-level text, however, some learners' scores increased.

In addition, when Daisy (L1 Chinese, L2 English) read the high-level text, the researcher-teacher noticed that she began using Google Translate. Later when asked why she had begun using it during the pre-test, she wrote:

> When too many new words appear in one sentence, I choose to use google translator instead of using dictionary to find the meaning of a single word each time. And French is the third language I learn. When using French-English dictionary, sometimes I still cannot fully understand the meaning of the word. The google translator can translate from different language, including my native language, which really helps a lot. I usually use it for reading. (personal correspondence, February 2, 2014)

In the case of the high-level text, from the video, she seemed to use it both for single words as well as longer passages. It was clear that when Daisy was not able to comprehend a word or section of the text, she felt she had no other recourse to use other than Google Translate. Daisy's use of Google Translate for parts of the high-level pre-test text likely affected her score, making it higher than it would have otherwise been. This may have slightly skewed her high-level pre-test results, which may reduce the significance of the difference between her pre- and post-test.

RS3

For RS3, the learners also read two texts for the pre-test and wrote summaries of each. Their two texts were: at a mid-level *Le Tableau*, and at a high-level *Le Gardien de L'Oubli*. This high-level text, although rated at the same level as *La Belle au Bois Dormant*, had roughly 1500 more words. *La Belle au Bois Dormant* was no longer used though for the reasons noted above. The summaries were rated by the researcher-teacher using the same rubric as noted above (see Appendix). Table 4.2 includes the scores on the summaries of both texts for RS3 and their names are listed in order of mid-level scores from lowest to highest. If learners were unable to finish reading the high-level text in the given time on both the pre- and post-test, they indicated the point in the text they had reached and wrote a summary for that portion of the text. Summaries were rated for the portion that the learner had read. During the pre-test, only five learners were able to complete the high-level pre-test in time.

Table 4.2 Pre-test summary scores for mid- and high-level texts for RS3

Pseudonym	Mid-level score	High-level score
Victoria	10	15
Hannah	10.5	17
Samantha	13	11
Christina	13.5	10
April	14	16.5
Annalise	14	18.5
Desiree	15	14.5
Edward	15	16
Maria	16	12
Sandra	16	16.5
Daphne	16.5	18.5
Lily	17	19
Lauren	17	16
Amy	19	20
Portia	19	17
Bill	19.5	13
Veronica	21	20
Evelyn	21	13
Barbara	21.5	15
David	22	19
Johann	22	13.5

As you can see from comparing the data in Tables 4.1 and 4.2, they were similar at the lower levels of scores; however, RS3 had learners that were more advanced than in RS1 and RS2.

Post-test scores RS1 and RS2

RS1 and RS2

For the post-test, RS1 and RS2 learners read *Le Roi et le Génie du Lac* for the mid-level text and *Le Gardien de L'Oubli* for the high-level text. Table 4.3 includes the scores for the learners' post-test summaries for both mid- and high-level texts. In the table, Daisy and Elizabeth do not have a score for their summary of the high-level text because they were unable to even begin reading this text in the time allotted for the post-test. As noted in Chapter 3, both post-test texts were nearly double in length from the pre-test texts for both mid- and high-level. Additionally, the mid-level post-test text was rated at a higher level of difficulty than the mid-level pre-test text, although it did not qualify as a high-level text. Given that

Table 4.3 Post-test summary scores on mid- and high-level text for RS1 and RS2

Pseudonym	Group	Mid-level score	High-level score
Marie-Claire	RS2	12.67	15.67
Elizabeth	RS2	14	–
Daisy	RS1	15.33	–
Ella	RS1	19.33	22.67
Claire	RS1	21.33	20.33
Gisele	RS1	22.33	19.33
Madeline	RS2	22.67	21.67
Sean	RS2	22.67	17

the mid-level post-test text was at a higher level of difficulty than the mid-level pre-test text, it may have lessened the significance of the difference between pre- and post-test. The names in Table 4.3 are listed in order of mid-level scores from lowest to highest.

RS3

For the post-test, RS3 learners read *Le Roi et le Génie du Lac* for the mid-level text and *Le Prince Blub et la Sirène* for the high-level text. Table 4.4 includes the scores for the learners' post-test summaries for both the mid- and high-level texts. As noted in Chapter 3, both post-test texts were quite a bit longer than the mid- and high-level pre-test texts. Given that the mid-level post-test text was at a higher level of difficulty than the mid-level pre-test text, it may have reduced the significance of the difference between pre- and post-test. The names in Table 4.4 are listed in order of mid-level scores from lowest to highest. If learners were unable to finish reading the high-level text in the given time, they indicated the point in the text they had reached and wrote a summary for that portion of the text. Summaries were rated for the portion that the learner had read. During the post-test, only seven learners were able to complete the high-level pre-test in time.

As you can see from comparing the data in Table 4.3 and 4.4, they were similar at the lower levels of scores; however, RS3 had learners that were more advanced than in RS1 and RS2. In general, the scores of the RS3 group are higher than the RS1 and RS2 groups.

Change in Mid-Level Text Summary Scores from Pre- to Post-Test

RS1 and RS2

As for the comparison of pre- and post-test mid-level text summaries, the scores and percentage of change for RS1 and RS2 are given in Table 4.5, in order from lowest to highest pre-test score. With the exception of

Table 4.4 Post-test summary scores on mid- and high-level text for RS3

Pseudonym	Mid-level score	High-level score
Victoria	20	18
Johann	21	22
Samantha	21.5	23.5
Bill	22	23.5
Daphne	22	23
Desiree	22.5	21.5
Hannah	23	21
April	23	24.5
Amy	23	22.5
Maria	23	22
Edward	23.5	22
Veronica	23.5	21.5
Portia	23.5	23.5
Barbara	23.5	23.5
Annalise	23.5	23.5
David	24	21.5
Lily	24	22
Christina	24	23.5
Lauren	24	22
Evelyn	24	21
Sandra	24.5	24

Elizabeth and Marie-Claire, all scores improved, some more dramatically than others. Gisele had the lowest score in the pre-test for either group, while her post-test score was among the highest for either group; her gain score was 12.66. Although Elizabeth and Marie-Claire's scores decreased slightly, this does not mean that they did not develop their L2 narrative literacy abilities. The extended length of the post-test text in comparison to the pre-test text and the higher level of difficulty should be considered. Additionally, as outlined in Chapter 2, development is not a smooth process, and these scores represent assessments at two points in time. In order to understand Elizabeth and Marie-Claire's L2 narrative literacy development, more data from the process of their development are needed. A graph of the mid-level pre- and post-test text summary scores can be found in Figure 4.1.

A paired samples t-test, on both RS1 and RS2 groups' scores, was run after verifying that normality had been satisfied, and the post-tests had a significantly higher score than the pre-tests ($t(7) = 2.86, p = 0.024, < 0.05$). The effect size for this analysis ($d = 1.56$) was found to exceed both

Table 4.5 Mid-level text summary scores for pre- and post-test for RS1 and RS2

Pseudonym	Group	Pre-test	Post-test	Gain score	% Change
Gisele	1	9.67	22.33	12.67	131
Claire	1	12.67	21.33	8.66	68
Sean	2	15	22.67	7.67	51
Ella	1	12	19.33	7.33	61
Madeline	2	15.33	22.67	7.33	48
Daisy	1	11	15.33	4.33	39
Marie-Claire	2	13.67	12.67	–1	–7
Elizabeth	2	17.67	14	–3.67	–21

Cohen's (1988) convention of a large effect ($d > 0.80$) and Plonsky and Oswald's (2014) updated L2 field-specific benchmarks for intragroup contrasts for a large effect ($d > 1.40$). In addition, $R^2 = 0.38$ was found to exceed Cohen's (1988) convention for a large effect (> 0.26) but would be considered a small (although nearly medium) effect by Plonsky and Oswald's (2014) updated figures ($>0.25, < 0.4$).

From this point on, for all Cohen's d and R^2 values below, the updated Plonsky and Oswald benchmarks will be used unless the scores do not meet these levels, in which case the more common Cohen guidelines will be used. In Cohen's (1988) guidelines, for Cohen's d the effect sizes are small = 0.2, medium= 0.5 and large = 0.8. For R^2, small ≤ 0.13, medium is $> 0.13, < 0.26$, large ≥ 0.26. For intragroup comparisons in the updated recommendations of Plonsky and Oswald (2014), for Cohen's d, the effect

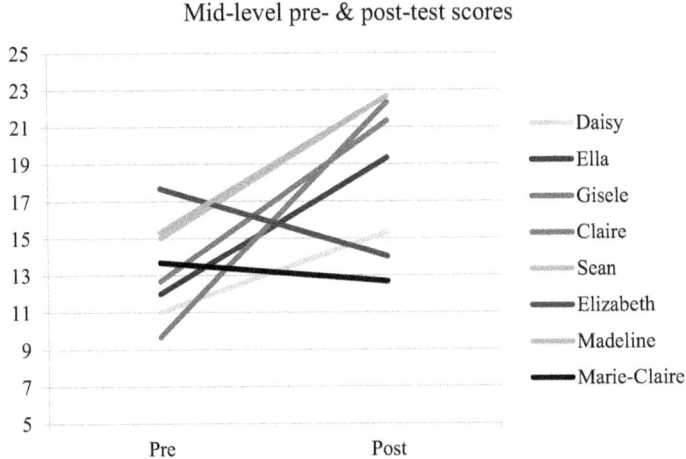

Figure 4.1 Graph of mid-level pre- and post-test text summary scores for RS1 and RS2

sizes are small = 0.6, medium = 1.0, large = 1.4. For R^2, small = 0.25, medium = 0.4, large = 0.6.

RS3

As for the comparison of pre- and post-test mid-level text summaries, the scores and percentage of change for RS3 are given in Table 4.6, in order from lowest to highest pre-test score. With the exception of Johann, all scores improved, some more dramatically than others. Hannah had almost the lowest score in the pre-test, while her post-test score was among the highest; her gain score was 12.5. Although Johann's score decreased slightly, this does not mean that he did not develop L2 narrative literacy abilities as he was already near the maximum possible high score, and it only decreased by one point. A graph of the mid-level pre- and post-test text summary scores can be found in Figure 4.2.

A paired samples t-test on RS3 learners' scores was run and the post-tests had a significantly higher score than the pre-tests ($t(20) = 8.16$, $p <$

Table 4.6 Mid-level text summary scores for pre- and post-test for RS3

Pseudonym	Pre-test	Post-test	Gain score	% Change
Victoria	10	20	10	100
Hannah	10.5	23	12.5	119
Samantha	13	21.5	8.5	65
Christina	13.5	24	10.5	78
April	14	23	9	64
Annalise	14	23.5	9.5	68
Desiree	15	22.5	7.5	50
Edward	15	23.5	8.5	57
Maria	16	23	7	44
Sandra	16	24.5	8.5	53
Daphne	16.5	22	5.5	33
Lily	17	24	7	41
Lauren	17	24	7	41
Amy	19	23	4	21
Portia	19	23.5	4.5	24
Bill	19.5	22	2.5	13
Veronica	21	23.5	2.5	12
Evelyn	21	24	3	14
Barbara	21.5	23.5	2	9
David	22	24	2	9
Johann	22	21	−1	−5

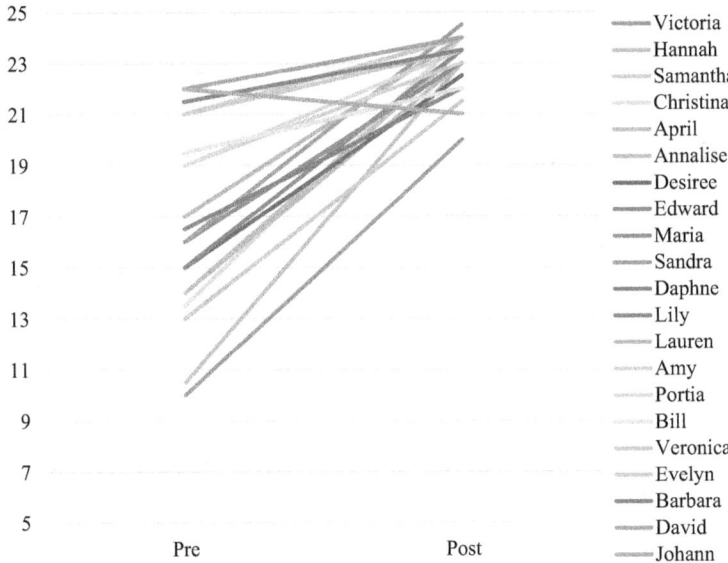

Figure 4.2 Graph of mid-level pre- and post-test text summary scores for RS3

0.0001, < 0.05). The effect size for this analysis ($d = 1.78$) was found to exceed Plonsky and Oswald's (2014) updated L2 field-specific benchmarks for intragroup contrasts for a large effect ($d > 1.40$). In addition, $R^2 = 0.57$, which would be considered a medium (although nearly large) effect by Plonsky and Oswald's (2014) updated figures (>0.4, < 0.6).

Change in High-Level Text Summary Scores from Pre- to Post-Test RS1 and RS2

As for the comparison of the pre- and post-test scores on the written summaries for the high-level texts, all RS1 and RS2 learners who had time to begin reading the post-test text improved their scores from pre- to post-test, as can be seen in Table 4.7. The names are in order from lowest to highest pre-test score. The changes in Claire and Ella's scores were the most dramatic with gain scores of 15 and 12.33 respectively. Although Madeline's gain score was the smallest, she had the highest pre-test score for high-level text summary and therefore had less room to improve. A graph of the high-level pre- and post-test text summary scores can be found in Figure 4.3 for those learners who started the high-level post-test.

A paired samples t-test, on both learner groups' scores, was run on the data in Table 4.7, again after verifying that normality had been satisfied. The high-level post-test scores were significantly higher than the pre-test scores ($t(5) = 4.62$, $p = 0.006$, $p < 0.05$). The effect size ($d = 2.47$ and $R^2 = 0.60$) was found to exceed Plonsky and Oswald's updated figures. In

Table 4.7 High-level text summary scores for pre- and post-test for RS1 and RS2

Pseudonym	Group	Pre-test	Post-test	Gain score	% Change
Claire	1	5.33	20.33	15	281
Elizabeth	2	7	–	–	–
Sean	2	9.67	17	7.33	76
Ella	1	10.33	22.67	12.33	119
Marie-Claire	2	11.33	15.67	4.33	38
Gisele	1	13.33	19.33	6	45
Daisy	1	15	–	–	–
Madeline	2	17	21.67	4.67	27

general, scores improved more in the high-level texts than they did in the mid-level texts in RS1 and RS2.

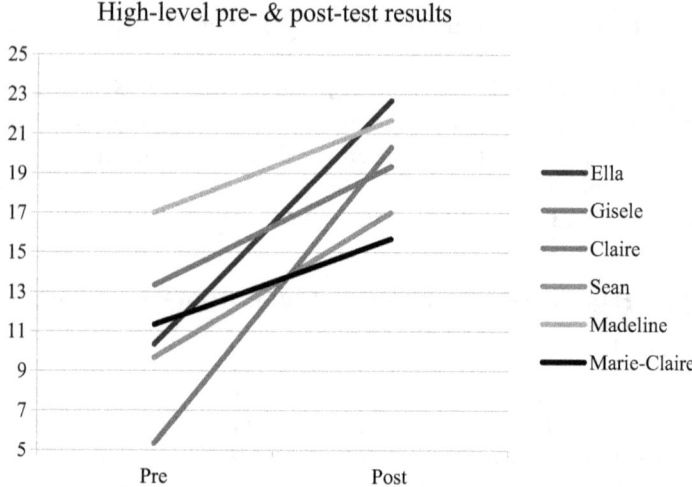

Figure 4.3 Graph of high-level pre- and post-test text summary scores for RS1 and RS2

RS3

As for the comparison of the pre- and post-test scores on the written summaries for the high-level texts, all RS3 learners improved their scores from pre- to post-test, as can be seen in Table 4.8. The names are in order from lowest to highest pre-test score. The changes in Christina and Samantha's scores were the most dramatic with gain scores of 13.5 and 12.5, respectively. The gain scores for David, Lily, Veronica and Amy were the smallest, as they had the highest pre-test scores for their high-level text

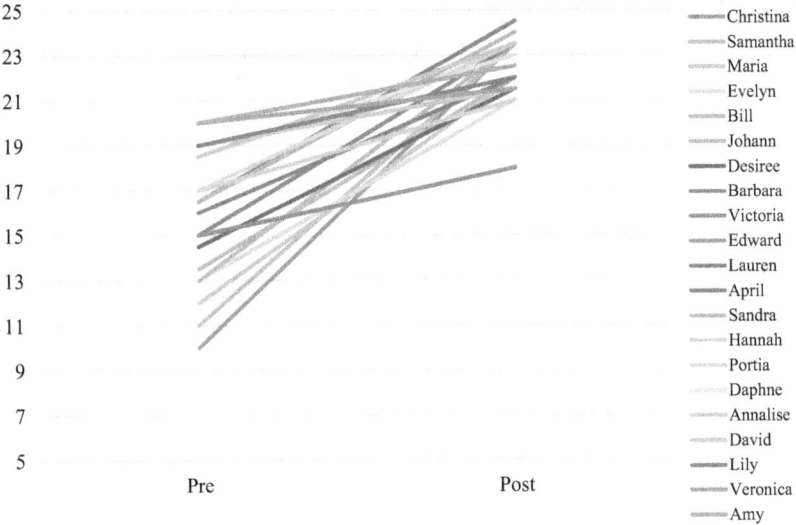

Figure 4.4 Graph of high-level pre- and post-test text summary scores for RS3

summary, and therefore had less room to improve. A graph of the high-level pre- and post-test text summary scores can be found in Figure 4.4.

A paired samples t-test, on RS3 learners' scores, was run on the data in Table 4.8. The high-level post-test scores were significantly higher than the pre-test scores ($t(20) = 9.09$, $p < 0.0001$, < 0.05). The effect size ($d = 2.88$ and $R^2 = 0.67$) was found to exceed Plonsky and Oswald's (2014) updated figures for a large effect size. In general, scores improved more in the high-level texts than they did in the mid-level texts in RS3. This may be because their pre-test scores were lower for the high-level texts than for the mid-level texts and hence they had more room for development.

Learners' Overall Change in Score and Percent Change from Pre- to Post-Test

RS1 and RS2

RS1 and RS2 learners' overall improvement for both mid- and high-level texts as measured in overall change in score and percentage of change are rank ordered in Table 4.9. Claire's development was the most significant, followed by Ella, Gisele, Sean and Madeline's development. Although Daisy's overall improvement can only be measured from the mid-level pre- and post-test texts as she was not able to begin the high-level post-test, her gain score was the next highest, followed by Marie-Claire. Elizabeth's development was the lowest but her change in score was also only calculated using the mid-level pre- and post-test texts, as was the case for Daisy. Both are marked with an asterisk in Table 4.9. In

Table 4.8 High-level text summary scores for pre- and post-test for RS3

Pseudonym	Pre-test	Post-test	Gain score	% Change
Christina	10	23.5	13.5	135
Samantha	11	23.5	12.5	114
Maria	12	22	10	83
Bill	13	23.5	10.5	81
Evelyn	13	21	8	62
Johann	13.5	22	8.5	63
Desiree	14.5	21.5	7	48
Victoria	15	18	3	20
Barbara	15	23.5	8.5	57
Edward	16	22	6	38
Lauren	16	22	6	38
April	16.5	24.5	8	48
Sandra	16.5	24	7.5	45
Hannah	17	21	4	24
Portia	17	23.5	6.5	38
Daphne	18.5	23	4.5	24
Annalise	18.5	23.5	5	27
David	19	21.5	2.5	13
Lily	19	22	3	16
Veronica	20	21.5	1.5	8
Amy	20	22.5	2.5	13

Table 4.9 Rank order of overall gain score and percentage of change for learners from RS1 and RS2

Pseudonym	Group	Gain score	% Change
Claire	1	23.67	349
Ella	1	19.67	180
Gisele	1	18.67	176
Sean	2	15	127
Madeline	2	12	75
Daisy	1	4.33*	39*
Marie-Claire	2	3.33	31
Elizabeth	2	−1.33*	−21*

general, learners' development from RS1 was higher than the learner development from RS2, although the learners in RS1 had the four lowest combined scores from the pre-test. As mentioned above, there was a significant difference for the mid-level pre-test summary scores between RS1 and RS2, but not for the high-level pre-test.

RS3

RS3 learners' overall improvement for both mid- and high-level texts as measured in overall change in score and percentage of change are rank ordered in Table 4.10. Christina's development was the most significant and Veronica's was the least. The percent change scores were generally about the same for RS1, RS2 and RS3.

Learning Potential Scores

RS1 and RS2

With the mid-level and high-level pre- and post-test summary scores, the learners' learning potential score can be calculated using Kozulin and

Table 4.10 Rank order of overall gain score and percentage of change for learners from RS3

Pseudonym	Gain score	% Change
Christina	24	213
Samantha	21	179
Hannah	16.5	153
Maria	17	127
Victoria	13	120
April	17	112
Sandra	16	98
Desiree	14.5	98
Annalise	14.5	95
Edward	14.5	95
Bill	13	94
Lauren	13	79
Evelyn	11	76
Barbara	10.5	66
Portia	11	62
Johann	7.5	58
Daphne	10	57
Lily	10	57
Amy	6.5	34
David	4.5	22
Veronica	4	20

Garb's (2002) equation: Learning Potential Score = (2 * post-test score − pre-test score)/Max score (121). Often the score from learners' independent performance on an assessment is the only consideration when investigating student performance or for placement in future educational experiences. By calculating the Learning Potential Score, teachers can incorporate the learners' 'openness to mediation' (Poehner & Lantolf, 2013: 329). It is possible for learners with low initial scores and high gain scores as well as learners with moderate initial scores and moderate gain scores to both exhibit a high learning potential. Whereas most researchers who calculate Learning Potential Scores do so with an actual and mediated score, in this case, the post-test scores, although completed independently, resulted from the internalized mediation from the C-BLI and DOLP, and therefore are used as a mediated score. The Learning Potential Scores and ratings for each RS1 and RS2 learner are given in Table 4.11, in rank order from highest to lowest mid-level LPS.

As for the mid-level texts, Gisele, Claire and Ella, each with low scores on the pre-test and significantly higher post-test scores, were rated as having high learning potential. High learning potential scores, according to Kozulin and Garb, are greater than 1.0, mid scores are between 0.71 and 1.0 and low scores are less than 0.71. Sean and Madeline, although they had moderate pre-test scores for mid-level texts, they also had moderate gains between pre- and post-test and therefore also generated high Learning Potential Scores. Daisy had a low to moderate score on the pre-test and had low to moderate gain score, which classified her as having a mid-level Learning Potential Score. Elizabeth and Marie-Claire, who had moderate pre-test scores, but made little gains, had low Learning Potential Scores. If Daisy had tried to finish two texts within the given time, it is possible that her Learning Potential Score for the mid-level text may have been classified as low.

As for the learning potential for the high-level pre- and post-test texts, Claire, Ella, Gisele and Madeline all earned high scores, while Marie-Claire and Sean earned mid-level Learning Potential Scores. The Learning

Table 4.11 Learning Potential Score for mid- and high-level text summaries for RS1 and RS2

Pseudonym	Group	Mid-level LPS	Rating	High-level LPS	Rating
Gisele	1	1.40	High	1.01	High
Sean	2	1.21	High	0.97	Mid
Claire	1	1.20	High	1.41	High
Madeline	2	1.2	High	1.05	High
Ella	1	1.07	High	1.40	High
Daisy	1	0.79	Mid	–	–
Marie-Claire	2	0.47	Low	0.80	Mid
Elizabeth	2	0.41	Low	–	–

Potential Score provides more information, especially to teachers, than do the pre- and post-test scores alone. Because of Marie-Claire and Claire's similar mid-level pre-test scores (13.67 and 12.67, respectively) and Marie-Claire and Ella's similar high-level pre-test score (11.33 and 10.33, respectively), they may have been expected to make similar gains on the post-tests. This was not the case, however. On the mid-level post-test, Marie-Claire's score was 12.67 while Claire's was 21.33 and on the high-level post-test, Marie-Claire's score was 15.67 while Ella's was 22.67. Both Claire and Ella can be considered as more open to mediation than Marie-Claire at this point in time. The learning potential scores could and should be used as a diagnostic tool to help inform future placement decisions or future instruction on literacy development for learners. Too often, only a single static score is used and as shown above, these do not provide enough information to determine their potential future trajectories.

RS3

The Learning Potential Scores and ratings for each RS3 learner are given in Table 4.12, in rank order from highest to lowest mid-level LPS.

As for the mid-level texts, all but two learners earned a high Learning Potential Score, with no learners earning a low Learning Potential Score. Although Barbara, Bill and Edward did not have high gain scores, they earned a decent Learning Potential Score because their pre-test scores on the mid-level texts were nearly at the maximum point value. As for the learning potential for the high-level pre- and post-test texts, six learners earned a mid-level Learning Potential Score, while 15 earned a high Learning Potential Score. Notably, the people who earned a mid-level Learning Potential Score on the mid-level texts all earned a high Learning Potential Score on the high-level texts. This could be something to further investigate. Again, those learners with low pre-test scores who had quite high post-test scores had very strong Learning Potential Scores. For the high-level texts, this time, those with high scores on the pre-test, while they did not have much room before reaching a maximum score, did not improve significantly and did not max out their scores, therefore earning them a mid-level Learning Potential Score. Finally, just as with RS1 and RS2, those learners with the same scores on the pre-test do not necessarily earn similar scores on the post-test, making the Learning Potential Score valuable for a diagnostic tool.

Scores on Pre- and Post-Test Summaries for both Mid- and High-Level Texts by Summary Category

RS1 and RS2

As the raters scored the pre- and post-test summaries using a rubric which contained five separate categories – main idea, (lack of) supporting

Table 4.12 Learning Potential Score for mid- and high-level text summaries for RS3

Pseudonym	Mid-level LPS	Rating	High-level LPS	Rating
Hannah	1.42	High	1	Mid
Christina	1.38	High	1.48	High
Annalise	1.32	High	1.14	High
Sandra	1.32	High	1.26	High
April	1.28	High	1.3	High
Edward	1.28	High	1.12	High
Lily	1.24	High	1	Mid
Lauren	1.24	High	1.12	High
Victoria	1.2	High	0.84	Mid
Samantha	1.2	High	1.44	High
Desiree	1.2	High	1.14	High
Maria	1.2	High	1.28	High
Portia	1.12	High	1.2	High
Daphne	1.1	High	1.1	High
Amy	1.08	High	1	Mid
Evelyn	1.08	High	1.16	High
Veronica	1.04	High	0.92	Mid
David	1.04	High	0.96	Mid
Barbara	1.02	High	1.28	High
Bill	0.98	Mid	1.36	High
Johann	0.8	Mid	1.22	High

details, synthesis, generalizations and accuracy – the change in learners' scores for each of the five categories for both mid- and high-level texts can be analyzed. Paired samples t-tests were run for each of the five categories and for both level of texts. Table 4.13 includes the p value and effect size using Cohen's d and R^2 for each of the five summary categories for mid- and high-level text summary scores. All p and Cohen's d values are reported for each category whether significant or not; however, R^2 is only reported when there is an effect for this statistic. In addition, a starred (*) value next to the figure indicates that the size of the value is based on Cohen's guidelines but not on the Plonsky and Oswald recommendations. The specific values for each are provided opposite. Only the RS1 and RS2 results by category will be provided.

Main idea

In terms of main idea, the post-test scores for both mid- and high-level texts were significantly higher than the pre-test scores. The effect sizes exceed the updated recommendations for a large effect. R^2 values were

Table 4.13 Mid- and high-level text summary scores for pre- and post-test by summary category for RS1 and RS2

Summary Category	Mid-level texts	High-level texts
Main idea	$p = 0.001$, $p < 0.05$ (significant) Cohen's $d = 1.49$ (large) $R^2 = 0.36$ (small)	$p = 0.009$, $p < 0.05$ (significant) Cohen's $d = 1.76$ (large) $R^2 = 0.44$ (medium)
Supporting details	$p = 0.355$, $p > 0.05$ (not significant) Cohen's $d = 0.38$* (small)	$p = 0.012$, $p < 0.05$ (significant) Cohen's $d = 1.95$ (large) $R^2 = 0.49$ (medium)
Synthesis	$p = 0.103$, $p > 0.05$ (not significant) Cohen's $d = 0.86$ (small) $R^2 = 0.16$* (medium)	$p = 0.011$, $p < 0.05$ (significant) Cohen's $d = 1.38$ (medium) $R^2 = 0.32$ (small)
Generalizations	$p = 0.185$, $p > 0.05$ (not significant) Cohen's $d = 0.76$ (small) $R^2 = 0.13$* (medium)	$p = 0.012$, $p < 0.05$ (significant) Cohen's $d = 2.20$ (large) $R^2 = 0.55$ (medium)
Accuracy	$p = 0.002$, $p < 0.05$ (significant) Cohen's $d = 2.04$ (large) $R^2 = 0.51$ (medium)	$p = 0.008$, $p < 0.05$ (significant) Cohen's $d = 2.40$ (large) $R^2 = 0.59$ (medium)

found to be small for mid-level texts ($R^2 = 0.36$) and medium for high-level texts ($R^2 = 0.44$). These results indicate that the learners developed in their ability to read French texts of mid- and high-level difficulty in terms of the main idea category.

A graph of the change in mid-level pre- and post-test text summary scores for main idea is given in Figure 4.5. The lowest score for each category is one and the highest is five. Gisele, Ella, Daisy and Sean showed the greatest improvement, while Claire and Madeline exhibited moderate

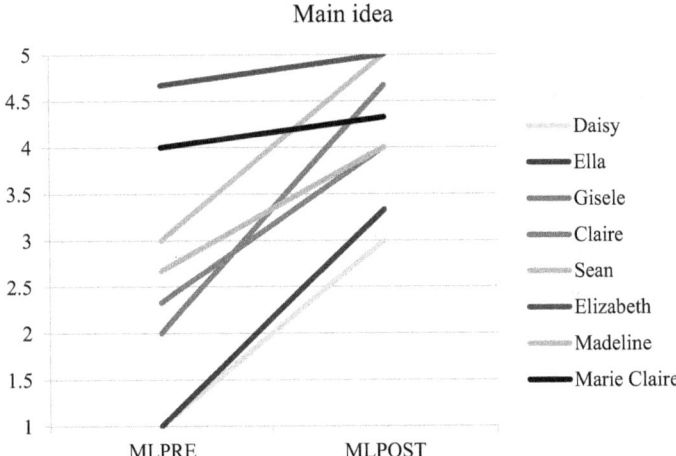

Figure 4.5 Graph of mid-level pre- and post-test summary scores for the main idea category for RS1 and RS2

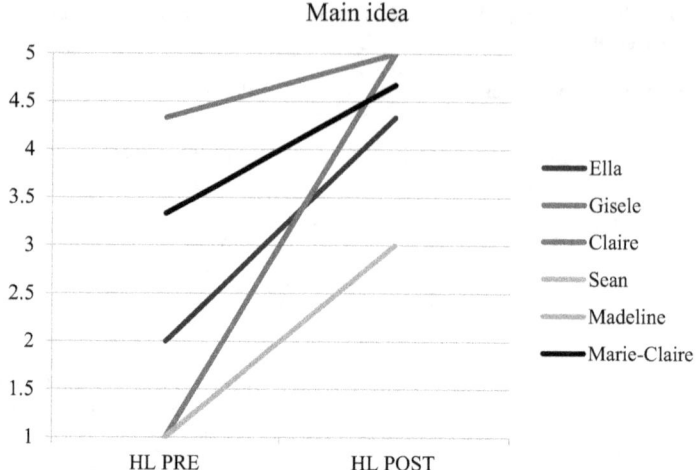

Figure 4.6 Graph of high-level pre- and post-test summary scores for the main idea category for RS1 and RS2

improvement, and Elizabeth and Marie-Claire, who had the two highest scores on the pre-test improved only slightly. Sean and Elizabeth scored the maximum of five points on the mid-level post-test text.

The graph of the change in main idea scores for the high-level pre- and post-test texts is given in Figure 4.6. Marie-Claire's line is superimposed on Madeline's line as they had the same scores on both pre- and post-test. Claire's score improved from the lowest on the pre-test (1) to the highest score (5) on the post-test. Sean, Ella and Marie-Claire also manifested a marked change in their scores from pre- to post-test. Gisele, who had a high pre-test score and therefore less room for improvement, still reached the maximum score possible on the post-test.

Supporting details

The statistics for supporting details indicated in Table 4.13 (p. 77) show significant improvement from pre- to post-test for high-level texts only. Although there was no significant change in performance on the mid-level texts, Cohen's recommended values show a small effect size. The graph in Figure 4.7 shows the change in pre- to post-test scores with regard to supporting details for mid-level texts. Gisele's development was the most notable. Daisy and Claire improved moderately, while Madeline, Sean and Ella improved only slightly (Madeline's line is superimposed on Sean's). Elizabeth and Marie-Claire's scores decreased from pre- to post-test. One possible reason, besides the increase in length and difficulty level for the two texts, is that sometimes as learners' reading ability improves and they are able to understand more of the text, they want to demonstrate their improved comprehension by including all known details. The

Developing Second Language Narrative Literacy 79

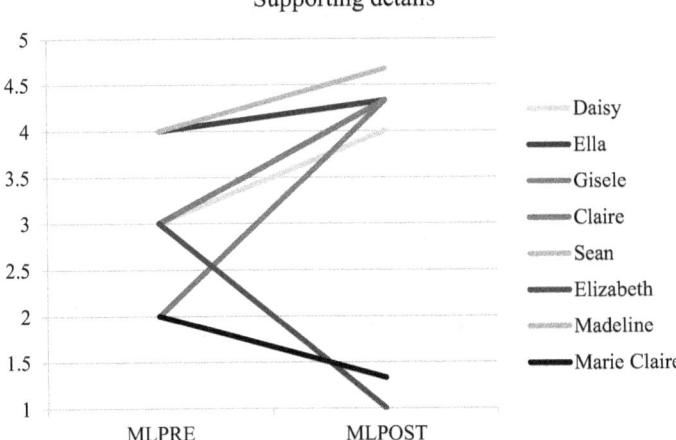

Figure 4.7 Graph of mid-level pre- and post-test summary scores for the supporting details category for RS1 and RS2

genre of a summary, the assessment for the current study, however, prioritizes main ideas over supporting details.

As for the difference in high-level pre- and post-test scores for the supporting details category, all learners except Marie Claire, improved, with Ella and Claire's growth showing the strongest improvement. Marie-Claire's score from pre- to post-test for supporting details remained at the same level. Perhaps she was able to understand fewer supporting details for the high-level text and therefore did not include them as she did in the mid-level post-test text summary. A graph of the scores can be found in Figure 4.8. Elizabeth and Daisy's scores were not included as they did not have time to start the high-level post-test text.

Synthesis

The statistics indicated in Table 4.13 for the synthesis category show significant improvement from pre- to post-test for high-level texts only. Although there was no significant change in performance on the mid-level texts, there was a small effect size ($d = 0.86$) according to the updated Plonsky and Oswald recommended values and a medium effect size for R^2 (0.16) according to Cohen's recommended values. The moderate gains in the synthesis category may have resulted from the indirect rather than explicit focus on how to provide a succinct, coherent and organized synthesis for the text summaries.

Figure 4.9 is the graph of the mid-level pre- and post-test scores for the synthesis category. The change in Gisele, Claire and Sean's scores was the most dramatic, while Daisy, Ella and Madeline also improved. Additionally, Madeline scored the maximum possible points for this category. Neither Elizabeth nor Marie-Claire improved (Marie-Claire's line

80 Second Language Literacy Pedagogy

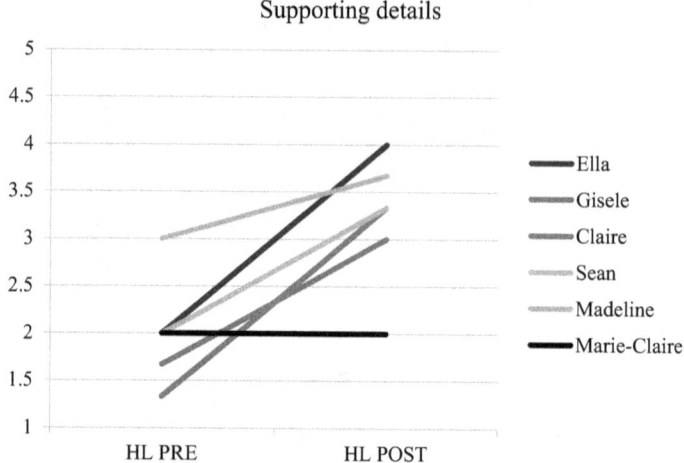

Figure 4.8 Graph of high-level pre- and post-test summary scores for the supporting details category for RS1 and RS2

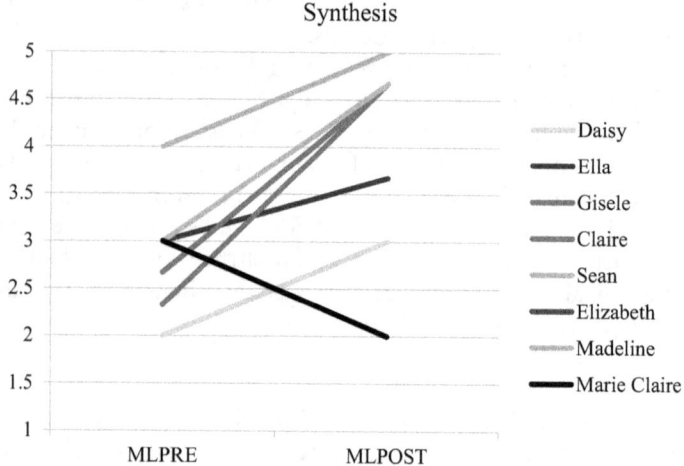

Figure 4.9 Graph of mid-level pre- and post-test summary scores for the synthesis category for RS1 and RS2

is superimposed on Elizabeth's). Again, the increased level and length of the mid-level post-test text may have played a role in the mid-level post-test text summary scores.

The graph showing the change in high-level pre- and post-test scores for the synthesis category can be found in Figure 4.10. Claire improved the most and Ella, Gisele and Sean improved significantly. Madeline and Marie-Claire improved, although only slightly.

The fact that the change in pre- to post-test scores was more significant for the high-level text summaries seems to confirm the effect that

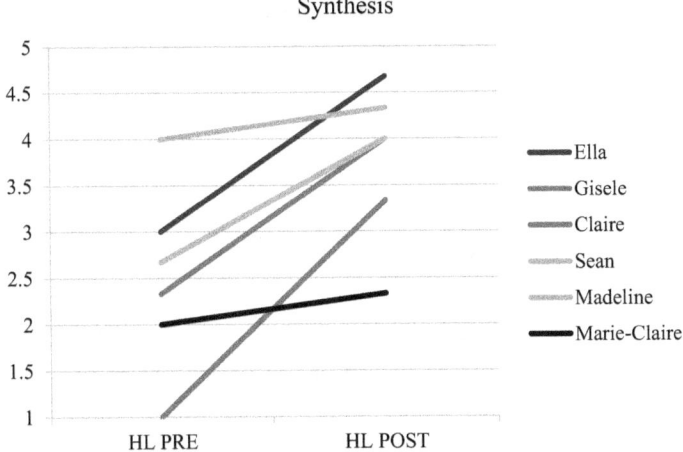

Figure 4.10 Graph of high-level pre- and post-test summary scores for the synthesis category for RS1 and RS2

Oded and Walters (2001) found in their study. The creation of a summary for a text correlated more strongly with more difficult texts than it did for less difficult texts. As they claimed, this may be due to the level of processing that the learners needed to do in order to read more difficult texts.

Generalizations

In the fourth summary category, generalizations, the statistics, as indicated in Table 4.13, show significant improvement from pre- to post-test for high-level texts only. Although there was no significant change in performance on the mid-level texts, there was a small effect for Cohen's d, using the updated Plonsky and Oswald recommended values, and a medium effect for R^2, using Cohen's recommendations. Although the use of generalizations was briefly discussed during the intervention phase of the current study, it was not the primary focus.

In Figure 4.11, the graph of the mid-level pre- and post-test summary shows improvement for Ella, Gisele, Claire, Sean and Madeline. Gisele's growth was the strongest and she scored the maximum possible points for this category on the post-test. Daisy, Elizabeth and Marie-Claire's scores did not improve. Again, the increased level and length of the post-test in comparison to the pre-test may have played a role. In addition, as Daisy's L1 is Chinese, she may have had less access to terms that could be used to generalize across text details.

Figure 4.12 is the graph of the high-level pre- and post-test text summary scores for the generalizations category. All learners improved, with Ella and Claire's growth being the strongest. Gisele, Sean and

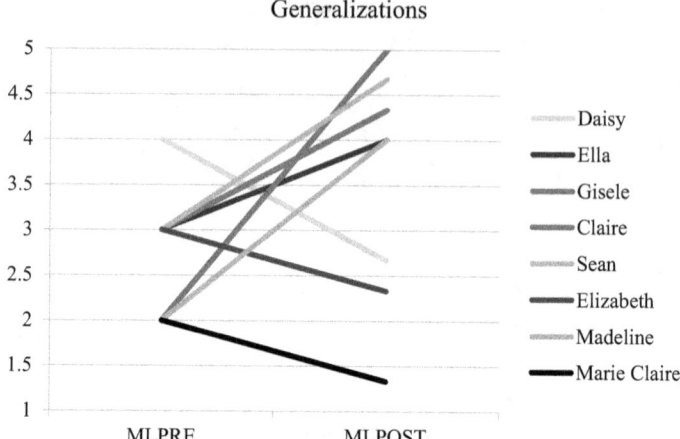

Figure 4.11 Graph of mid-level pre- and post-test summary scores for the generalizations category for RS1 and RS2

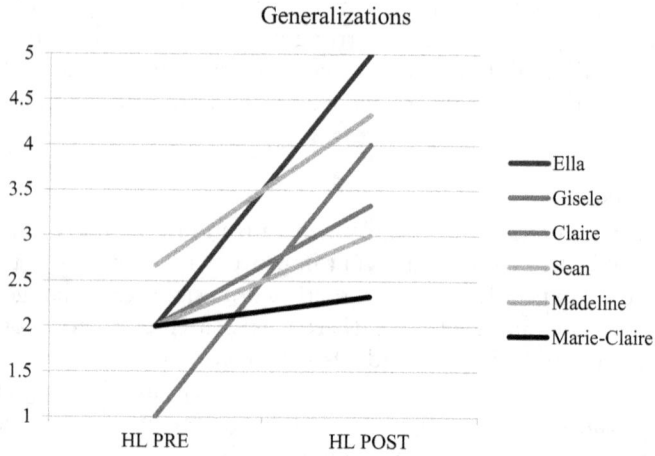

Figure 4.12 Graph of high-level pre- and post-test summary scores for the generalizations category for RS1 and RS2

Madeline's improvement was moderate, while Marie-Claire's was minimal. Ella scored the maximum possible points for this category on the post-test.

Accuracy

The statistics for accuracy, indicated in Table 4.13, show significant improvement from pre- to post-test for both mid- and high-level texts. The effect sizes exceed the updated Plonsky and Oswald recommendations for a large effect and R^2 values were medium for both mid- and

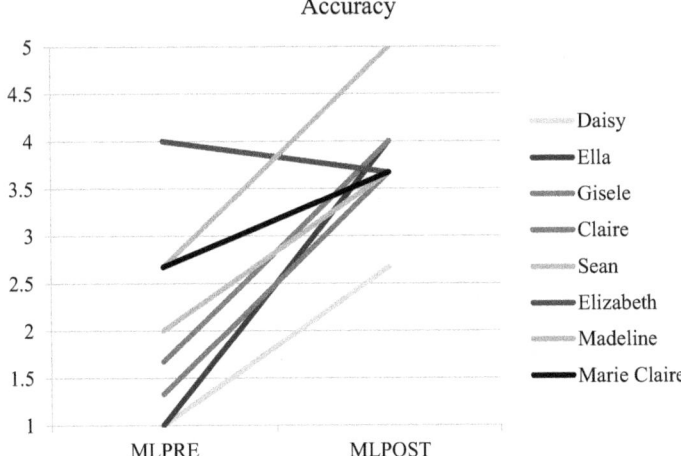

Figure 4.13 Graph of mid-level pre- and post-test summary scores for the accuracy category for RS1 and RS2

high-level texts. These results indicate that the learners developed in their ability to read French texts of mid- and high-level difficulty in terms of accuracy.

Figure 4.13 shows the graph of the change in mid-level pre- and post-test summary scores for the accuracy category. All learners improved, except for Elizabeth who had a slight decline. Gisele, Claire and Madeline's improvements made the most significant improvements. Madeline scored the maximum possible points on the post-test for the accuracy category. Even though the improvements were significant, the longer length and more difficult rating for the pre- and post-test mid-level texts may have played a role in the amount of improvement for the post-test text summaries. For the pre-test, a majority of the learners scored a two or below for the accuracy category, which were the lowest scores in any of the categories. As Elizabeth was the highest scorer for the mid-level pre-test text summaries in the main idea and accuracy categories and therefore had less room for improvement and these two categories were the ones most directly affected by the C-BLI, this may also explain her lower rate of improvement.

The graph of the change in pre- to post-test scores for the accuracy category for the high-level texts can be found in Figure 4.14. All learners improved, although Claire, Ella and Marie-Claire's scores improved the most. Sean made moderate progress, while Gisele and Madeline improved only slightly. As Madeline's pre-test score was fairly high, she had less room for improvement.

There is more to investigate in terms of the breakdown by rubric category for mid- and high-level pre- and post-test scores. As working on

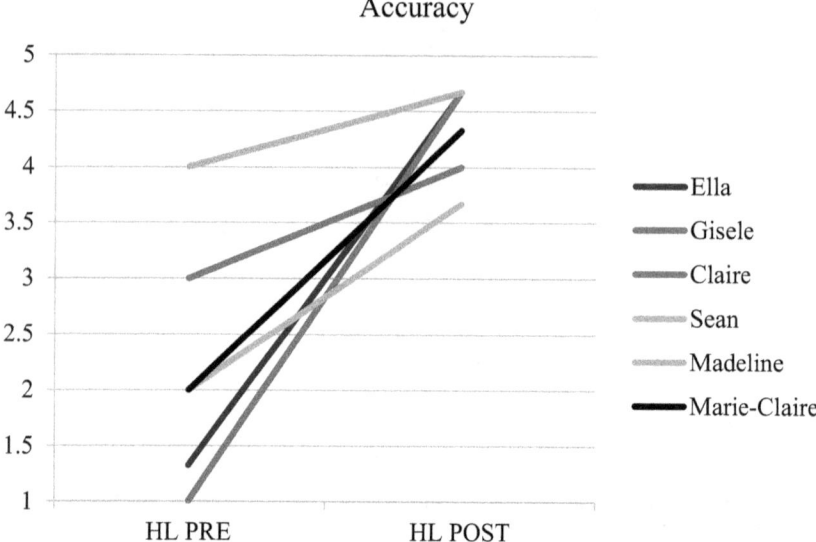

Figure 4.14 Graph of high-level pre- and post-test summary scores for the accuracy category for RS1 and RS2

finding main ideas is a critical part of the C-BLI, it makes sense that learners would improve significantly in this category. In addition, with L2 literacy, L2 learners, when they are not sure or cannot make sense out of enough of the discourse, will fill in with ideas from their L1 schemas and scripts. This often leads to inaccurate statements about what happened in the text. Given this, it is also not surprising that with the help of the C-BLI, learners had more tools and did not only have to rely on their L1 schemas and scripts, hence why the accuracy category also showed a significant difference. While there were some gains for mid-level texts and significant gains for high-level texts for supporting ideas, generalizations and synthesis, there may have been more if the pedagogy had incorporated some focus on these ideas or the activity of summary writing, making the literacy connection between reading and writing more explicit.

Overall Results RS1 and RS2

In this section, the overall results showing both product and process will be presented. In Figure 4.15, the scores from not only the pre- and post-test summaries for both mid- and high-level texts are given but the scores from the low- and mid-level summaries produced by the learners during instruction are also included. In general, the scores decrease from the mid-level to the high-level during the pre-test phase. There are a couple exceptions, which may be due, as mentioned above, to the similarity of the high-level pre-test story to a well-known text. The scores on the

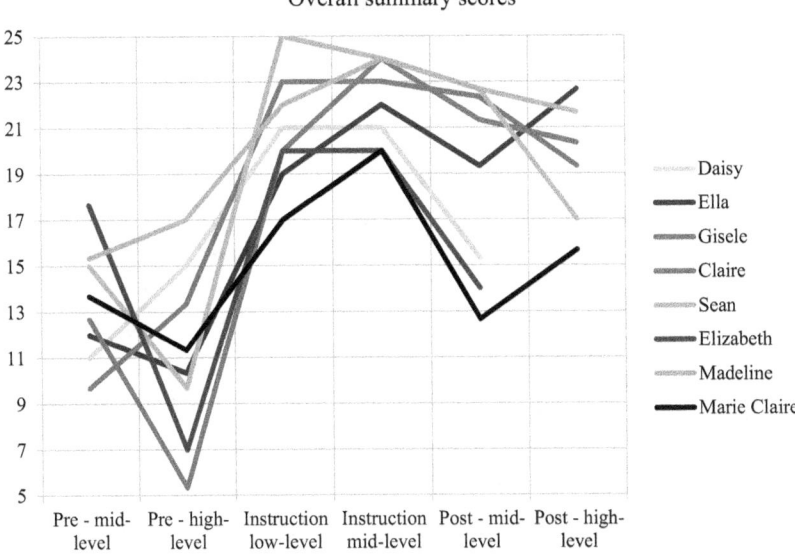

Figure 4.15 Graph of all summary scores including instructional texts for for RS1 and RS2

low-level instructional text summaries then increase sharply followed by a slight decline, increase or stable score for the mid-level instructional text. As the text level is more difficult, but at the same time learners are developing their L2 narrative literacy ability, none of the changes in scores for the second instructional text are surprising. Development is not a process that unfolds smoothly and continually in a monotonic way. It is, as Vygotsky (1987) described, erratic and revolutionary. Finally, for most learners, the scores from the mid-level post-test summaries are higher than the high-level post-test summaries, which again is not unexpected.

In Figure 4.16, we can see a graph of only the scores for the mid-level summaries from pre-test to instructional text to post-test. Essentially, the scores improve from pre-test to instructional text and then decrease for the post-test. Again, they do not return to the level of the pre-test, with the exception of Elizabeth and Marie-Claire. The mid-level post-test text was more difficult and almost double in length from the mid-level pre-test text, which may have played a role in Elizabeth and Marie-Claire's results.

Figure 4.17 is a graph of the scores from only the instructional text summaries. Ella, Claire, Madeline and Marie-Claire's scores increase, while Gisele and Daisy's scores remain the same. Sean and Elizabeth's scores decrease slightly. As the mid-level text was more difficult, it is not surprising that some scores would decrease slightly, although this does not mean that the learners were not developing throughout the instructional phase of the study. Importantly, to better understand the nature of the

86 Second Language Literacy Pedagogy

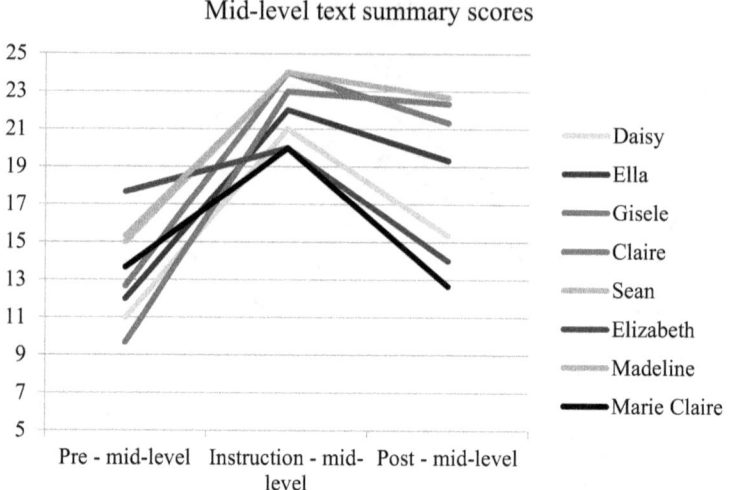

Figure 4.16 Graph of mid-level text summary scores including instruction for RS1 and RS2

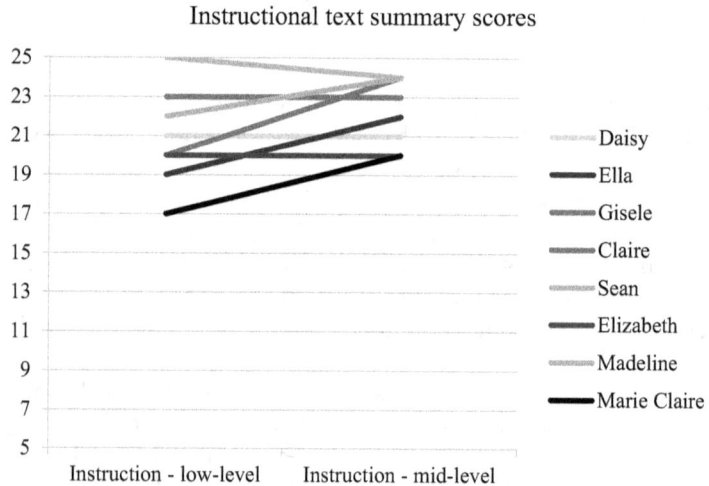

Figure 4.17 Graph of instructional text summary scores for RS1 and RS2

learners' development, it is necessary to investigate the process of their development along with the product of their development. I will analyze the process in Chapter 6.

Conclusion

Learners in RS1, RS2 and RS3 had quite typical backgrounds for intermediate L2 learners. In this chapter, learners' summary scores were traced throughout time, throughout the learners' development and in activity, as is necessary from a V-SCT perspective (Rubenstein, 1940; Vygotsky, 1978). Through the C-BLI and DOLP pedagogy, learners were able to significantly develop their L2 literacy abilities as documented through quantitative ratings of their pre-test, instructional and post-test text summaries. While their development was not smooth or always incrementally improving, this is to be expected from a V-SCT perspective (Vygotsky, 1987). Learning Potential Scores importantly documented how open to mediation learners were over time and help to paint a more nuanced picture of learners' development than static scores alone (Kozulin & Garb, 2002; Poehner & Lantolf, 2013). Learners who had the same pre-test scores sometimes had drastically different post-test scores and their development took different paths. Through these data, we begin to understand learners' ZPD-in-activity (Vygotsky, 2012). We learn what they are able to do independently and what they are able to do with mediation.

The learners' scores improved the most in the mid-level texts for the main idea and accuracy categories, followed by the high-level texts in the same categories. It is not surprising that scores would increase in these two categories first, as L2 narrative literacy can only be built on a foundation of accurately understanding the main ideas. Once learners have developed in these two areas, they are better able to focus on more subtle features such as producing a succinct, coherent and organized synthesis, using generalizations and not including supporting details. Given that these three areas did not comprise an explicit focus of instruction, these results are not surprising. These results could be used as a diagnostic for designing future *obuchenie*, which will be outlined in Chapter 7. By looking at how individual learners developed overall, as well as in each of the summary categories, highly attuned mediation can be used to address areas that may now be ripe for development. Future *obuchenie* for L2 narrative literacy could and should include a more direct writing component, as reading and writing, from this perspective, are dialectically linked in literacy. In Chapters 5 and 6, a more in depth look at the process of the learners' development will be investigated.

Note

(1) There was no statistical difference between groups for any other test.

5 Developing Awareness in Literacy Concepts

Introduction

In this chapter, I will focus on the qualitative analyses of learners' verbalizations about their understanding and use of the three scientific concepts (Foundation, Organization and Genre) that make up the overall concept of L2 literacy during the three semester-long studies. This chapter answers the second part of the first research question: (1b) To what extent does L2 learners' conceptual understanding of narrative literacy concepts – Foundation, Organization and Genre – improve as determined by changes in the quality of their verbalizations?

Verbalizations

Reading/Literacy

RS1 and RS2

In RS1 and RS2, learners were asked to 'describe the nature of second language reading from your experience'. The learners' responses are remarkably similar to one another at the outset of the study. They expressed some ease with understanding the gist or the main idea of a text, but not the specific details. Gisele mentioned that for her, L2 reading happened in a classroom, for an extended period of time and involved completing exercises to display understanding. This is not a surprising description given that this is the most common experience for most classroom L2 learners. They wrote about their L2 reading challenges including having 'difficulty' (Claire), becoming 'flustered' (Sean), being 'really stuck' (Madeline), having 'trouble comprehending' (Marie-Claire), 'being pretty slow' (Elizabeth) and 'need[ing] to find out every single word' (Elizabeth) before being able to understand a text. Madeline wrote that when she has no other recourse to understand a text, she uses a translator (online). For Daisy, the L1 Chinese participant, however, L2 reading involved 'understand[ing] what the text expressed or is about', investigating the 'purpose' and 'feel[ing] the emotion of the author'. In general, learners felt like they could understand the main idea of a text but that the experience was challenging and frustrating.

Learners were asked the same question partway through the study. Claire mentioned that the three concepts were needed to fully understand a text. For Sean, however, he only mentioned the elements of Foundation. Gisele highlighted that L2 reading required a more in-depth analysis than she had used in previous L2 reading experiences. Elizabeth noted that these concepts are similar to what she would use in her L1 reading. Ella wrote about the progress she was making – that it was difficult but that she could understand the main idea. Marie-Claire mentioned that using context clues, dictionaries and learned L2 knowledge guides her. Madeline discussed L2 texts she might read such as subtitles, textbooks and current events. Finally, Daisy had a different perspective than the others. She wrote that L2 reading is about 'communicat[ing] with native speaker[s]' and learning different information about different cultures, including the way people live, as well as what they eat and do. Her view of the nature of L2 reading is more advanced and broader in focus than the L1 English participants in the study. Several learners had incorporated the use of literacy concepts or components into their understanding of the nature of L2 reading. It is noteworthy that Elizabeth recognized that these concepts were similar to those she would use in her L1 reading. Some of the concepts were likely implicitly understood prior to this study.

Finally at the end of the studies, learners in RS1 and RS2 again described the nature of second language reading from their experience. Claire wrote 'I now feel more comfortable with second language readings and have been able to analyze literature', which is also evident in the marked improvement in her scores from pre- to post-test. Elizabeth also mentioned that the study definitely helped her to improve what was 'a difficult and time-consuming' process, by 'teaching [her] to be more efficient'. Sean wrote that L2 reading involves 'taking what I know about reading in my native language and applying it to French, through different approaches'. What was once implicitly used in L1 reading can now be applied to reading in French. Both Ella and Daisy focused on using the concepts and components of the study to read L2 texts. Madeline again mentioned types of L2 texts. Marie-Claire wrote that L2 reading requires the use of context, practice and knowledge of verb conjugations. As this was the predominant focus of the researcher-teacher's mediation with Marie-Claire because of her needs, this was not surprising. Gisele, however, was frustrated because, 'the content is simple but getting there is a hassle'. She mentioned during the instructional phase that she was frustrated that she had difficulty reading texts in an L2, which L1 readers could read easily and at a younger age. For her, the comprehension and analysis process required much more work to reach the same understanding, which she found tedious. While this is important to address, it would be helpful for Gisele to know the progress that she was in fact making. In general though, learners felt more confident and comfortable about their L2 reading and knew how to investigate the text for comprehension and analysis.

The learners' verbalization on the nature of L2 reading from their experience in general shifted dramatically from the outset to the completion of the study. At the beginning, they wrote about their difficulties as well as their need to use online translators, while at the end, they felt that their L2 reading had improved, they were more comfortable reading L2 texts and they had the tools to 'analyze literature' (Claire) and investigate textual elements. Overall, there was a progression from reporting a limited understanding of texts, especially the supporting details, with reading being difficult and confusing to improvement and comfort in reading and analyzing texts. The change in Claire's response, from 'hav[ing] difficulty putting together entire concepts' and 'understand[ing] certain concepts but hav[ing] difficulty piecing [them] together' to 'feeling more comfortable' and 'being able to analyze literature' was perhaps the most salient shift out of any of the learners. In general, they began to understand L2 reading as a process where they could use concepts from the study as their guides. For some of the learners, L2 reading became much more like L1 reading in terms of what they were able to do and in terms of the complex concepts that they could use in order to read and analyze French texts; a significant shift from 'becom[ing] flustered' (Sean) and 'need[ing] to find out every single word' (Elizabeth).

RS3

In RS3, learners were asked to 'explain your understanding of reading and how you use/plan to use your understanding to guide your reading of texts in French'. In this study, learners were grouped based on the type and amount of mediation they were predicted to need based on their pre-test results. There were three people in the higher-level group, six in the middle-level group and 12 in the lower-level group. For most of the analyses, there was no discernable pattern of differences between the levels other than for how they wrote about reading/literacy. For that reason, I will present their data for this verbalization area by group, while the remaining verbalizations will be discussed as a full group.

In the higher-level group at the outset of the study, their answers included: (a) signals of strength: 'my understanding in reading French continues to excel' (David); (b) an interest in reading: 'big fan of reading in general and I'm very optimistic that this class will help me to cultivate that fandom' (Bill); (c) an awareness of reading/literacy's importance: 'reading is very important, that's the basis' (Amy); (d) an awareness of one's ability level: 'at intermediate level' (David); but still (e) some focus on correctness and pronunciation: 'having this understanding will help me to write with correctness' (David) and 'understanding how to speak the words being read, I can try to read out loud and make sure my pronunciation is correct' (Amy).

In the middle-level group, there was a focus on: (a) using context clues: 'I work a lot with context clues, I focus on what I know' (Lily); (b) using what you know: 'I use words I already know and words that look like English words to read' (Edward); (c) using learned grammar: 'I have a fairly decent grasp on French grammar, so I plan to use that in my readings' (Desiree); (d) using L1 reading: 'how well one can use skills they learned from their first language and use those skills when reading a second language' (Lauren); (e) vocabulary: 'words I don't know might have a different meaning just definition wise than how its [sic] used in text' (Victoria); (f) fluency: 'one doesn't have to be fluent in a language in order to understand what they are reading' (Lauren); (g) awareness that translation is not the best strategy: 'I found that reading in French is easier to understand, while saving time, if I don't translate word by word or sentence by sentence' (Victoria); and (h) that it is a challenge: 'Reading in French is harder than english [sic] since its [sic] my second language' (Victoria).

In the lower-level group, there was a focus on: (a) using cognates: 'find cognates and infer the text' (Hannah); (b) using what you know: 'Reading in a second language is difficult but it is important to take your time and identify words that you do know' (Samantha); (c) the relation to L1 reading: 'Literacy can be difficult in a second language depending on your proficiency of literacy in your first language' and 'Comprehending texts has always been one of my weaknesses in English, so I'm sure it will be more difficult in French' (Samantha); (d) learning vocabulary and grammar: 'reading allows you to improve you [sic] vocabulary' and 'the more you read the more grammar structures you can recognize and see how to use them in writing or speaking' (April); (e) translation: 'I personally would translate and try to memorize the most important words' (April); (f) challenges: 'I am perhaps a touch intimidated by reading large sections of French frequently, but I hope that I can improve my ability by the end of the course' (Portia); (g) main idea: 'I might be able to get a general idea of what the story is about' (Samantha); (h) an (perhaps misguided) evaluation of level: 'I'm pretty good at reading' (Hannah) and 'at the moment I think my reading skills are a little above average compared to the general learner' (Evelyn); and (i) the importance of reading: 'Reading in a second language literacy is important for being able to expand one's vocabulary and practice without others' (Sandra).

Overall, across the levels, there is some understanding of reading/literacy's importance and that you should use the tools that you have to help (cognates, learned vocabulary/grammar, context clues). However, at the middle and lower-levels, the main focus is at the word and sentence level and on the challenges that they may face.

During the middle of the semester, I asked learners to write verbalizations specifically for the concepts of Foundation, Organization and Genre; however, some learners at each level additionally talked about reading/literacy at a more general level in their verbalization. I will discuss the changes in how they talked about reading/literacy at this point of the study. One of the higher-level learners wondered about the goal of learning about the concepts in French: 'are we doing these types of exercises to (eventually) be able to do it subconsciously or is it just to better our comprehension skills? And is it only for works of literature? I think I subconsciously do some of this stuff when I am reading a novel in English' (Amy). Her statement is quite interesting because we may use many of the concepts that I was teaching them subconsciously when reading in our first language. How they learned to read and what they use to read successfully in their first language is rarely open to conscious inspection before teaching them explicitly about it, but can become open to conscious inspection with instruction. Amy made the connection between what she uses to read successfully in her L1 and what she was being taught to use in her L2.

In the middle-level group, the few learners mentioning reading/literacy at this midway point in the study wrote about how the process felt foreign and difficult at first but that it is helpful, and some parts are becoming easier. In the lower-level group, one learner indicated that reading in an L2 had not yet caught her interest and that she did not enjoy doing these types of analyses in her first language. However, she liked how we worked on the analyses together and that she felt like she had made significant progress. Other learners mentioned that they have a much better understanding now and one indicated that they will use this method to read and analyze French texts in the future.

At the end of the semester, some learners again addressed reading/literacy in general in their verbalizations of the concepts. A learner in the higher-level group remarked about how this method was very helpful to understand L2 texts. In the lower-level group, learners again mentioned that it was challenging at first but became easier to comprehend. One learner commented about how the three concepts are different but that they allow readers to 'analyz[e] texts from all perspectives' and that this allowed for developing 'a full understanding of the story'. In addition, they mentioned that 'these methods develop reader's critical thinking skills and brings the surface level reader to the deep thinker' which was echoed by another learner. Another learner mentioned that using the concepts was 'helpful in understanding French texts because they force us to go out of our comfort zone and really learn how to analyze the text rather than just reading and translating it'.

Overall, although they were not specifically asked about reading/literacy in later verbalizations, they mentioned it becoming easier, that it was helpful, that it helped them to better understand, develop critical thinking skills, analyze texts and no longer rely on translation.

Foundation

RS1 and RS2

For RS1 and RS2, learners were asked at four different times to share their understanding of the concept of Foundation and how they plan to use it to guide their thinking/reading. The first time was at the beginning of the second session, before being introduced to the concepts; the second was just after being introduced to the concepts; the third was approximately halfway through the C-BLI process; and the fourth was after completing the post-test assessment.

During the first verbalization learners shared their understanding of Foundation, before being introduced to the C-BLI concept and was likely based on what they thought was foundational to reading a text in French. They provided similar information as they had when they defined reading above and focused on vocabulary, grammar, learned L2 knowledge, main points of the story and the setting. As for how they use it, they mentioned translating and paying attention to vocabulary, verb tenses, main characters, setting and main points.

In the second verbalization after the researcher-teacher's explanation of the concept and the SCOBA, learners shared their understanding of the C-BLI concept of Foundation. Not surprisingly, they mentioned what they had just learned. This is the start to appropriating the explanation and forming their own understanding of Foundation. Overall, the learners shifted from just knowing that somehow vocabulary, tenses, characters, main idea and setting are important to knowing what components to investigate and how they might go about doing so. They were starting to develop a sense that Foundation can serve as a tool to make the task manageable, eliminate confusion, prepare their roles for the next concept as well as to gain a fuller understanding of the text.

For the third verbalization about halfway through the C-BLI, learners again shared their understanding of the Foundation concept. They mentioned the four roles/elements of Foundation which they had been using to read and also referred to Foundation as the 'main concepts' (Ella), 'basic elements' (Daisy) and the 'building blocks of the story ... [which] form the basis of our understanding' (Elizabeth). The learners understood that these were the foundational tools that would allow them to understand and make meaning from texts. In their verbalizations about how they are using Foundation to guide their thinking/reading, they again mentioned the roles and how each role allowed them to better understand the stories. Madeline mentioned that 'learning why verb tenses are used is also very helpful to understanding the story'. In fact, previously most of the learners thought that a specific tense/aspect/mood must fill particular grammatical slots and did not realize that tense, aspect or mood could be chosen to create particular effects in the story. They spent a fair amount of time during the instructional phase of the study focusing on how to identify verb tenses/aspect and how they are used to create specific types of effects on a reader. They also began to perceive reading as an interactive process with different elements making both unique and interdependent contributions to understanding.

At the end of the study, they provided their final verbalization on their understanding of Foundation and how they used the concept to guide their thinking/reading. Although learners once again mentioned the four roles, they wrote about them differently at this time. They mentioned what the roles/elements of Foundation allowed them to do; for example, 'better understand the meaning of vocab[ulary] and the usage of grammar' (Claire) and 'how and what the vocab and grammar are conveying' to a reader (Sean). In this way, they developed a different sense of the purpose of lexical and grammatical elements in the text and that the connotation of words and how the grammar was used were more important than simply knowing an English equivalent for them. For Sean, these roles now allowed him to 'make an educated prediction'. This is important to note because at the outset of the study, Sean would offer increasingly fantastical predictions using his L1 schemas and a great deal of imagination, but he came to be able to offer informed predictions based on his comprehension of the text. Elizabeth also mentioned that work on the other concepts would not be possible without the work on Foundation as she understood the interdependent nature of the concepts. For Daisy, Foundation allowed her to 'pay more attention to [the] details', 'sense the emotions' and understand the effect that particular words had on readers. She also mentioned that it helped her to better predict future events and better understand the author's intentions.

At the outset of the study, learners knew that they needed to use their understanding of vocabulary and grammar, whether it was from previous knowledge or from using resources, in order to read a text. By the end of the study, they realized that understanding the vocabulary and grammar of a text allowed them to identify and interpret the main ideas in order to create summaries and to use this information to make educated text-based predictions regarding the events described in the narrative rather than on the basis of L1 story schemas. They felt that Foundation helped them to better understand texts, be able to pay attention to the details, make predictions and know the author's intentions based on the language choices that they made when they created the story. Ella and Madeline understood that this concept could be used not only for narrative texts, but for all pieces of writing, and in any language. In other words, their understanding of the concept was recontextualizable. Madeline understood that reading is not a passive process of extracting meaning, but an interactive meaning-making activity. There was also a growing awareness of the interdependent nature of the concepts. All of this in turn increased their confidence in their ability to read L2 texts.

RS3

In the full classroom study, learners were asked three times to verbalize their understanding and use of the concept of Foundation to guide their thinking/reading – once before the C-BLI concept was explained, once in the middle of the semester and once at the end of the semester. At the beginning of the semester and before being introduced to the concept of Foundation through C-BLI, most learners mentioned vocabulary, grammar/syntax, L1 reading and main idea/plot foundation. A few mentioned that Foundation was based on past French courses, Spanish or Latin knowledge. Three mentioned that it was needed before other things or, in other words, serving as a foundation. Two learners mentioned either that they were not sure or that their understanding was limited. These verbalizations are in line with the initial verbalizations from RS1 and RS2 for Foundation.

Midway through the C-BLI process, learners were again asked to verbalize their understanding and use of Foundation and their responses generally focused on four areas: definition, evaluation, process and outcome. In terms of how they defined Foundation, it included the four roles – that it was the basis, first lens, first layer, ground form, or meat of the story – and that it helped them to better understand what the text was about. Most learners indicated that it was the easiest or most obvious concept and that they felt they were getting better at doing the roles, while some said that it was 'extremely important' or the most helpful. One of the same learners also pointed out that 'one learns the least in foundation; I won't really learn much from French literature if all I read are the words' (Johann). In other words, while Foundation is important to understand what is happening in the text, it is not sufficient for analyzing it, which the other concepts allow you to do. Other learners seemed to feel satisfied at this point that Foundation was sufficient to help them understand what they wanted to understand with French texts. In terms of the process, learners outlined how they used the roles as well as how they brought the pieces of Foundation together. Learners also pointed out how they brought their understanding from Foundation to bear in terms of the other concepts – Organization and Genre. One learner also noted that what they learned in Foundation forms the majority of the summaries that they write. Finally, one learner recognized that they also use Foundation in their first language but that they need to do it more 'actively' in their second language (Amy).

At the end of the study, learners verbalized their understanding and use of the Foundation concept a final time, after completing the posttest. Their answers were prolific and can be categorized in the following six areas: definition, evaluation, process, outcome, other concepts and SCOBA. Learners once again mentioned the four roles and the importance of each in the process of understanding what they are reading.

Many indicated that the concept of Foundation was aptly named as it was the foundation, basis, basic principles, backbone, base or first lens which they use to read and understand a text in French. They wrote that 'after fully understanding vocab and grammar, the main idea can be put together. Then predictions can be made' (Amy). They mentioned that this was a way to begin investigating an author's use of grammatical tenses to shape the main idea, but that 'it is not enough to understand all the ideas that [the] author has reflected in his [sic] story' (April). Some pointed out that they had used the ideas of Foundation in their L1 reading and now use it in their L2 reading – what was once done subconsciously has now been done consciously and will become fully internalized again for this new language and context. In terms of evaluative comments, they wrote that it helps with the most obvious aspects of the story, it is the easiest concept to use first, sometimes may be sufficient depending on what you want to do with the text you are reading, but other times it is the basis for the other concepts which allow you to go deeper. They said that it is very helpful and the most important aspect. 'Despite how basic the concepts may be, they are still vital to understanding' (Bill). In terms of the process, their answers mirrored the order of the roles, with vocabulary first, then grammar, main idea and finally prediction. As for their discussion of the outcome of Foundation, they mentioned that Foundation is needed for understanding the text before working on Organization and Genre. They also wrote that without each element of Foundation, a reader would not get the full understanding of the text. As for the SCOBA, they were asked to reconsider what their version of the SCOBA for Foundation would be. Some learners offered different configurations for the roles – a flow chart, a Venn diagram, or a series of concentric boxes with vocab in the largest one, then grammar in the next smaller one, followed by main idea and finally prediction in the smallest one. One learner's verbalization best represents the overall sentiment of the learners about Foundation at the end of the semester:

> The foundation of a text concerns the vocabulary, grammar/discourse, main idea, and prediction throughout the story. The language and vocabulary that author's [sic] use is purposeful and paying attention to these aspects can really help you when reading in a different language to better understand the story. Taking into consideration the type of vocabulary and language that author's [sic] use can really give insight into the type of language that should be used when conveying a certain message. Certain vocabulary have connotations that can arouse certain emotions within the audience to allow the narrative to have a bigger impact. Obvious challenges and questions can arise when concerning the foundation if readers do not know the vocabulary the author chose. It can also be confusing for the audience if it is not apparent why certain words were chosen and why they are important to the plot. (Veronica)

Organization

RS1 and RS2

For the first verbalization on Organization in RS1 and RS2, the learners shared their implicit basic understanding that narratives or stories have a beginning, middle and ending. They also mentioned that Organization involved 'piec[ing] together parts of text' (Claire), first understanding sentences then paragraphs, the roles the characters play and 'keep[ing] ideas in order in a sensible way that can be translated to the reader' (Gisele). There was no mention, however, that authors can choose to order events in different ways or the nature of the effects that these different textual structures can have. In terms of how they used Organization during the pre-test before being introduced to the concept, they looked for the beginning, middle and end of the texts, they used what they knew and looked up what they did not know, they assumed a chronological sequence and they recognized that it was a fictional text. While these are all fine, none is particularly helpful in terms of understanding how authors organize texts and what effects their organization may have on readers.

After learners were introduced to the concept of Organization, their verbalizations included a variety of elements from the explanation such as: the roles or the full list of elements from Mandler's story grammar, the Cuisenaire rods, the connection to other concepts such as building on Foundation, the sequencing of events instead of necessarily using chronological order, the effect events have on other events, the way elements of the story organization are linked together and the characters' actions and reactions. At this stage, learners are generally imitating the researcher-teacher's explanation and the SCOBA, but with time they will internalize their understanding of the concept of Organization. They planned to use the concept Organization to better understand the sequence of events and what is happening in the text, how the episodes are connected, know where they are in the text, or as Elizabeth stated, 'so I get a sense of what's going on, when things are going on and why they're in that order'.

Midway through RS1 and RS2, learners again verbalized their understanding of the Organization concept. At this point in the instructional phase, the learners have moved beyond listing the component parts of Mandler's story grammar or the roles that comprise Organization for the most part. Instead, they wrote about how stories can be divided into parts, that these parts are interdependent and that the author can choose how to sequence the events and does not therefore have to relay events in chronological order. For some learners, Organization includes being able to see and manipulate the elements of a story. Two learners also made reference to the use of the Cuisenaire rods. Although learners used Foundation to develop a basic understanding of the text, through investigating the components of a story's organization, they were able to develop a much deeper understanding of the text. Interestingly, for Gisele, Organization allowed her to divide the story into the component parts, which helped her 'set aside the content and see the building blocks of the reading'. In other words, the materialized representation allowed them to see the organization of stories visually (Gisele) as well as in their mind (Ella). In spite of the fact that Marie-Claire wrote that she used the concept to identify the parts of the story, she admitted that she did not use it while she read, but 'after we're done with the reading'. For her, at this point in time, reading still had a somewhat narrow definition and only included the first pass through a text. At this point, the learners were investigating Organization during the second pass through a text.

At the end of RS1 and RS2, in the learners' final verbalizations about Organization, they understood that stories can be broken down into component parts (Claire, Gisele, Madeline, Marie-Claire and Elizabeth), that events can be sequenced and that they are connected (Ella, Sean and Daisy), and that these component parts allow them to understand the details of the events. For Elizabeth, the elements of Organization show 'how they [the characters] get themselves through certain situations'. Both Sean and Madeline made reference to a chain or timeline, again likely influenced by the use of the Cuisenaire rods. Although the Organization drew the learners' attention to the structure of the story, it is significant that they understood that authors can be creative in the structuring of a text in order to create particular effects. At this point, some learners wrote that Organization helped them to understand how events led to, or caused, other events (Claire, Sean, Madeline) and how stories develop and shift (Gisele, Daisy). Ella wrote: 'I use organization to create a clear picture of the events of a story in my mind'. It is not clear whether in her mind, she is able to clearly comprehend the events of a story or whether the clear picture is of the episodic structure of the events. Elizabeth mentioned the use of the Cuisenaire rods explicitly however when she wrote, 'when using the blocks, I would carefully look at each character's reaction[,] how they dealt with that [and] made goal paths when just reading the story w/o [without] blocks, it kind of comes naturally'. For Elizabeth, the concept and the materialized representation allowed her to not only investigate events and sequences of events in detail, but she also was able to internalize this mediating tool.

When learners first wrote about how they used Organization to read the pre-test texts, some commented that they identified the beginning, middle and ending of stories. After they were introduced to the concept, they planned to use it to understand the story grammar components, the sequence of events, the story in general, and more details about the events, including how the events are connected. As the study progressed, they were able to accomplish what they had planned. By the end of the study, they had a deeper understanding of the concept and how they could use it to guide their thinking and reading of L2 texts. They understood how events can be sequenced, how stories develop, how story grammar components are connected and interdependent. They were able to understand nuances related to the events and their understanding not only built on their Foundation work, but it also helped with their work on Genre as we will see below. Finally, the use of the blocks was mentioned by a few learners as being helpful in seeing the textual organization and later, for some, being able to do it in their mind, having internalized the mediating power of the Cuisenaire rods.

RS3

For RS3, at the beginning of the semester learners wrote about their understanding of Organization before being introduced to the concept as part of the C-BLI. The majority of the learners mentioned elements related to their own personal organization while they are reading texts in terms of organizing the information as they read, sentences that flow in a logical order when they write, L2 sentence structure, and rules for French verbs, nouns and tenses. One person mentioned that it is 'how one part of the text relates to another [which] helps... to understand the content of the text' (Amy). Another indicated that it needs to be clear why the text is organized as it is. One learner focused on verb tenses and said that texts can be organized by the tense they are written in: 'one text might focus strictly in the present while another may first focus on something in the future, jump to the past and finally reach the present' (Daphne). Two learners indicated that the organization of French texts might be different than in English which might make it more difficult. Finally, two learners indicated that the text's organization might help them to understand the text or even to predict the message of the text. While some of these can be helpful, such as how parts of a text relate to others, the role that tenses may play in the organization, that English and French texts may be organized differently, or that the organization might help them to understand the text, there is more to the Organization concept that will allow them to understand, interpret and analyze texts more deeply.

At the midway point of the semester, learners verbalized their understanding of the Organization concept and how they used it to guide their thinking/reading. Many of them pointed out that Organization deals with how the story is structured, listed the roles and indicated that it helped them understand how the text was developed. For some learners, Organization is 'when the reader starts to understand the deeper meanings within the story' (Lauren), 'what the character is trying to accomplish, has accomplished, or a reaction from the character' (Lily) and that it allows you to 'analyz[e] the motives of the characters and ultimately the author' (Annalise). Two learners discovered something unexpected through Organization: (a) 'I learned a lot about... pacing. I had some preconceived notion that settings were only a line or two while, attempts were single sentences, and other things like that... this preconceived notion was completely blown out of the water' (Johann) and (b) 'I have been amazed twice now at how directly the organization shapes the less obvious elements of the text...the way the story was set up has lent itself to a specific purpose on the part of the author' (Portia). Importantly, learners realized that 'some text[s] proceeds [sic] through time, others proceed by progression through reactions to previous actions, while others proceed by a combination of both' (Barbara) instead of being organized chronologically as they indicated in their first verbalization. Although many learners found it helpful for improving and shaping their understanding of the text, they still found Organization a challenge because they had never used this concept specifically and explicitly before in their L1 or in French. One learner pointed out that the Organization concept helped to clarify issues that may not have been fully resolved through Foundation. Another learner made reference to the visual aspects of Organization (the Cuisenaire rods): 'It allows me to visualize the setup of the story which really helps me because I feel that the visual is what makes the most sense to me. I can really see the progression' (Lily).

In RS3, learners' final verbalizations on Organization extended their thoughts from the midway point of the semester. In addition to providing the component parts and roles, learners indicated that it helps 'mak[e] a text more understandable' (David), 'helps you see how the author structures a story to achieve a desired outcome' (Daphne), allows them to 'follow the sequence of events in a story' (Edward) and that 'being able to see all the parts that the author intentionally created helps the reader like me see her [sic] development in characters and themes as well' (Victoria). Several learners mentioned that the materialized form through the Cuisenaire rods helped them to visual the authors' organization. For example, 'it's easier for me to see the progression that way then [sic] to just see it on paper' (Lily) and it makes it 'easier to see if the story moves horizontally through several episodes or vertically with just one episode' (Lily). Understanding Organization allowed the readers to 'see how the author structures a story to achieve a desired outcome' (Daphne), and to 'discover the underlying purpose and intended message of the story' (Veronica). As one learner eloquently wrote, 'it really encouraged me to look at the story's structure as a purposeful element of the author's vision' (Portia). The learners generally felt that Organization was the most difficult of the concepts because they had not yet done something similar in their L1. Organization took more practice and 'a lot of brain power' (Evelyn) before it became easier, but it did help them to better understand the events of the text. In fact, one learner indicated that 'looking into organization is a really great critical thinking skill' (Portia). In relation to Foundation, some learners felt like it helped them to understand remaining issues, go deeper, 'realize parts of the story that I didn't understand when only looking at foundation' (Lauren), and that it 'helps me to realize which main ideas from foundation are maybe more important to the story' (Lauren). One learner summed up well one of the most important elements that they had learned:

Analyzing the organization of French texts has allowed me to see the various possibilities of ways authors can form a story. A certain text could have twenty different episodes, while another could only have one. Analyzing the organization of various texts has given me a different perspective of how a certain story is presented and what the author is trying to accomplish with the formation of episodes and their placement in the text. (Barbara)

Genre

RS1 and RS2

The verbalizations for the final concept of Genre in RS1 and RS2 took place at the same time intervals as the ones above. At the beginning of the studies, the learners mentioned text types such as 'folklore', 'fantasy', 'non-fiction', 'mystery', 'romance' and 'horror'. Some even listed elements unrelated to Genre such as 'setting' or 'key words'. One mentioned that the kind of story it is tells you 'how it's supposed to make you feel' (Ella). Another learner mentioned that different genres are written in different ways and have different purposes. At the outset of the study, they have a very basic, implicit, everyday, non-systematic and incomplete understanding of the concept of Genre. In terms of how they used their understanding of Genre for the pre-test texts, they indicated that discovering the text type helped them understand if their 'idea of the story was a correct one' (Ella). For Gisele, from the emotions in the text, she could guess what kind of genre it was. Marie-Claire only focused on identifying if the text was fiction or non-fiction.

After the researcher-teacher's explanation of the concept of Genre, the learners provided details from the instruction and SCOBA such as the four roles and what they are as well as how you might investigate them in texts. Marie-Claire wrote: 'I can use genre to help figure out why a piece of work was written, who it was intended for, all based on the interactions between characters'. At this point, they are imitating what they understood from the researcher-teacher's instruction.

At the midway point of the study, the learners again verbalized their understanding of Genre. Some of their verbalizations reveal how development is neither a smooth nor an incremental process; instead, it is revolutionary, which means it can include backtracks and pauses. Both Ella and Elizabeth's responses are similar to what they wrote prior to being introduced to the concept and once again included exemplar text types. Claire, Gisele and Marie-Claire listed the roles that comprise Genre, which is fairly common. Sean wrote about 'the type of language and how it's used ... [and] constructed' which shows some understanding that authors choose and use language for different effects. Daisy wrote, 'Genre is the language style of the article. The meaning above what the words look like. And it may reflect some cultural beliefs'. Her response was the most developed at this point in time. In terms of how they use the concept of Genre to guide their reading/thinking, for Daisy it helped her to 'dig more into the article [text]' to better understand the author's language and style choices, as it did for Sean as well. It also helped Daisy and Ella to develop a deeper understanding of the text. Madeline specifically commented on the importance of investigating an author's use of different tenses as well as Genre helping her to comprehend the reason behind characters' behavior. For Gisele and Elizabeth, it quite simply helped them to develop an overall feel of the story or 'what the story is actually about'. Although learners included some of their everyday understanding of Genre or simply listed roles that comprise the concept, there was some progression. Learners in general not only identified what and where to investigate to understand more, but also that there was more to understanding a text than they previously had thought. Language usage, style and even tenses could be revealing in ways that they had never considered before.

In general, the learners' final verbalizations were much more nuanced and developed than on any of the three previous occasions. Claire and Madeline wrote that Genre concerns the authors' purpose and the style of the language. Daisy expanded this idea by adding that the authors' use of language may have additional meanings and evoke certain emotions as well as how the 'author wants to relate to readers'. Sean also wrote about language and style but for him, Genre included the reason why the words and style were chosen. Gisele and Marie-Claire included the metalanguage for the roles and elements from the SCOBA, and Marie-Claire added an explanation of field, tenor and purpose. Elizabeth wrote that 'Genre allows us to see the story in a certain category in order to understand it better. We look at how it's written [and] how the character relationships are portrayed'. While she included some appropriate information, misunderstandings remained, and some details are missing. Ella's response only addressed tenor, and she included characters in the author-reader relationship. In terms of how the learners used Genre to guide their reading and thinking, Genre helped them to 'garner a better understanding' (Gisele), make texts simpler (Marie-Claire) (i.e. easier to understand), and because genres have a common way of being written, it 'made it easier to understand and predict things' (Elizabeth). Finally, learners commented on the authors' language and style choices including that they were able to 'see why a certain style was used' (Claire, Sean and Madeline) and how the author's choices help to convey the point of the story (Sean).

Genre helped learners to investigate and understand the role that language plays in texts (Marie-Claire) i.e. 'why an author switches from *passé composé* to *imparfait* to *passé simple*'. During several one-on-one mediation sessions between the researcher-teacher and Marie-Claire, they investigated tenses, the use of tenses, and the effect that using different tenses had on the story. At the outset of the study, Marie-Claire had difficulty identifying the root or stem of the verb, the infinitive and the tense/

aspect/mood of a verb. She also did not realize that authors could choose to use tenses for particular effects, nor did she appreciate the nature of those effects on the story. Most of the time in one-on-one mediation sessions with Marie-Claire was used to develop these abilities because of the importance of understanding authors' use of tense/aspect/mood in narratives. Her understanding of the verb conjugations and tense/aspect/mood shifted, but most importantly her view of language changed and how we can make choices to use language in the way that we want.

The learners' understanding of Genre no longer includes exemplar text types and instead began to incorporate the idea that authors make language and style choices for particular purposes and therefore there are deeper meanings behind their word choices. Genre also allows them to investigate the author/reader relationship through the language of the text. Their understanding of Genre was not yet systematic or complete, but it had developed throughout the study.

RS3

At the outset of RS3, the learners verbalized their understanding of Genre before they were introduced to it through C-BLI. While some indicated that it was the 'category of text – romance, mystery, or non-fiction' (Sandra), there were fewer mentions of this overall. They wrote that genres would provoke different feelings, would consist of different writing styles, may differ in their ability to be understood, may have different lexicon and may differentially impact the readers' attention. Veronica wrote that Genre was 'a category that recognizes similarities between writings' which was the most advanced definition provided at this point. A few people indicated that they did not have much experience with different genres but were open to learning about and from different genres. Others indicated their comfort with Genre but did not further specify how or what their understanding was. A few learners wrote about whether certain genres were similar or different to genres in other languages and how. In terms of the outcome of Genre, a few learners indicated that knowing the genre might help them to make predictions, understand the text, or read more efficiently.

At the midway point, after learners were introduced to the concepts and were using them to guide their reading of French texts, they included a variety of ideas in their verbalizations. Some included the roles of Genre such as Field, Tenor, Mode and Purpose and how they defined and used each of these in their reading. Some people focused specifically on ones that they found especially helpful or that they needed more practice with. Many people wrote about how the concept of Genre concerned analyzing the text to find deeper meanings, the main idea, the themes, the style and purpose, and it is through the analysis that you can 'identify the methods or ways the author tries to engage the reader with the story' (David). In terms of investigating the Genre elements in a text, one learner wrote:

> The language that an author uses in their stories is purposeful, which may not be apparent to someone reading in a language that is not their first, so taking these aspects into consideration and really paying attention to the formula of the story and the specific traits that the author chose can help you understand the language better. (Veronica)

This was echoed by other learners as well; their biggest revelation was that authors choose the language they write with for particular purposes and for a particular audience. Many learners wrote that Genre is where they felt they learned the most, that it was the 'main analytical step' (Lily) and allowed for a deep dive into the text. A couple of learners at this point felt that they still needed more practice with it. One learner mentioned that Genre reminded them of a creative writing class that they took in their L1. Finally, one learner wrote 'as with organization, I have been struck with how well genre brings out the nuances of the text I failed to see prior' (Portia).

After completing the post-tests, the learners in RS3 verbalized their current understanding of each of the concepts including Genre. Many of their verbalizations echoed their midway verbalizations but some built further on their understandings. They again mentioned the roles, how they defined them, and how they used them in analyzing the texts. For example, one learner wrote:

> Genre, the typical ways of engaging rhetorically with situations that recur, allows us to see how the author is trying to convey the text to the reader. The field of a text shows the reader the general themes presented in the story. Tenor shows how the author uses language to create a specific relationship between himself [sic] and the reader, such as the use of a formal/informal tone. For example, a children's story will contain a different type of language than that of a philosophical novel. Mode shows the role language plays in the type of text intended by the author in terms of whether it is an oral or written story. Verb heavy texts usually tell a story, while noun heavy texts usually present information. The purpose of a story is usually the overall idea the author wants to convey. It addresses why the text was written, who the text was written for, and who uses the text. (Barbara)

One learner summed up their thoughts on Genre, in addition to listing and defining the roles of Genre, by writing:

> The final step in the process, this aspect helps us to analyze the author's intents [sic] of writing the story as well as the audience for whom the story was intended... This is the final step in the process of analyzing a story and is meant to 'tie up' all the loose ends... prior to this class, I treated genre as a one-facet concept ('what kind of story is it?'). Now though, I understand that it goes deeper. (Bill)

Other learners emphasized that 'Genre is found using the language of the story' (Amy) through 'the patterns in the text and why the author may have chosen to write it a certain way' (Desiree). This idea of choice was echoed by many learners as this was a novel idea to them that authors can make choices about which words they want to use in order to create different effects for the reader. One mentioned that 'Field and tenor can really draw the audience into the story and make them part of the plot, experiencing things along with the characters' (Veronica). They also noted that Genre helped them to 'solidify the meaning of the story that I have been developing through foundation and organization' (Lauren) This helped some learners 'when creating [their] summaries – it helped [them] to take out the extra fluff that [they] had previously been adding, and helped [them] get to the point' (Desiree). One learner even mentioned that Genre helps them to understand 'the story from a 'French speaker's perspective rather than a 'French learner's perspective' (Evelyn). A number of learners expressed their enjoyment at using genre and that it is similar to what they might do in L1 reading; one learner wrote:

> I really enjoyed using genre. I think that with genre, for the first time, I began looking at French texts for some of the elements I might search for in English. When examining genre I felt like I was reading at a higher level than I had been. I have always enjoyed exploring the author's choices regarding how to craft the story, and I think genre truly hits on that, whether it be by forcing you to look at the passive/active voice in the story, probing for thematic elements, or examining the story's dialogues/interactions. (Portia)

Finally, one learner shared a poetic and imagistic version of her view of C-BLI, the concepts, and SCOBAs:

> If you were to put the three [concepts] together, I picture it as a tree. Foundation would be the roots. Without the roots, the tree (story) cannot grow and live. The trunk would be organization. The branches represent the goals, attempts, and simple reactions of the story. Off of the organization trunk would be genre as the leaves. The leaves (genre) grow through as their own and change with seasons (perspective). (Maria)

The learners' understanding of the concept of Genre and how they used it to guide their reading of French texts developed throughout the course of RS3. At the outset, they provided text types and some ideas about how it might be useful for them but at a generic or undeveloped level. They soon came to understand the concept of Genre through the C-BLI and by the end of the study were aware of how it could better help them not only to more thoroughly understand texts, but also to dig in more deeply into the language of the text. They, like the learners in RS1 and RS2, came away with a new understanding that people make choices about language, that using language is not a slot-filling exercise with one right answer, and that these choices have an effect on our interlocutors. The learners understood how Foundation, Organization and Genre were interdependent and how each one contributed to the understanding of texts.

Conclusion

Prior to the instructional phase of the studies, the learners in RS1, RS2 and RS3 felt that reading was an arduous, confusing, overwhelming task that yielded at best a limited understanding of a text in the L2. They believed that their only resources were Google Translate or their previous vocabulary and grammatical knowledge, which was not sufficiently robust for the purposes of reading. Outside of this study, they would likely have continued to struggle with reading and perhaps thought that one solution would be to wait until they had a sufficient amount of the L2, as many reading researchers and L2 teachers have believed. One learner expressed feeling the need to know every word in order to develop any understanding of a text. They had limited ways to attempt to comprehend a text. They had an implicit understanding that texts had a beginning, middle and end, but felt that events were placed in chronological order in narratives. Their L1 understanding was implicit and not yet able to be used as a tool for thinking (Hudson, 2007; Lantolf & Thorne, 2006; Mandler, 1984). They could use their everyday or beginning understanding of Genre to list exemplar text types, which could be used to determine if their understanding was appropriate. They had no understanding that authors make language and style choices when writing texts and that they are not constrained to using a specific tense/aspect/mood in a particular grammatical slot. For learners whose goal was to minor in French and who would therefore need to be able to successfully participate in upper-level literature classes, their verbalizations of the nature of L2 reading, Foundation, Organization and Genre at the outset of the study, showed little hope of them having the tools that they would need to accomplish their goal.

Once learners were introduced to the concepts, they first imitated the researcher-teacher's explanation and the elements of the SCOBAs, but as they used these concepts to participate in practical goal-directed activities in the instructional phase of the study, their verbalizations of the concepts and the nature of L2 reading as well as their use of the concepts shifted a considerable degree. They became more confident because they had developed the capacity to use tools to help them make meaning from texts and analyze the texts from a literary perspective. They were more comfortable investigating textual elements and using the concepts to guide their thinking and reading. L2 reading became more like L1 reading and they were able to use complex concepts like they would in their L1. Reading became a process of meaning making and not an impossible extraction process and it allowed them to be able to communicate with people in another language/culture. They had developed a conceptual understanding of the literacy concepts and they could use the concepts as tools for thinking and to change their literacy practices as well as their understanding of texts (Vygotsky, 1997; Vygotsky & Luria, 1994).

As for Foundation, the learners understood that it is the main or foundational concept that helped them to understand a text and that comprehension of a text was possible through the investigation of vocabulary and the author's grammatical usage. It was then possible to identify not only the main ideas of a text, but to also pay attention to the smaller details. They were now able to make educated predictions instead of using their imagination and L1 story schemas. Foundation was recontextualizable to other types of texts and in other languages. The learners began to appreciate how the concepts were connected and interdependent.

Concerning Organization, at the end of the study, the learners understood that authors choose the manner in which to sequence events in order to create particular effects on readers and that the elements in a narrative rely on each other, are linked and are interdependent. They were able to identify narrative elements, sequences of events and more details and nuances in the story. They could identify how Organization was interdependent with Foundation and Genre. For some, the materialized form of Organization was internalized, allowing them to determine the structural form of a narrative while reading, without using the blocks, but in their minds. Even though there was no evidence of development in Elizabeth's quantitative performance on the post-test, she was able to develop her understanding and use of the concepts, particularly for Foundation and Organization, as evidenced by the shifts in her verbalizations and her internalization of the Cuisenaire rods.

As for Genre, the learners came to realize that authors make language and style choices and do so for specific effects and purposes. They were able to investigate the author–reader relationship through the language of a text (Tenor) as well as the functional use of language for Field, Mode and Purpose. Overall, through the learners' verbalizations, their understanding of the concepts and how they use them as tools for thinking and learning became more explicit, abstract, systematic, recontextualizable and complete, although further development is possible and necessary. The learners were able to appropriate and initiate some control over the three relevant concepts. In other words, they were developing into higher psychological functions for the learners, which would allow the learners to continue developing into independent readers.

6 Tracing Literacy Development

Introduction

This chapter addresses the second and third research questions. The second question is: Does a Division-of-Labor Pedagogy result in learners' appropriation and internalization of the four roles that comprise each of the three concepts: (1) Foundation – vocabulary, grammar/discourse, main idea and predication; (2) Organization – beginning, complex reaction, goal path and ending; and (3) Genre – field, tenor, mode and purpose. The third research question is: How does mediation change over time as learners' L2 reading ability develops. As the learners appropriate and internalize the roles, they need less mediation; therefore, these two questions are interdependent. The analyses contained in this and the two previous chapters, together, provide a thorough picture of learners' L2 narrative literacy development.

Three key terms for the chapter, appropriation, internalization and mediation will be briefly explained again to best appreciate the analysis. In addition, I will present a brief overview of the ZPD to remind the reader of the relevance of this concept for learner development. In the three studies, using C-BLI and DOLP, learners were co-regulated, meaning that as a collective they shared a common goal and used a division-of-labor to guide their 'joint coordinated interaction' where they 'exchanged the products of activity' and were prolepted into their future independent abilities through the 'interdependence' of the collective (Petrovsky, 1985: 183). They were also co-regulated through the researcher-teacher's (henceforth, RT) mediation. According to Lantolf and Poehner (2014), '[i]t is through co-regulation that individuals appropriate and ultimately internalize the forms of mediation available in a social environment and in this way eventually attain self-regulation (i.e. agency)' (2014: 158). The RT's mediation must continually be attuned to the collective as well as the individual learners' ZPD-in-activity. The ZPD-in-activity is a metaphor for the 'activity in which individuals function collectively, working toward a shared object and wherein forms of participation and contribution may shift as new capabilities are formed' (Lantolf & Poehner, 2014: 158). As the learners' participation and contributions shift, so too must the nature of the RT's mediation.

Appropriation of the roles, in this case, involves the ability to understand the roles, use them in practical goal-directed activity, articulate rationales, share the role preparation appropriately and integrate and use the roles and concepts as tools for thinking when reading French texts. For internalization, the 'key aspect... is where the locus of control resides: in others, in the self, or distributed between the self and others (including the artifacts that they have created)' (Lantolf & Poehner, 2014: 48). Internalization is a transformative process, where the collective or interpsychological functioning becomes intrapsychological. What was once necessary for learners to do as a collective, through DOLP, will become possible for them to do independently. Once the concepts and roles have been appropriated and internalized, learners will be able to use them independently, in a wide variety of contexts, and to suit their own needs in addition to being able to 'monitor and evaluate the effectiveness of their [own] performance' (Haenen, 2001; Lantolf & Poehner, 2014: 68). As learners appropriate and internalize the various forms of mediation, therefore developing L2 narrative literacy, the amount and forms of mediation must change. It is a contingent relationship in which the mediator attempts to identify the learners' needs and provide an appropriate level of mediation but 'the mediator him/herself is [also] guided by the learner' (Lantolf & Poehner, 2014: 158) particularly with regard to the learner's responsivity to the mediation offered (see Poehner, 2008).

Given the approximately 75 hours of audio and video data accumulated for these three studies, it is not possible within the constraints of this book to analyze each moment in each learner's developmental process. Instead, select moments have been chosen and will be analyzed here as a complement to the analyses in Chapters 4 and 5. To demonstrate an in-depth analysis of what is possible to learn about L2 literacy development and changes in mediation during the three semester-long studies, I will present an analysis of key moments of Claire's developmental process. Claire's developmental profile was chosen as she exhibited the most extensive level of development throughout all three studies. Keep in mind that she was placed in the lower scoring of the two small groups based on the pre-test scores, in RS1. In addition, she was particularly responsive to mediation. Although the focus here is on Claire, the other learners also showed evidence of development and their profiles surely merit equal attention. To be sure, the analysis of Claire's profile is, in my view, more than adequate to illustrate how development unfolded over the course of the intervention and in order to respond to the second and third research questions. According to Marx and Engels (1985), 'The steam engine was the most convincing evidence of the fact that mechanical movement can be obtained from heat. A hundred thousand steam engines did not prove this more convincingly than did one engine' (as cited in Vygotsky, 1997, https://www.marxists.org/archive/vygotsky/works/1931/research-method.htm).

Claire's Perspective on the C-BLI/DOLP Process

Claire voiced her perspective on the instructional process throughout the study either on her own volition or as a response to a question by the RT. Her perspective will be analyzed first to provide a background against which the remaining analyses can be anchored.

During the second instructional session and when learners were beginning their role preparation for the first page of the first French text, Claire quietly evaluated the process, with her gaze down on her text. See line 1 of the transcript, given in Excerpt 6.1 below. The transcript conventions can be found in Table 6.1.

Table 6.1 Transcription conventions

+	short pause
++	long pause
+++	very long pause
(2.0)	timed pause (2.0 seconds or more)
.	falling intonation
,	slightly rising intonation
?	rising intonation (not necessarily a question)
(word)	uncertain hearing
(xxx)	unable to transcribe
word	in French
hh	out-breath or laughter
::	stretched sound
(( ))	gesture/gaze descriptions or loose description
-	abrupt cutoff
=	latched utterance
[	onset of overlapping speech
°	markedly softer speech
LH	left hand
RH	right hand
R	right
L	left

Excerpt 6.1 Session 3-2 – Commentary about process 1

```
1 Claire   °this is a little bit harder in French.°
          ((gaze down))
2         +
3 RT      wh- yeh hh
4 Claire  °°just a little bit°°
```

In line 3, the RT agreed and laughed slightly. Claire then provided an even quieter further evaluation, with an ironic tone to her utterance in line 4.

During the first instructional session and the beginning of the second, learners were introduced to the concepts and practiced with an English text. Claire realized within two minutes of preparing her role for the first French text that it was more difficult than with the English text.

Almost 14 minutes later, as the learners continued to prepare their roles, Claire once again provided a quiet evaluation with her gaze facing downward. The transcript is given in Excerpt 6.2 below.

Excerpt 6.2 Session 3-2 – Commentary about process 2

```
1  Claire   °this is gonna to take a lo::t longer°
            ((gaze down))
2           °to do one story than°
3  RT       yes.
4  Claire   °ok.°
5           I'm just making sure I'm not like slow
6           and you're all like
7           [ahead of (me)
            ((gaze shifts up to RT then Gisele))
8  RT       [you're doing just fine
```

In lines 1–3, Claire was concerned that the length of time it would take to complete the process for one story would be longer, but she did not indicate the shorter alternative. Once the RT acknowledged the longer timeframe, Claire, in a normal volume but with gaze remaining down, provided a second concern – that she was taking more time to prepare her role than the other learners in the collective. However, at this point, the others were not yet finished with their role preparations either. Once the RT confirmed to Claire that she was not delaying the group, she returned to preparing her role.

During the third instructional session, on page three of the first instructional text and Claire's first time preparing the prediction role, during a pause in the RT's one-on-one mediation session with Daisy, Claire once again offered a quiet evaluation with her gaze down. As can be seen in line 1 of the transcript, in Excerpt 6.3, she offered a positive evaluation of the prediction role.

Excerpt 6.3 Session 4-3 – Commentary about process 3

```
1  Claire   °I like the prediction°
            ((gaze down))
2  RT       (you good)
3  Claire   °this is° yeh it's,=
            ((gaze shifts up))
4  RT       =have you gotten to do it yet,
5           I can't re[member.
6  Claire             [no I haven't done it [yet.
7  RT                                       [ok. good.
```

As this was the first positive commentary from Claire about the process, the RT clarified that it was the first time that Claire had been assigned the role of prediction. This was in fact the case and the RT accepted Claire's evaluation with 'ok. good.'.

During the fourth instructional session, on the final page of the first instructional text, during one-on-one mediation between the RT and Claire and after Claire was able to successfully determine the tense of a verb and provide an appropriate justification for her selection, she again provided a quiet evaluation of the process, again with her gaze lowered. The transcript is given below in Excerpt 6.4.

Excerpt 6.4 Session 5-4 – Commentary about process 4

```
1  Claire  °this is getting a lot easier as you go along.°
2  RT      good
```

During the final page of the first instructional text, Claire had the opportunity to prepare the grammar/discourse role for the second time and she remarked that the process was becoming easier for her. In fact, this was the first time that she had taken responsibility for any role for a second time. The RT accepted Claire's evaluation in line 2 of the transcript.

During the sixth instructional session, in response to the RT's question about whether the group should focus on half of the first page of the second instructional text or the entire first page, Claire voiced her confidence in the collective's ability to focus on the entire first page of the text. As the second instructional text was a mid-level text, while the first was a low-level text, the RT needed to determine an appropriate length of text to focus on for the more difficult second text. Claire's response in lines 1 through 4 of the transcript, in Excerpt 6.5 below, began with a slightly rising intonation but she then restarted in line 2, ending her utterance with falling intonation. She provided two other variations of her confident assurances in lines 3 and 4, again with falling intonation.

Excerpt 6.5 Session 7-6 – Commentary about process 5

```
1  Claire  no we can-,
2          we can do this.
3          we'll get it done.
4          we got this.
```

During the seventh instructional session, while waiting for Daisy to complete her role preparation, Gisele launched into a discussion about the types of texts that French L1/English L2 learners would read in English when they read at the same level as her in French. The discussion then focused on the types of texts that are read in the fourth semester French reading class at the university. The RT provided the names of two texts that had been on the syllabus the previous year and some of the learners indicated that these were no longer on the syllabus. In fact, they said that now there were only excerpts of texts assigned in the class. The RT replied that in the recent past, learners had to read several full-length texts for the course. Claire responded to this fact saying, 'I'd almost rather do that. I feel like just kinda like + going through the class'. The RT alerted Claire to the fact that in her next French class she would have to read full-length texts. Claire responded, 'and like I don't have that kind of experience'. The RT assured her that she would be ready and would have that experience as a result of participating in the research study ('that's why you're here.'). Claire agreed but felt that the nature of the instruction and practice that occurred in the research study should also be happening in her class: 'I feel like + this is the stuff + that I should be doing in class'. She then indicated that the intervention was in fact providing her with the experience she desired, 'and like this I mean this helps more than anything else'. From Claire's response, the type of instruction she was experiencing was necessary and helpful and was what she had expected to be part of her fourth semester bridge class in order to prepare her for the upper-level literature courses.

During the eighth instructional session, as the learners were preparing their roles for Organization for the second instructional text, Claire again offered a quiet evaluation, with her gaze on the text, as can be seen in line 1 of Excerpt 6.6 below.

Excerpt 6.6 Session 9-8 – Commentary about process 6

```
1  Claire   °this story is a [lot less complex°
            ((gaze on text))
2  RT                         [((gaze shifts to Claire))
3  Claire   [°than the other one° ((gaze on text))
4  RT       [((LH moves to nose))
5           +
            ((Claire's gaze shifts to RT))
6  RT       [((shakes head back and forth once))
7  Claire   [you can already tell
8           there's going to be a lot less episodes [though
9  RT                                               [((shakes
            head up and down several times))
10          uhhuh
```

Claire indicated that the second instructional text was from her perspective less complex than the first. At first the RT was checking Gisele's role preparation and was not immediately attuned to Claire's response. Her gaze shifted to Claire midway through Claire's evaluation in line 1. Given that the second text was at a higher level of difficulty than the first, although the learners were not overtly made aware of this, it was not immediately clear to the RT whether Claire was referring to the difficulty level or the text structure. In line 6, the RT shook her head back and forth once with her left hand on her nose as she thought about this information. As the RT shook her head, Claire clarified in lines 7 and 8 that the story was less complex due to the episode structure of the text. At the end of her clarification, the RT nodded affirmatively several times and confirmed Claire's evaluation.

Approximately 35 minutes later, once the learners had finished with Organization, the RT solicited comments about the nature of Organization for the second instructional text and referred to the Cuisenaire rods (blocks) as can be seen in lines 1, 3, 5 and 6 of the transcript in Excerpt 6.7 below.

Excerpt 6.7 Session 9-8 – Commentary about process 7

```
1   RT        so ++ what's the nature of our story
2             +
3   RT        (well) you see it + right there
4             ++
5   RT        what do you think + about our blocks this time,
6             any thoughts? comments?
7   Claire    it's + le- less episodes,
8   RT        [umhm
9   Claire    [it's shorter, um it's more (I would) say
10            it's more simple in its structure,
11  RT        [(°°ok°°)
              ((nods))
12  Claire    [but I mean it kind of + is,
13  RT        ok,
14  Claire    just because there are less stories
15  RT        less epi[sodes,
16  Claire            [or less episodes,
17  RT        yeh.
18  Claire    uh
19            +
20  Claire    but there's like a clear
21            [+
22  RT        [((gaze shifts down))
23  Claire    [((RH metaphorically holding episode in air,
              taps down on table, and moves to R once to
              represent 2 episodes))
24  RT        could you feel the- like- +
25            get the sense as you were-
26            as we were reading through it?
27            or not necessarily.
28  Gisele    no
29  RT        not not until we looked at it.
30  Gisele    yeh
31  Claire    yeh like +
32            not when I was doing all the rest of it
33            but when I looked at it again
```

```
34            right before this
35            I could tell
36            it was just going to be like two things
37  RT        ok.
38  Claire    it's a lot easier to understand.
```

During the RT's solicitation to the learners, she continually shifted her gaze from one learner to the next in order to invite any of the learners to respond. In lines 7, 9, 10 and 16, Claire responded that there were fewer episodes, that it was shorter, and simpler in its text structure due to the fewer number of episodes. In line 23, Claire represented the structure of the Cuisenaire rods that was still present on the table additionally with her right hand. Her thumb and fingers were about four inches apart and above the table as if metaphorically holding the episode structure in the air. She tapped her hand down on the table, moved it to the right and tapped it down again to represent the two episodes and the way that they were connected. The RT's gaze, however, was not on Claire while she was gesturing. In lines 24–27, the RT asked the learners if they were able to begin to sense the episode structure during their first pass through the text (when they focused on Foundation). Gisele responded in line 28 that she could not and confirmed the RT's comment that it was not until they began Organization that she could sense the structure (line 30). In lines 31–38, however, Claire indicated that although she was not able to sense the structure during Foundation, she was able to do so before beginning Organization. In addition, she provided an evaluation in line 38 by expressing that 'it's a lot easier to understand.'.

In the final session, before beginning the post-test, the RT and learners discussed the study, and the RT asked the learners to articulate the helpful elements in the intervention as well as to suggest any changes. During the discussion of the Foundation concept, Claire compared the nature of her reading before the intervention to reading during the intervention and how she anticipated it would be after the program was completed. The transcript is given in Excerpt 6.8 below.

Excerpt 6.8 Session 12 – Commentary about process 8

```
1   Claire   I definitely thought it was helpful
2            +
3   Claire   um + you know- if- if I would've just read that
4            I would've been like
5            well I don't know
6            this word and this word and
7            this word and this word
8            and I just would've made a list
9            and I would've uh + looked em all up,
10           and then I + would've just moved on.
11  RT       [umhm
```

```
12  Claire   [and I wouldn't have tried to like understand
13           what I was reading,
14           but ++ going about it the way that we did +
15           using context clues and trying to find out
16           the words
17           then seeing how the grammar + changes that
18           because I would've just looked it up
19           and I would've been like well it means this.
20           but in this form it doesn't mean this.
21  RT       u[hhuh uhhuh
22  Claire   [or something like that.
23           +
24  Claire   and then ++ as we moved on to each part
25           we kind of had a main idea and a prediction
26           and it helped us better + prepare
27           for what was coming next when we were reading.
28  RT       umhm
29  Claire   so even though it was like
30           a longer process of reading,
31           I mean ++ if we were to do it like by ourselves
32           it might not take as long.
33  RT       [umhm
34  Claire   [or like and you know
35           if you're not- you're not writing everything
36           down.
37           but still + it helps you understand + the
38  RT       ok
39  Claire   text
40  Gisele   umhm
41  Claire   ten times better.
42  RT       ok
```

In line 1, Claire provided a positive evaluation of the Foundation concept. In lines 3–10, she described her reading process prior to the study. She indicated that there would have been many unknown lexical items, she would have made a list, looked up every word and 'just moved on.'. In lines 12–19, she clarified her previous comments, indicating that prior to the study she was not concerned with understanding the text, using context clues to determine the meaning, or investigating how the form of the word changes the meaning. In line 20, she alluded to the fact that when she investigated unknown words at the end of the program she knew that if a word was in a different form, it may not have the same meaning as she would have thought before when she did not consider the form of the word. In lines 24–27, she included the main idea and prediction roles and said that it helped the collective to 'better prepare for what was coming next when we were reading.'. In lines 29–32 and 34–36, she acknowledged that the process took more time than what she had previously done but if they were to use it on their own, it would take less time because they do not need to write down their role preparations. In line 37, 39 and 41 she said that it (Foundation or entire process) helped her to understand the text significantly better.

Claire's comments throughout the process, whether solicited or unsolicited, changed significantly throughout the intervention. At the outset, she lacked confidence and worried about delaying the collective's progress, but as she developed a better understanding of the roles, was able to prepare her role(s) confidently and appropriately, she began to offer more positive evaluations of the process. Although the narratives continued to have a higher difficulty rating, as she developed her L2 narrative literacy ability, she was able to shift the locus of control and take on more responsibility, while sustaining a growing confidence in her ability to read in French.

Claire's Understanding of the Concepts and Roles

Vocabulary and grammar/discourse

During the second instructional session, while learners were preparing their roles for the first page of the first instructional text, Gisele, who was assigned the role of vocabulary, was having difficulty determining the meaning of the words in the title, *Le Champ du Lièvre* (The Rabbit's/Hare's Field). She was able to determine that an appropriate English equivalent in the text for *champ* was 'field' and she asked the RT for help with *lièvre*. The one-minute one-on-one mediation included instruction on how to best use a bilingual dictionary and Gisele determined that 'hare' was the most appropriate equivalent from the dictionary entry. She was unsure, however, how that equivalent fit into the context of the story.

As Gisele had written in her notebook, 'field of hare', the RT asked her for an appropriate English equivalent. Even though learners may have appropriate English equivalents for each word, they are often unable to decipher what the words mean in combination. The RT, in this case, asked Gisele for the equivalent of 'field of hare' in order to verify if it was possible for her. First, Gisele provided 'field of bunnies'; the researcher then asked if *lièvre* was plural and Gisele admitted that it was not. She then provided 'field of the rabbit' which is a word-for-word translation of the title, but it was still not clear that she understood what these words meant when collocated. She then offered 'field of the vegetarians' which makes less sense, but she attempted to use the context of the story at the expense of her vocabulary and grammatical knowledge, as she knew that *lièvre* did not mean 'vegetarians'. Even though Gisele was able to determine the meaning of the individual words, it was in fact an illusion of knowing. She was object regulated at this point and was unable to make sense of these words together and in the context of the story. As the remaining issue at this point in the mediation was that *du* signals possession (i.e. the rabbit's or hare's field), and not the English equivalents of *de* 'of' plus *le* 'the' and therefore a grammatical difficulty, the RT encouraged Gisele to ask the learner in charge of the grammar/discourse role (Claire) for assistance, which she provided.

Gisele told Claire what she had understood so far and asked, 'what *du* would make that?' 'field of hare like how?' Claire was not able to respond immediately and included it in her role preparation. When it was time to share their role preparation, Gisele repeated what she had been able to decipher. Claire then added her understanding; the transcript is given in Excerpt 6.9 below.

Excerpt 6.9 Session 3-2 – *Champ du Lièvre*

```
1   Claire   I got that it says the field of the hare,
2   RT       meaning what.
3   Claire   that it's possession.
4   RT       ok. so how would we say that in everyday English
5   Claire   the hare's field
6   RT       [ok.
7   Gisele   [((nods))
8            ++
             ((Gisele writes in her notebook: the hare's field))
9   Claire   does that sound right?
10  RT       no that's that's [correct.
11  Claire                    [(that's right)
12  RT       so- or the rabbit right,
13  Gisele   [yeh.
14  Claire   [((nods))
15  RT       the rabbit's field + um +
16           why is the title the rabbit's field,
```

In line 1, Claire too offered 'field of the hare' which again comprised the word-for-word English equivalent for *champ du lièvre*. In line 2, the RT asked Claire what 'field of the hare' meant; in other words, to explain how the grammar affected the meaning of the individual words to create a meaning beyond the sum of the individual words. In line 3, Claire was able to offer that *du* indicated possession and the RT prompted her further to determine if she was able to apply that understanding to the individual English equivalents for the title of the text. In line 5, Claire was able to provide an appropriate equivalent for the title of the story: 'the hare's field,' which the RT accepted in line 6 and Gisele accepted with a nod at the same time. Gisele then wrote 'the hare's field' in her notebook.

Although Claire's equivalent was appropriate and accepted by both the RT and Gisele, she was not confident about her response and asked in line 9 'does that sound right?' with rising intonation. The RT confirmed her response in line 10 and Claire overlapped her utterance and accepted that it was appropriate. The RT also offered that rabbit was also an appropriate equivalent for *lièvre* and both Gisele and Claire accepted at the same time, with verbal and bodily responses respectively. The RT then continued the mediation to determine if the learners were able to understand how their equivalent fit into the context of the story and why it may have been chosen as the title.

The above analysis demonstrates the necessary temporary, but artificial separation of the vocabulary and grammar/discourse roles as well as the importance of the RT to further investigate learners' responses. Although it may have seemed obvious that Gisele would understand that 'field of the hare' meant 'the hare's field,' as seen above, this was not the case. If the RT had not followed up with Gisele or later with Claire, they would not have been appropriately mediated and their illusion of knowing may have continued.

During the fourth instructional session, Claire was assigned the vocabulary role for the first time for the fourth page of the first instructional text. Before the excerpt shown in the transcript in Excerpt 6.10 below, Claire had been preparing her role.

Excerpt 6.10 Session 5-4 – *Souffler*

```
1   RT       what is going here what is
2            [what are they blowing out
3   Claire   [souffler
4            uh I me- I think it meant like they
5            + like it said
6            like + blow out or to +
7            what I got from it was like that they were like
8            + blown out like ++ physically
9   RT       ok let's look at that
10           ((5 seconds later))
11  Claire   °°sou (xxx)°°
12           ((6 seconds later))
13  Claire   to blow out to blow to whisper [(t)
14  RT                                     [hmmm
15           +++
16  RT       so if we look at this to blow
17           and then we have in parentheses air
18  Claire   yeh. + uh- I me-
19           oh to l-
20           they like huffed and puffed kinda [thing
21  RT                                        [umhuh umhuh
22  Claire   yeh.
23  RT       yeh that seems like it would make more sense
24  Claire   ok yeh.
25  RT       in this
26           +
27  RT       that goes along with this one [right
28  Claire                                 [yeh exactly
29           [yeh.
```

```
30  RT      [ok any questions for me,
31  Claire  nope
32  RT      ok you're ready,
33  Claire  thank you.
```

In lines 1 and 2, as the RT looked over Claire's list of chosen vocabulary to investigate along with their English equivalents, she noticed that Claire's equivalent for *souffler* (from *soufflaient* in the text) was not appropriate and asked her to explain what she meant by 'blowing out'. Although *souffler* can mean 'to blow out' if it is used in reference to a candle, it was not appropriate for the context of the story, where 'to huff and puff' or 'to be winded from breathing heavily' were more appropriate. In lines 4–8, Claire attempted to explain the reason 'blow out' was an appropriate equivalent, but her explanation was unclear and remained inappropriate. The RT indicated in line 9 that they should investigate this word further and Claire began to look up *souffler* in the dictionary, using private speech in line 11 to select the appropriate dictionary entry. In line 13, she began to list the English equivalents for *souffler* from the dictionary entry. At the beginning of the fourth equivalent, the RT overlapped Claire's utterance with 'hmmm,' indicating that Claire needed to select the appropriate equivalent. Notice that the first equivalent that she read from the dictionary was the one that she had previously selected. This is common behavior for most L2 learners when using a bilingual dictionary; they select the first equivalent in the dictionary entry without determining the appropriateness of the equivalent for the context.

After a lengthy pause and no response from Claire, the RT provided further mediation, in lines 16 and 17, by calling her attention to a particular equivalent and the collocational information provided. Claire acknowledged the RT's suggestion in line 18 with 'yeh.' and after several false starts in lines 18 and 19, she was able to provide an equivalent for *souffler* that was appropriate to the story, using the collocational information in the dictionary: 'they like huffed and puffed kinda thing'. In line 22, she was more confident with her answer ('yeh.') after the RT accepted her equivalent. The RT provided the reason that 'huffed and puffed' was appropriate for the context in lines 23, 25 and 27, while Claire continued to agree in lines 24, 28 and 29. Claire did not have any further questions and indicated that she was prepared to share her role with the collective.

During the sixth instructional session, Claire was assigned the role of vocabulary for the second time (along with grammar/discourse). During the fourth instructional session, she was assigned the role of vocabulary for the first time and had already used a bilingual dictionary to investigate the meaning of many words before the mediation session with the RT. For her second time preparing the role, the RT wanted to determine if Claire was able to select an appropriate amount of vocabulary to investigate after having determined if she could decipher the meaning of any words from the context. Their one-on-one mediation concerning this topic will be analyzed in the following three excerpts.

In lines 1, 3, 4, 6, and 7 of Excerpt 6.11 below, the RT reminded Claire to carefully select words to investigate before she began using the dictionary to look up each word with which she was unfamiliar. Claire acknowledged and agreed in lines 5, 8 and 10.

Excerpt 6.11 Session 7-6 – Vocabulary selection 1

```
1  RT       so as long as you-
2           +
3  RT       select first what you want to look at
4           before you start looking up
5  Claire   looking (xxx) up
6  RT       because otherwise
7           you start looking [up everything
8  Claire                     [yeh.
9  RT       ok
10 Claire   alright cool
```

Three and a half minutes later, the RT noticed that Claire had a lengthy selection of words to investigate. Claire responded that some words were for her vocabulary preparation while others were for her grammar/discourse role preparation. The RT suggested that they look over the list together and Claire responded by acknowledging that there were many unfamiliar words in the text. Forty-five seconds later, they began to look over the list. The transcript is given in Excerpt 6.12 below.

Excerpt 6.12 Session 7-6 – Vocabulary selection 2

```
1  RT       any that- that you can guess + from context
2  Claire   oh ++ yeh
3  RT       let's try that first. + narrow some of this down.
4  Claire   alright.
5           ++
6  Claire   I feel like
7           I have a lot of vocab words in here umm,
8  RT       °yeh you do.°
9  Claire   and that's like weird um,
10 RT       no it's- it's not weird.
11          it's just + you might be here for + hours.
12          +
13 RT       so let's try to get what we can from context.
14          + and [then
15 Claire        [ok
16 RT       use this for the ones we really have no idea.
17 Claire   (xxx) um
18          (13.0)
```

```
19  Claire   um.
20           (2.0)
21  Claire   u- I thi- ok. so from
22           +
```

In line 1, the RT asked Claire directly if there were any words that she could decipher on the basis of context. Claire responded with surprise in line 2 ('oh'), even though the RT had previously provided mediation on this topic, and Claire agreed ('yeh'). The RT then explained why she should first use the context to eliminate some of the words that she needed to investigate. In lines 6 and 7, Claire acknowledged that she had selected many words and in line 8, the RT quietly agreed. Claire became aware that what she did was not appropriate for the role preparation but labeled it as 'weird' in line 9. In lines 10, 11, 13, 14 and 16, the RT assured her that it was not 'weird' and explained why she needed to determine the meaning of as many words as possible from context before using a dictionary. From Claire's response 'um,' followed by a thirteen second pause, another 'um' and a two second pause, it appeared that she was not readily able to narrow down the list. Starting in line 21 and continuing for the next two minutes and forty seconds, she was able to, with mediation, determine the meaning of the first word on her list from the context as well as identify a number of words that she planned to investigate for the grammar/discourse role preparation.

In the excerpt in Excerpt 6.13 below, the RT continued asking Claire about specific words on her list to ascertain whether she was able to understand their meaning from the context.

Excerpt 6.13 Session 7-6– Vocabulary selection 3

```
1   RT       fauteuil?
2   Claire   oh I know that.
3            yeh. alright.
             ((erases))
4            I don't know why I did that one
5   RT       anorak?
6   Claire   oh. and I knew that and
7            I could figure that out from (it)
             ((erases))
8            but I was just-
9   RT       puni?
10  Claire   ok so maybe I was on a roll
11           with just [underlining things,
             ((erases))
12  RT                 [I think so.
13           I think so. voix?
14  Claire   yeh. I- ++ (I-) ++ yeh.
             ((erases))
```

```
15            I was just on a roll with underlining things.=
16    RT      =éclate?
17            +
18    RT      éclate d'un rire?
19            (2.0)
              ((erasing))
20    Claire  yep
21    RT      umkay ++ tremblotante?
22            (2.0)
23    Claire  [uhh
24    RT      [une main + tremblotante?
              ((points to her hand))
25    Claire  oh a hand trembling, oh ok.
              ((erases))
26            (3.0)
27    RT      and you already [got this.
28    Claire                  [is that?
29            +
30    Claire  oh yeh we already have that too.
              ((erases))
31            [(3.0)
32    RT      [((points to another word))
33    Claire  (and xxx)
34            (4.0)
35    RT      grimaçant un sourire?
36            +
37    Claire  yeh you can figure that out from context.=
              ((erases))
38    RT      (xxx)
39            +++
40    Claire  alright.
```

In line 1, the RT asked Claire about *fauteuil* (chair) and Claire immediately realized that she knew the meaning of the word ('oh I know that.') and erased her underlining of the word in the text. In line 4, she indicated her uncertainty about why this particular word was on her list. the RT then asked about *anorak* (anorak), as it is the same in both French and English, although there may be more common English equivalents. Again, Claire was surprised ('oh.') and informed the RT that she already knew the word and, in any case, could determine its meaning from the context, as observed in lines 6 and 7. She again erased her underlining of the word in the text. The RT continued on with another word from her list, *puni* (punished), in line 9. Once again, Claire knew the word and expressed that she may have been overzealous in her vocabulary selection (line 10) and erased the underline under the word once more. The RT agreed, in lines 12 and 13 and continued with another word that Claire likely knew, *voix* (voice). Claire was familiar with this word or could determine the meaning from context, as attested to in line 14. Claire continued to convey to the RT that she was aware that she had unnecessarily selected words to look up in a dictionary (line 15).

Claire may not have needed further mediation to continue to pare down the list if the remaining words had been of equal difficulty as the previous words had been. The RT, however, began to ask about words that were likely more difficult for Claire. In line 16, the RT asked about *éclate* (bursts) but when Claire did not respond, the RT provided more context: *éclate d'un rire* (bursts into laughter). Claire's response was simply to erase her selection and say 'yep' in line 20. The RT then asked about *tremblotante* (trembling), which was not only a more difficult word, but was in the form of a present participle, which the collective had previously investigated for the grammar/discourse role. Claire did not respond for two seconds and in line 24, the RT pointed at her hand as she provided more context, *une main tremblotante* (a trembling hand). The extra context, and potentially the pointing at the hand (although *main* is a word that learners generally learn in a first semester French class), was sufficient for Claire to determine the meaning of yet another word on her list.

There was then a lengthy pause (line 26), but Claire failed to offer candidates for elimination from the word list. The RT continued in lines 27 and 32 and Claire once again was able to eliminate these words from the list (lines 28, 30, 33). In line 36, once again the RT paused to allow Claire to continue paring down the list on her own, but she did not do so. In line 35, the RT offered another possibility for elimination, *(en) grimaçant un sourire* ((while) forcing a smile). The form of *grimaçant* is not only a present participle, but with *en* is a gerund, which the learners had been investigating for the grammar/discourse role as well. In line 37, Claire also determined that she could figure it out from context and erased her underlining. When Claire was asked in the previous two excerpts to determine if there were words whose meaning she could determine from context, with the exception of one phrase between Excerpts 6.12 and 6.13, she was unable to eliminate any of the words in her list until the RT asked her about specific words. After this excerpt, Claire and the RT found a word for which Claire needed some slight mediation after which point, she returned to preparing the role on her own. Claire not only acknowledged that she in fact knew the above words or could figure them out from context, but importantly she also provided appropriate English equivalents when sharing her role preparation.

During the seventh instructional session, Claire did not have any words on her list that she could have determined from context, nor did she need to be reminded how to prepare her role. She did however ask for verification on her English equivalents for *gémit*, *gamin* and *patience*. She had appropriate equivalents but needed the RT's confirmation.

During the ninth instructional session, each learner had all four roles for Foundation. Claire and Gisele discovered that they were both having difficulty with *croisa* (met) when they each asked the RT for assistance.

The transcript is given in Excerpt 6.14 below. Prior to the excerpt with some mediation from the RT, Claire and Gisele were able to determine that *croisa* was not related to the verb *croire* (to believe) as they had thought and was formulated in the tense *passé simple*. *Passé simple* is used in formal writing such as literature and is therefore considered a literary past tense. From their knowledge of the formation of *passé simple*, they were able to determine, with mediation, that *croisa* was an inflected form of the verb *croiser*. They did not, however, know the meaning of *croiser*.

Excerpt 6.14 Session 10-9 – *Croisa* 1

```
1   Claire   to cross + to fold one's arms + to pass. + to meet.
                 ((slight head tilt after 'to meet.'))
2            (2.0)
3   RT       which [one °do you think°
4   Claire         [so ((looks at text))
5            it's
6            +++
7   Claire   I think it's to meet
                 ((looks at dictionary, gaze shifts to RT))
8   RT       because,
9   Claire   because
                 ((gaze shifts to text))
10           ++
11  Claire   le géant croisa un enfant
12           +
13  Claire   so they meet
14  RT       umhm
15  Claire   (ok)
16  Gisele   whos- looked lost,
17  RT       umhm,
18           +
19  Gisele   good.
20           (2.5)
21  Gisele   (xxx) hh
22           (2.0)
23  RT       so since it's passé simple
24           ++
25  RT       it's
26           +++
27  RT       that or something [(else),
28  Claire                     [he met
29  RT       umhm
```

Claire looked up *croiser* in a bilingual dictionary and in line 1 she listed the possible English equivalents. Her voice changed slightly with falling intonation on 'to pass.' and 'to meet.' and after the final and correct equivalent (to meet), she nodded her head slightly. After a two-second pause, the RT attempted to verify that Claire and/or Gisele were able to determine the correct English equivalent, in line 2. Claire overlapped with the RT after 'which' and the RT finished the remainder of the question in a quieter voice. Claire did not provide the appropriate equivalent during the overlap but used 'so' and 'its' in lines 4 and 5 to hold the floor while she shifted her gaze to the text. After a fairly lengthy pause, as Claire shifted her gaze back to the dictionary, she provided an appropriate equivalent for *croiser* for the context, 'to meet'. In line 8, the RT immediately asked for the reason why 'to meet' was appropriate for *croiser* in this context. Claire shifted her gaze back to the text and once again held the floor ('because'). After a pause, she read the relevant text segment: *le géant croisa un enfant* (line 11). Following a short pause, she provided an English equivalent for the phrase. It was not completely appropriate though because *croisa* was in *passé simple* and therefore should have been 'met'. The RT accepted Claire's response thus far in line 14 in terms of the English equivalent matching the context. After a short interaction with Gisele in lines 16–21, the RT attempted, in lines 23, 25 and 27, to determine if the learners were able to provide the appropriate equivalent both in form and meaning for the context. Her mediation was fairly implicit and included pauses in which the learners could respond. In line 28, Claire overlapped with the RT's third prompt and provided the appropriate equivalent in form and meaning, which the RT accepted in line 29.

Later when Claire presented her role preparation to the collective, she provided the French word from the text, *croisa*, the infinitive *croiser*, the tense *passé simple* and the appropriate English equivalent 'met' as indicated in lines 1, 3 and 7 of the transcript in Excerpt 6.15 below.

Excerpt 6.15 Session 10-9 – *Croisa 2*

```
1  Claire   croisa,
            ((gaze down))
2           +
3  Claire   is croiser,
4           +
5  Claire   um
6           +
7  Claire   and it's in passé simple so it means met
```

From this point on, Claire was able to select words to investigate using a bilingual dictionary that she was unable to understand from the context and identify appropriate English equivalents for the context without further mediation from the RT.

Passé simple

During the second instructional session and six minutes into the initial role preparation for the first page of the first text, Claire, who was assigned the grammar/discourse role, needed a reminder about what the grammar/

discourse role entailed. When she shared her preparation with the RT, it turned out that she had prepared Genre rather than Foundation. The RT reminded Claire what the grammar/discourse role entailed and then began to provide examples of grammatical or discourse elements from the text with which may have caused her problems, thus requiring further investigation on her part. In Excerpt 6.16 below, the transcript of the one-on-one mediation session is given.

Excerpt 6.16 Session 3-2 – *Passé simple* 1

```
1  RT      or + um + the fact that that's prit,
2          +
3  RT      and déclara,
4          ++
5  Claire  yeh I was kinda confused by that one
```

In lines 1 and 3, the RT selected *prit* and *déclara*, both of which are verbs that are in *passé simple*. *Passé simple* carries a similar meaning as *passé composé* and can be used in conjunction with *imparfait* in the same way that *passé composé* can. By fourth semester, learners have generally been introduced to the tense but for purposes of recognition only. In line 5, after pauses, Claire acknowledged that she 'was kinda confused'. She added these verbs to her list to investigate. Just under fifteen minutes later, she said "°*déclara*°" quietly to herself (i.e. private speech) and began using a grammatical resource (*501 French Verbs* book, Kendris, 1996) to investigate it. Four minutes later, during her time to share her role preparation, she read the phrase from the text in French which contained both *passé simple* verbs and provided an English equivalent for the phrase before continuing on with the next items on her list, as indicated in lines 1, 3 and 5 of Excerpt 6.17 below. Although they were appropriate equivalents, the role preparation and sharing entails more than simply providing an appropriate equivalent. The RT then began a lengthy exchange with the three learners present (Daisy was absent).

Excerpt 6.17 Session 3-2 – *Passé simple* 2

```
1   Claire  and the lion- le lion prit le parole et déclara
2           +
3   Claire  uh he took the floor and declared
4           +
5   Claire  and then um
6   RT      how do you know + that's + past tense.
7           (2.0)
8   Claire  uhh
9           +++
10  RT      or what- + past tense is it,
11  Claire  past s- + simple, + passé simple
```

```
12  RT      yeh what is that
13          +
14  RT      do you know do you know what passé simple is,
15  Gisele  [uh
16  RT      [all three of you
17  Gisele  I can- + y- yes hh
18  Claire  uh yes and no [hh
19  Gisele                [hh
20  RT      have you ever heard of it
21  Claire  [yes=
22  Ella    [yes=
23  Gisele  [yes=
24  RT      =yes
25          ++
26  RT      what do you know about it
27          +++
28  Gisele  the endings
29          +
30  Gisele  I can tell from the endings
31          on the prit and déclara
32  Claire  yeh
33  RT      ok
34  Claire  that's about it hh
35  RT      and what- + what + is it used for
36          +
37  RT      why might they be using the passé simple here
38          +++
39  RT      versus [any other tense
40  Gisele         [(passé xxx)
41  Claire  cuz it just happened + right + no
42          (3.0)
43  Claire  cuz it's just like a one time act,
44          ++
45  RT      ok, so is it different
46          or the same as passé composé,
47          +++
48  Claire  °different,°
49          +
50  Gisele  it seems like relatively the same
51          from what I can tell
52          ++
53  RT      ok,
54  Gisele  but passé composé has a preceding
55          avoir or être hel[ping [verb
56  RT                       [ok
57  Claire                         [(yeh)
58          ++
59  RT      so::
60          ++
61  Claire  wait
62  RT      yeh
63  Claire  I- I know this
64          +
65  Claire  and I like have it on the tip of my tongue
```

```
66              ++
67   Claire     what like + why we used it.
68              (3.0)
69   Claire     °I don't know°
70              it's not because it's a one time thing.
71              cuz I think I said
72              like the opposite of what I wanted to say.
73   RT         ok
74              ++
75   Claire     uh + because + it's
76              (2.0)
77   Claire     °I don't know.°
78              (2.0)
79   Claire     °it's like a° general
80              (2.0)
81   Claire     I don't know.
82   RT         I think you're trying
83              to think of imparfait maybe
84   Claire     [maybe I'm thinking
85   RT         [passé composé and imparfait,
86   Claire     maybe that's what I'm thinking [of.
87   RT                                        [and the diff-
88              the difficulties between
89              [when you use which of those
90   Claire     [yeh maybe
91              yeh maybe I'm getting it wrong=
92   RT         =but then [we have passé simple
93   Claire               [that's
94              yeh I don't know.
95              +++
96   RT         do you know when passé simple is used Ella,
97   Ella       I do but ++ ok let me just get this straight
98   RT         ok
```

The RT first asked, in line 6, how Claire knew these verbs were in a past tense. After a lengthy pause, Claire's attempt to hold the floor ('uhh'), and another lengthy pause, the RT modified her question, asking in which tense in the past the verbs were. In line 11, Claire appropriately labeled the tense as *passé simple* but offered no further information. The RT then asked Claire, in line 12, what *passé simple* was and after a pause and no response, she asked the collective if they knew what the tense was. Gisele and Claire responded with considerable uncertainty and vagueness as indicated by hesitations, false starts and laughter, as well as stating both 'yes' and 'no', in lines 15, and 17–19. In line 20, the RT decided to verify that the learners had in fact heard of the tense before. They all responded that they had in lines 21–23, which overlapped. In line 26, the RT tried again to determine what they knew about the tense and after a lengthy pause, Gisele responded that she was aware of the endings. Claire agreed in line 32 stating that she recognized the endings of the two verbs in question, *prit* and *déclara*. She had not recognized them though in the previous excerpt, or at least did not indicate that she had. Although in line 34, Claire said that the endings comprised the extent of her knowledge of *passé simple*, the RT asked about how the tense is normally used (lines 35, 37 and 39). In lines 41 and 43, Claire began to explain her understanding of the usage of *passé simple*; her explanation was filled with pauses and exhibited superficial 'rules-of-thumb' knowledge typical of most textbook presentations of *passé composé*.

In lines 45 and 46, the RT asked whether *passé simple* was similar or different than *passé composé*. Claire responded that they were different, while Gisele answered that they were 'relatively the same from what I can tell' in lines 50 and 51. Gisele clarified that the two tenses differed in their form though and Claire agreed (see lines 54, 55, and 57). In line 61, Claire said, 'wait,' which appears to serve both a social, floor-holding function, and as private speech in which she told herself that she may have determined an appropriate explanation. In lines 63–72, she aimed to express her understanding of the usage of *passé simple* but again her explanation was filled with hesitations, pauses, false starts, and ended with an acknowledgement that she did not in fact know and that she was confused. In lines 75–81, she continued, but twice more acknowledged that she did not know.

From her attempted explanations: 'a one time act' (line 43) and 'a general' (line 79), which are parts of the oft-used rules of thumb for *passé composé* and *imparfait*, the RT indicated in lines 82, 83, 85, 87–89 that perhaps Claire was thinking of the usages of these two tenses instead of *passé simple*. Although *passé composé* and *imparfait* are the two most commonly used tenses in the past in learners' textbooks, their usages are quite difficult for English-speaking learners of French to understand, particularly given that they are used in conjunction in narrative texts. Claire overlapped the RT's utterance in lines 84, 86, 90, and 91 and acknowledged that she had likely been confusing the tenses. In line 92, the RT returned to ask again about *passé simple* and Claire admitted for a final time that she did not know. As Ella had been silent through the exchange to this point, the RT asked her what she knew about the tense in question. In line 97, she indicated that she did know how it was used but had a question before she shared her understanding.

Following the excerpt, Ella asked about another verb form that had not yet been part of the discussion – the conditional. For the next three minutes, the RT responded to Ella's question and mediated Claire's use of a different grammatical resource book than she had used previously. Ella also asked for a list of verbs from the text in *passé simple*. As a response, the RT listed all of the verbs in this section of the text and asked Gisele and Ella to determine which were in *passé simple*. She provided this level of mediation to determine if the learners were in fact able to identify verbs in *passé simple* from their endings. Claire then explained her understanding of *passé simple* from what she had located in the grammar resource book. The RT and the collective then compared *passé simple* and *passé composé*, *passé composé* and *imparfait*, and *passé simple* and *imparfait*. They also discussed if and why there would be *passé simple* and *passé composé* in the same text as well as how to form the *passé simple* for verbs that end in ER, IR and RE.

Two instructional sessions later, Claire was assigned the grammar/discourse role for the second time. When the RT sat down next to Claire to check in with her, Claire immediately commented, with no prompting, that there were verbs in the *passé simple* in the text for which she provided appropriate examples, as can be seen in lines 1, 3, and 4 in Excerpt 6.18 below.

Excerpt 6.18 Session 5-4 – *Passé simple* 3

```
1  Claire  °alright° ++ so + we already know + passé simple=
2  RT      =ok=
3  Claire  =and then you see a couple situations
4          where it's there
5  RT      ok
```

Throughout the brief excerpt, Claire's gaze was lowered, she did not use rising intonation, both of her utterances were latched with the RT's, indicating that she had confidence in her knowledge and therefore did not need to wait for the RT's confirmation. After the five-line exchange, she continued with a new topic for her grammar/discourse role preparation. This was a significant shift from the previous excerpt where Claire (and others) was only able to identify that the tense of two verbs was *passé simple*. In this excerpt, she did not need mediation, was confident in her role preparation and she was, importantly, correct in her evaluation.

One and a half minutes later in Claire's role preparation for grammar/discourse, she pointed out that a particular verb was in *passé simple*, as seen in line 1 in Excerpt 6.19 below. Although Claire showed considerable confidence in her ability to deal with *passé simple* in the previous excerpt, she was not yet fully in control as can be seen from this and the following excerpt.

Excerpt 6.19 Session 5-4 – *Passé simple* 4

```
1  Claire  I think this is passé simple
2  RT      sure,
3          ++
4  Claire  uh + oh no cuz that's got a thing before
5          it oh so that's passé composé.
6  RT      umkay.
```

It is unclear from the video, which verb Claire and the RT were discussing, as it was never overtly identified. The RT asked if Claire was 'sure,' with slightly rising intonation. After a pause, Claire was able to indicate that it was not *passé simple* but *passé composé* and was able to provide the reason it was the latter tense. Her gaze was on the text, and she produced falling intonation at the conclusion of her utterance; the RT accepted her claim and reasoning as appropriate in line 6.

Two minutes and forty-five seconds later, the RT noticed that Claire wrote 'P.S.' next to a verb on the last page of the first text. The verb, *répondit*, was conjugated in the *passé simple*, but has the same conjugation as an IR verb would in the present tense; however, *répondre* is an RE verb. In Excerpt 6.20 below, the RT decided to verify that Claire was able to be confident in her determination of *passé simple* for the verb in question.

Excerpt 6.20 Session 5-4 – *Passé simple* 5

```
1    RT       sure that that's passé simple,
2             (3.0)
3    RT       it can be
4             ++
5    RT       can it be anything else,
6             ++
7    Claire   um::
8             (6.0)
9    Claire   °could it just be° + future,
10   RT       how do you form future
11   Claire   I mean no + no it's not future.
12   RT       ok,
13            (3.0)
14   Claire   I mean + it could be + present, he responds
15   RT       how do you do ++
16            that [type of conjugation in the present
17   Claire        [(but there wouldn't be)
18            (2.0)
19   Claire   °répondre° R E verbs
20            (3.0)
21   Claire   ohh I think uh
22            +++
23   Claire   I think- it's not passé simple (xxx)=
24   RT       =sure=
25   Claire   =no (xxx) sure
26            now you're making me [question it.
27   RT                            [hh
28            ++
29   Claire   um
30            (5.0)
31   Claire   I think it is
32   RT       what's the p- you were hesitating with present
33            what's the present conjugation
```

34	**Claire**	that's what I'm trying to like ++ remember
35		+
36	**Claire**	with R E verbs
37		(3.0)
38	**Claire**	I'm gonna look up +++ °répondre°
39	**RT**	Daisy can we have your 501 French verb book
40	**Claire**	can I see that book
41	**RT**	(°thank you°)
42	**Claire**	thank you
43		(26.0)
		((Claire searches for *répondre* in the 501 French verb book))
44	**Claire**	um
45		++
46	**Claire**	°u- like-° it's *passé simple*.
47		++
		((RT nods her head))
48	**Claire**	it definitely is then.
49	**RT**	yeh.
50	**Claire**	ok.
51		++
52	**Claire**	yeh I knew th-
53		I knew that it wasn't right for present
54		but I wasn't sure then
55		cuz then I started ques[tioning myself
56	**RT**	[it makes
57		this makes you think
58		that it could be I R present tense
59	**Claire**	yeh [but then it's not [R E though.
60	**RT**	[(xxx) [(xxx)
61	**RT**	yeh
62	**Claire**	ok.
63	**RT**	good
64	**Claire**	alright I'm good

In line 1, the RT asked if Claire was confident about her identification of the verb tense. Following a three second pause, the RT indicated that Claire could have made the correct determination, but after another pause, she probed further, asking if the verb could be in any other tense. Claire first suggested the future (line 9) but once the RT asked how the future is formed (line 10), she quickly dismissed this option (line 11). In line 14, Claire selected the present tense as an option and once again, the RT asked her to verify her determination with the present tense conjugation. From line 17 to 26, Claire quietly provided the infinitive (*répondre*), that it could be classified as an RE verb, and rejected her original and correct designation of *passé simple*. In line 24, the RT asked her if she was confident about her new tense determination. Claire responded that she was unsure, and that the RT's questions made her second-guess her original selection.

She continued to think about the issue and in lines 32 and 33 the RT asked her about her previous label of present tense and again asked her for the present tense conjugation of *répondre* in order to help her determine that *répondit* was not its present tense form. In lines 34, 36 and 38, Claire attempted to determine the present tense conjugation but was unable to do so and indicated that she would need to look up the conjugation of *répondre* in one of the grammar reference books. In lines 46 and 48, after using the reference book, Claire returned to her original choice of *passé simple*, and the RT confirmed in lines 47 and 49 with 'yeh.' and head nods. In line 55, Claire expressed that she had started questioning herself. In lines 56–58, the RT explained the reason that the tense of this particular conjugation was challenging, and Claire confirmed that RE verbs in the present tense do not have the same endings as IR verbs do. Although Claire's work on *passé simple* had changed dramatically, it was important to determine if she had a full understanding of the tense and if she had confidence in her tense determination. Although she was still unsure, by this point she had improved significantly from the second instructional session.

By the ninth instructional session, Claire was able to be confident about *passé simple* and was even able to assist Gisele with regard to the verb *croisa* (*croiser* in *passé simple*) as noted earlier. She also selected to share her role preparation for *passé simple* with the collective. At this point, the learners had each prepared all four roles. Claire listed examples of verbs conjugated in *passé simple* from the final page of the text, explained the reason *passé simple* is used, that *passé composé*, *imparfait* and *passé simple* could be used in the same text, and that in this particular text, *passé simple* was used for the narrator/author. She was correct, gave a full explanation and was confident.

Especially for the grammar/discourse role, there is a tension between the grammatical elements that are beyond learners' ability at a particular point in time and those that they are able to learn in the process of reading a text, accompanied by mediation. In the case of *passé simple*, the learners had previously been introduced to the tense, at least cursorily, and that the tense is prevalent in literature. Although their understanding was minimal at the outset of the study, they were, with mediation, able to understand *passé simple* and its usage in narrative texts by the end of the study.

Understanding the roles

The learners needed mediation to fully comprehend what each role entailed, how to investigate textual elements, which resources to use and how to use them, and how to share their role preparation. Several examples will be provided to illustrate the change in Claire's shifting understanding of the roles throughout the study.

At the outset, the reading process was deconstructed into its component parts to enable learners to understand, practice, appropriate and internalize each component before the process could be carried out in its entirety by each learner. Because the vocabulary and grammar/discourse roles are tightly linked and interdependent, it was difficult for learners to disambiguate them at the beginning of the study. As explained above, during the second instructional session, Gisele was unable to determine the meaning of the title of the first text *Le Champ du Lièvre*. She investigated the meaning of *champ* and then *lièvre* with the RT's mediation, but when it was determined that Gisele's remaining difficulty was one that concerned grammar/discourse, the RT said, 'maybe you can ask your grammar person to work on this part'. As explained above, Gisele did so, and Claire investigated the use of *du* in the title. Later in the same session, Gisele needed to investigate the verb *demanda*, which is in *passé simple* for the infinitive *demander*. Gisele said that she would investigate the verb, but the RT reminded her, 'why *demander* + what it is if she [Claire] wants to do why it's *demanda*, + she can'. Although investigating the meaning of *demander* separately from the meaning and usage of *demanda* may seem artificial, it was necessary, at the outset, for vocabulary and grammar/discourse to be artificially divided. At this point in the process, learners were not yet able to investigate the interconnected meaning of both the vocabulary and grammar/discourse function of a word.

During the second instructional session, Claire's first role preparation (grammar/discourse) for the first text, and a mediation session between Claire and the RT, Claire informed the RT what she had learned thus far. It was not appropriate for the role that she was assigned, however. The RT attempted to redirect Claire's focus to what the grammar/discourse role entailed as shown in Excerpt 6.21.

Excerpt 6.21 Session 3-2 – Understanding the roles 1

```
1  RT  any + thing that you don't understand
2      (3.0)
3  RT  the way that grammar or discourse is used
4      (3.5)
5  RT  so just for example.
6      +
7  RT  like something like à ceux qui,
       ((points to text))
8      ++
9  RT  or
```

In lines 1 and 3, the RT asked Claire if there were any grammatical or discourse elements in the text that she did not understand. During the lengthy pause between and following the RT's question, Claire did not respond. The RT then began to list elements in the text that may have caused problems for Claire, and which would therefore be appropriate to investigate for the grammar/discourse role (lines 5 and 7). Following Excerpt 6.21, the RT asked Claire about two verbs (*prit* and *déclara*) in *passé simple* and Claire expressed her confusion, as was seen in Excerpt 6.16 above. Following Excerpt 6.16, the RT provided another possibly difficult textual element, *vive*, which is a form of the verb (*vivre*) in the subjunctive mood. The RT listed examples in order to redirect Claire's focus to first select textual elements that she needed to investigate. If Claire needed mediation in order to investigate the selected elements, they could then focus on how to study these elements. Claire was able to express the meaning of the verb *vivre* but not *vive*. In lines 1, 3, 5 and 7 in Excerpt 6.22 (21 seconds after Excerpt 6.21), the RT emphasized how the vocabulary and grammar/discourse roles differ.

Excerpt 6.22 Session 3-2 – Understanding the roles 2

```
1  RT    so are they any things
2        ++
3  RT    that are
4        +++
5  RT    not just the meaning of the word but
6        +
7  RT    the form it takes
```

About 20 seconds later, the RT identified another possible difficulty, in which Claire was able to determine that *en mangeant* is derived from the verb *manger* but did not recognize its form nor did she understand its use. The RT again clarified the difference between the vocabulary and grammar/discourse roles, in lines 1 and 2 as shown in Excerpt 6.23 below and introduced Claire to the available grammatical resources in lines 4 and 7.

Excerpt 6.23 Session 3-2 – Understanding the roles 3

```
1  RT       so the fact that it's in
              ((pointing to text))
2           + the form en mangeant versus manger
              ((pointing to text))
3  Claire   yeh that confuses me then
4  RT       right. so you might need + some of these
                                          ((pointing to
                                           grammatical
                                           resources))
5           +
6  Claire   [(ok)
              ((nods))
7  RT       [resources + to get to the bottom of that
8  Claire   ok
              ((nods))
```

9	**RT**	ok.
10		+
11	**RT**	to help you
12		+
13	**RT**	not only + understand the basic idea
14		but the very particulars
15		of how language is used
16	**Claire**	ok
		((nods))
17	**RT**	to paint a particular picture.

Again, the RT attempted to assist Claire in determining appropriate textual elements that caused grammar/discourse difficulties in her comprehension of a particular section of the text and encouraged her to investigate these further. After Claire expressed her confusion (line 3), the RT identified the resources she might use and the nature of what she needed to investigate while using the resources (lines 11, and 13–15). Claire acknowledged the RT's suggestions with 'ok' and head noddings (lines 6, 8 and 16). Not surprisingly, Claire needed mediation from the RT to appropriately use the grammatical resources to investigate the elements they had jointly selected.

Four instructional sessions later, when Claire was once again assigned the role of grammar/discourse (along with the role of vocabulary), she was no longer unsure about what the grammar role entailed, nor did she need the RT's mediation for how to investigate textual elements, what resources to use, how to use them or how to share her role preparation. She also no longer focused solely on the tense, aspect or mood of the verbs in the text, although these were an important part of the grammar/discourse role. For example, in the sixth instructional session, when the collective was focused on the first page of the second instructional text, the RT asked Claire 'why do we have this + statement with + pronouns and we don't even know who they are when we first read this first sentence'. The first sentence of the text was '*Elles lui ont joué un sale tour, vraiment*' (They played a dirty trick on him, really). *Elles* and *lui* are both cataphoric pronouns; therefore it was not yet clear to the reader to whom the pronouns referred, nor why the author might have used this as the first sentence of the text. Claire responded immediately, 'it's like an attention grabber,' which the RT accepted. Claire then continued 'you want to know, °what dirty trick they played.°' 'who's sh- who's he,' 'really,' and the RT again accepted Claire's explanation, which was appropriate.

The above examples focused on the vocabulary and grammar/discourse roles are similar in nature to the developmental process for each of the other roles. For example, when Claire was first assigned the main idea role, she needed the RT's mediation to fully comprehend, appropriate and internalize the role. In the third instructional session, during a one-on-one mediation session and after Claire had shared the main idea that she had prepared for the collective, the RT asked her to abridge her summary, including only the main ideas, and to use generalizations, as shown in Excerpt 6.24. In order to maintain focus on the RT's mediation of Claire's knowledge regarding the main idea role, some elements of the interaction are loosely described in double parentheses instead of closely transcribed.

Excerpt 6.24 Session 3-2 – Understanding the roles 4

```
1    RT   can you + boil that down even more.
2         ((Claire agreed))
3    RT   doesn't have to be one sentence.
4         ((Claire provided updated summary))
5    RT   what are the key like
6         the key + elements for this page.
7         ((Claire listed key elements))
8    RT   why 10 steps,
9         ((Claire provided appropriate reasoning but not
          an appropriate generalization))
10   RT   it's not so much that they took 10
11        ((Claire condensed the summary but not sufficiently))
12   RT   but it's that the- the 10 steps
13        +++
14   RT   will + like everyone will have something
15        + that matches
16        ((Claire again mentioned the ten steps))
17   RT   that matches with thei- their n- needs right,
18        ((Claire revised her summary))
19        ((24 seconds of discussions about the summary))
20   RT   you might need to write down like in a bullet form
21        +
22   RT   the main ideas
23        ((10 seconds of discussions about the summary))
24   RT   and how to boil it down to
25        +
26   RT   more like- generalizations
27        where it's like it's not about the 10
28        but it's about their needs.
29        and then put it back together.
```

In lines 1 and 3, the RT asked Claire to condense her summary and clarified that it 'doesn't have to be one sentence.'. After Claire provided an updated summary, the RT asked her to identify the main ideas (lines 5–6), which Claire did, adding that each animal was asked to take 10 steps. In the story, the lion asks each animal to mark the edges of their field with ten steps on each side (to make it fair for each animals' needs). They each did so, except for the rabbit, which jumped (as rabbits do) instead of walking, therefore marking out a field larger than its fair share. In the summary, the main ideas, concerning the topics in question, are as follows: the plan to determine an appropriate field size for each animal by gait as well as the animals' unhappiness with the rabbit's bending of the rules. The fact that 10 steps were chosen as opposed to any other number of steps, however, was not an important detail that Claire had included in her summary. Claire was not able to determine, even with mediation (see lines 8–11), which of these were main ideas and which were supporting details. The RT then explained to Claire, in lines 12, 14, 15, and 17, that the 10 steps represent that the size of each animal's field would match their needs, which Claire accepted.

Notice that Claire did not respond appropriately during any of the pauses or restarts in lines 12–17. The RT later advised Claire to create a list of main ideas so that she did not write a word-for-word translation of the events in the text and could begin to select only the main ideas for the text (see lines 20 and 22). The RT also suggested that Claire use generalizations (lines 24 and 26) and provided an example of what she meant by generalizations (lines 27–29). Claire was able to provide an appropriate summary by the time that she shared her role preparation and continued to do so from this point in the study forward. She did not need any further mediation regarding preparation of the main idea role.

Claire was assigned the role of prediction for the first time during the third instructional session. After she shared her role preparation with the RT, the latter began to mediate Claire's understanding of the nature of the prediction role. The RT first asked Claire 'how do you think they'll they do that?,' as it was unclear how the animals would be likely to do what she had predicted. When Claire was unable to provide an appropriate reason based on the text, the RT clarified the prediction role: 'the most important thing for making a prediction + is to have + a prediction, but also to have it point out in the text where + where your ideas are coming from what makes you think that that is what's going to happen + otherwise it's like you know it can become any ending or any future'.

About three minutes later when the RT checked in with Claire once more, she was still unable to provide an appropriate text-based prediction. The RT then asked, 'what in the text though makes you ++ makes that a relevant ++ a realistic possibility ++ is there any clues that are in there?,' but Claire provided a general and not a specific text-based response: 'because (5.5) usually ++ like a children's story has like a moral + or something'. The researcher then stated, 'but (in) this particular page,' making it clear that Claire needed to locate something in the language of the particular page on which they were currently focused to inform her prediction. Claire was able to point to specific and appropriate language in the text but was later unable to use it to improve her prediction on her own. She presented the latest version of her role preparation for prediction to the collective but immediately afterwards stated: 'but now I'm starting to rethink it,' after which she provided an appropriate text-based prediction. When the RT asked for her reason for changing her prediction, Claire responded: 'because they're not just gonna happen upon him by chance and I think they're kind of they have this idea in their head ++ that the rabbit's working like too hard for what he should be working,' which was an appropriate text-based reason that supported her prediction. The RT confirmed Claire's response, 'ok I think that's wh- yeh. ++ that's th- key there. ++ that that's ++ just super human. + or super-,' Gisele completed the RT's utterance 'super rabbit hh'. Finally, the RT accepted Gisele's humorous contribution and continued to agree with Claire's reasoning: 'super rabbit right, + so that's unusual. so they might + they might try to get to the bottom of it.'. For the remainder of the study, Claire was able to provide appropriate text-based predictions without further mediation needed.

As for Organization, during the fifth instructional session and Claire's first assignment of the role of 'complex reaction,' when she shared her role preparation, the RT noticed that Claire had confused goal and attempt. Goal is one of two components for complex reaction and attempt is one of two components for goal path, which was assigned to Gisele. The portion of the text that Claire shared for goal was in fact a combination of the goal and attempt. The RT alerted Claire to this fact: 'we have to be very careful between goal and attempt + so his goal is' and then when Claire did not respond during a 2.5 second pause, the RT clarified the difference between the two elements of the episode structure by providing their definitions: 'to resolve [some issue and then attempt is how he's going to actively put that into place.'. The difficulty with this particular goal was that it had to be inferred, as it was not explicitly stated. Claire was able, with mediation, to determine the implied goal for this section of the text. During the eighth instructional session, and the learners' role preparation for Organization for the second instructional text, Claire included information that was not explicitly mentioned in the text, but instead was what she imagined the characters may have done. The RT reminded Claire, 'don't think about ++ this in + real life how this would play out. + like ++ hey we're going to have this plan bla bla bla and here's how we're going to do it da da da + you just have the words in the text. +++ and they have to fit into different spots. ++ so we only are classifying what we can see here.'. From this point in the study, Claire used only the textual elements to identify the Organization of the text.

As for Genre, during the fifth instructional session and Claire's first practice with the role of tenor for the first instructional text, she needed mediation in order to provide appropriate language of the text as evidence of the author's relationship with the reader. Claire had indicated that at the end of the text, the author/narrator warns the readers that if they see the rabbit they should not reveal that the author/narrator told them the story. The RT asked for evidence of how the author talks to the reader, using the language of the text. Claire discussed the author's use of *vous* when he addressed the reader at the end of the text and indicated that therefore the author considered the reader to be 'an authority figure' and 'he's not talking down to us necessarily.'. The RT asked Claire to consider that the author's use of *vous* could be used as a plural second person pronoun instead. Given that the author of the text is known for being an oral storyteller, his use of *vous* as a plural address form was a more likely possibility. Claire then suggested that although the author was warning the reader, he did not use 'a very formal voice necessarily' and again the RT asked for language of the text that served as evidence of her assessment. For both Organization and Genre, the learners needed mediation to understand the concepts, what the roles entailed and especially that they needed to use the language of the text as evidence for their role preparation.

Throughout the research study with the RT's mediation and the collective's participation in the C-BLI/DOLP reading process, Claire (as well as the others) was able to appropriate the roles for each concept, internalize them, use them as tools for thinking to guide her thinking and reading process, provide appropriate role preparation to the collective, be confident about her understanding, and required less mediation as the program progressed. Her scores improved dramatically from pre- to post-test and her verbalizations changed significantly from Time 1 to Time 4.

Change in Mediation

To analyze the change in mediation as instruction moved forward, some previously discussed excerpts along with a few new ones will be analyzed. By carefully transcribing bodily movements including gestures and gaze as well as verbal elements including the volume of speech, the content, pausing and intonation patterns among others, it is possible to identify the quality of the RT's mediation, assess the learners' responsivity to it and identify changes in mediation that occurred over time. Learners may not be aware that they need mediation; they may recognize that they need mediation but are unable to ask for the specific assistance that they need; or they may realize that they need mediation and are able to identify the type that is most appropriate for their development. Mediation must be sensitive to the learners' needs allowing them to have maximum responsibility and agency depending on their ZPD-in-activity. As they develop, they will be able to take on more responsibility. Throughout this process, learners are developing the ability to be solely responsible for their performance and be able to monitor, evaluate and repair any difficulties that arise.

As has already been noted, following mediation for a particular (part of a) role, Claire did not need further mediation other than what has been analyzed above. It is important to mention as well that after learners had had practice with each of the roles several times (as in the case for Foundation and Organization), the RT asked the learners to select the roles they would prepare first, based on which roles they felt they needed more practice with. Each time, Claire quickly chose the roles with which she needed further development. Throughout the mediation sessions, Claire was responsive to the RT's efforts: she used utterances to hold her place, overlapped the RT's utterance when she was able to respond without further mediation, applied what she had learned from mediation when preparing her roles independently, and responded to mediation as soon as she was able to, thus allowing the RT to better attune her future mediation.

During the fourth instructional session, Claire was assigned the grammar/discourse role for the second time, and as noted above, was developing her understanding of *passé simple*. During mediation, the RT asked Claire if she knew the tense of an uncommon verb that appeared in the text. See line 1 of the transcript in Excerpt 6.25 below. As the construction was quite challenging because of the adverb positioned between the auxiliary verb and the past participle and because of a reflexive infinitive after the tense in question (*Ils ont bien failli se battre*), it was used to assess Claire's developing ability with the grammar/discourse role.

Excerpt 6.25 Session 5-4 – Mediation 1

```
1    RT       know what tense this is,
2             ++
3    Claire   that was the one I-
4             that was- um something I was going to look up
5    RT       any clues,
6             ++
7    Claire   um
8             (6.5)
9    Claire   it's not passé simple,
10   RT       it's not,
11   Claire   it's not passé-,=
12   RT       =ok.
13            ++
14   Claire   is it c- I think it's passé comp-
15            is it passé composé,
16   RT       how do you know
17            ++
18   Claire   because the bien + is going before it
19            but + they use avoir
20            and um that would be the end of an + I R verb,
21   RT       yep.
22            ++
23   Claire   so faillir. I don't know what that means.
24            but ++ yo-
25            you can say that it's passé [composé.
26   RT                                   [umhm umhm
```

In lines 3 and 4, Claire replied that she needed to investigate it because she was not sure. Although she may have needed to do so, the RT attempted to verify whether she would be able to resolve her confusion with some implicit mediation. The RT asked, in line 5, if there were any clues as to the tense in the context. After several pauses, Claire determined that the verb was not in *passé simple*, the tense that she was preparing earlier in the session. To verify if Claire was certain, the RT asked in line 10 'it's not,' with slightly rising intonation. By lines 14 and 15, Claire asked the RT if it was *passé composé*, which was the correct tense. To be sure, the RT asked for Claire's reasoning, which she provided in lines 18–20, accompanied by a comment on the challenging nature of the construction. The RT accepted her reasoning in line 21. Claire then provided the infinitive of the verb in question (*faillir*) and although she was not familiar with the meaning of the verb, with implicit mediation, she was able to determine the tense.

In Excerpts 6.11, 6.12 and 6.13 earlier for the sixth instructional session and Claire's second turn with the vocabulary role, the RT mediated Claire's understanding of the role preparation and how to use the context to determine the meaning of unknown words before using a bilingual dictionary to investigate the remaining words. In Excerpt 6.11, the RT reminded Claire to 'select first what you want to look at' but she did not indicate how Claire might accomplish this task. Later, in Excerpt 6.12, the RT asked if there were any words for which Claire was able to determine the meaning from the context. This slightly more explicit information was needed as Claire was unable to appropriately select the words to investigate with a bilingual dictionary, by first eliminating the ones that she could resolve using the context. The mediation in Excerpt 6.12 focused on the way in which Claire should begin preparing her role. After lengthy pauses, she failed to identify any words whose meaning she could figure out from the context. In Excerpt 6.13, the RT then provided more explicit mediation by asking about specific words that were either easier to understand from the context or that she likely knew from her previous French coursework. Only at this level of mediation was Claire able to determine that she knew the meaning of six words from her original list.

As the lexical items became more challenging for Claire, the RT provided some implicit mediation along with identifying the words. For example, with *une main tremblotante* (a trembling hand), as hand was likely quite familiar to Claire, but trembling was not, when she did not respond to the addition of more context (first, *tremblotante* and then *une main tremblotante*), the RT pointed to her hand and Claire was able to provide an appropriate equivalent (although using French word order) for the phrase. It should be noted that the RT did not move her hand to demonstrate the trembling and kept the focus on the part that Claire was likely to know – *main*.

In Excerpts 6.10 and 6.14 above, the RT mediated Claire's use of the bilingual dictionary to find the most appropriate English equivalent for *souffler* and *croiser*. In Excerpt 6.10, after Claire listed several equivalents from the dictionary entry, the RT simply said 'hmmm,' but after a lengthy pause and no response from Claire, she provided more explicit mediation concerning the collocational information provided in the dictionary. In

Excerpt 6.14, after Claire once again listed several dictionary entries, the RT asked which was appropriate ('which [one °do you think°'). After 'which,' Claire overlapped the RT's utterance and began to determine the appropriate equivalent for the context. She was then able to do so on her own, and after prompting from the RT ('because,'), she was able to explain her reasoning.

From Excerpt 6.16 to 6.17, Claire successfully identified that the tense of *prit* and *déclara* was *passé simple* but she, as well as the other members of the collective, did not know anything about the function of the tense. The RT provided extensive mediation with the collective concerning *passé simple*, *passé composé* and *imparfait* and their usage in narrative texts. Two instructional sessions later, Claire identified verbs in *passé simple* on her own (Excerpt 6.18). In Excerpts 6.19, 6.20 and 6.25, the RT assessed Claire's developing understanding of *passé simple* in more complex constructions, and although she needed some mediation, her understanding of the tense and its usage significantly developed following the mediation in the second instructional session. She needed minimal mediation for *passé simple* in the ninth instructional session (see Excerpt 6.14 above, lines 23–28 for *croisa*) and was able to assist another learner in the collective as well as provide thorough information when she shared her role preparation (see Excerpt 6.15 above).

After brief mediation with the RT for the summary and prediction roles in the third instructional session outlined above, Claire no longer needed mediation to understand how to prepare the summary role and appropriately used the language of the text as evidence for making predictions. With Organization, Claire also needed some mediation concerning complex reaction and goal path (in the fifth instructional session) as well as the importance of using the language of the text to identify the components of the episodes (earlier in the eighth instructional session). She was, however, able to prepare her Organization roles with only minimal mediation as can be seen in two excerpts from later in the eighth instructional session, as shown in Excerpts 6.26 and 6.27 ahead.

Excerpt 6.26 Session 9-8 – Mediation 2

```
1   Claire   I- I have an idea,
2   RT       ok,
3   Claire   but I guess I have to wait
4            to see where they finish,
5   RT       write down what you think so far
6            and then you can always
7            ++
8   RT       are you at the end or the beginning
9   Claire   I'm the end this time.
10  RT       ok so make sure ++ you see what's before you
11           to see you're starting at the right spot.
12  Claire   umhm
```

Claire was assigned the roles of 'goal path' and 'ending' and needed less than two minutes with no mediation to complete her role preparation. In lines 1, 3, and 4, she alerted the RT that she had completed the task. The RT then reminded her to write down her role preparation. Following the verification of her role assignment, the RT advised her to corroborate her role preparation with the sections of the text for the roles prior to hers (lines 10 and 11). Less than four minutes later, as the RT completed a one-on-one mediation session with Gisele, Claire handed her notebook to the RT for verification, which initiated a brief mediation session with Claire (see Excerpt 6.27).

Excerpt 6.27 Session 9-8 – Mediation 3

```
1    Claire   ((hands her notebook to RT as RT finishes up
              mediating Gisele))
2             °I might have too much°
              ((gaze down))
3             (9.0)
4    RT       you have a little bit too much too.
5    Claire   in the beginning,
6    RT       umhm.
7             do you see [why,
8    Claire              [so would the first part
9             of what I said in the beginning
10            ++ be ++ part of the goal,
11   RT       uhhuh.
12   Claire   and the second part's + her=
13   RT       =umhm=
14   Claire   =attempt. ok.
15   RT       umhm.
16            +++
17   RT       exactly + good job.
18            ++
19   Claire   °that's what I couldn't decide°
              ((gaze down))
```

In line 2, Claire acknowledged quietly and with her gaze lowered that she may have included 'too much' for her roles of goal path and ending. The RT may not have been attuned to Claire's comment given the minimal volume and the RT's gaze on Claire's notebook entry, not on her. In line 4, the RT pointed out that Claire had more information than was appropriate for her roles and Claire was able to pinpoint where she had included too much information (line 5). As the RT began to ask if Claire understood the reason, Claire overlapped her utterance, providing a thorough and appropriate reasoning in lines 8–10, 12 and 14, which the RT confirmed in lines 11, 14 and 15. The RT then praised Claire's developing ability in line 17 to which Claire responded in a quiet voice and lowered gaze that she had been unable to decide, but implied that as soon as the

RT indicated that there was an issue (with minimal mediation), she was able to resolve it. Claire did not need further mediation for the Organization role.

Conclusion

As the analysis in the above excerpts shows, Claire required less mediation for many of the concepts and roles as instruction progressed. If appropriately attuned mediation had not been provided to Claire, it is unlikely that she would have improved her performance on the post-tests. Moreover, the effects of mediation were also manifested in changes in the quality of Claire's verbalizations, which ultimately resulted in her appropriation and internalization of the conceptual knowledge. At the outset, Claire was co-regulated by the collective, DOLP and the RT, but from the mediation in the C-BLI and DOLP she was able to internalize the roles for each concept, she became more self-regulated, and was therefore able to read much more independently than she did at the outset of instruction. By the end of the instructional sessions, Claire understood the roles, used the concepts as tools to guide her thinking and reading, articulated rationales, shared her role preparation appropriately and took on the responsibility for more roles at one time even as the difficulty level of the texts increased. The locus of control shifted from the collective and the RT to Claire (Lantolf & Poehner, 2014). Over time, Claire's responsivity to mediation changed, and she became more agentive in her interactions with the RT and the collective. The RT continually had to re-attune her mediation to be appropriate to Claire's changing needs (Vygotsky, 1997; Vygotsky & Luria, 1994). As she became more confident and independent, she monitored and evaluated the effectiveness of her performance and needed less confirmation from the RT. As noted in Chapter 4, Claire's Learning Potential Score was high, and her openness to mediation was clearly demonstrated throughout the analysis of her participation in the C-BLI and DOLP (Kozulin & Garb, 2002; Poehner & Lantolf, 2013). Although her L2 narrative literacy development was not complete at the end of the study, it had significantly improved. Finally, although the analysis in this chapter focused on Claire's developmental process, the other learners in RS1, RS2 and RS3 responded similarly to mediation and likewise showed development from the outset to the completion of the study. Each learner had their own unique path, and although the percentage of change in their scores from pre- to post-test may not have been as remarkable as Claire's was, each learner was able to significantly develop their L2 narrative literacy ability.

7 Future Developments in Vygotskian Second Language Literacy Pedagogy

Introduction

These three studies investigated the extent to which L2 learners of French were able to develop narrative literacy abilities using C-BLI implemented through a Division-of-Labor Pedagogy. The developmental process was carried out through two primary forms of mediation: systematically organized conceptual knowledge of the literacy process and dialogic interaction between a researcher-teacher and the learners. It is widely acknowledged that in most university foreign language programs a significant gap exists between courses where the focus is on language learning and courses where the goal is to interpret and analyze literary texts in the L2. Consequently, the present studies sought to design an effective instructional approach that would make a significant contribution to closing the gap. Specifically, the studies had the following research questions:

(1) To what extent does a C-BLI approach to L2 narrative literacy give rise to learners' conceptual understanding of the Foundation, Organization and Genre concepts, and through these concepts promote the development of L2 literacy abilities?
   (a) To what extent does L2 learners' ability to read a text improve, as measured by the difference in scores on written summaries from pre-test to post-test as assessed by independent raters?
   (b) To what extent does L2 learners' conceptual understanding of narrative literacy concepts – Foundation, Organization and Genre – improve as determined by changes in the quality of their verbalizations?
(2) Does a Division-of-Labor Pedagogy result in learners' appropriation and internalization of the four roles that comprise each of the three concepts: (1) Foundation – vocabulary, grammar/discourse, main idea

and prediction; (2) Organization – beginning, complex reaction, goal path and ending; and (3) Genre – field, tenor, mode and purpose?
(3) How does mediation change over time as learners' L2 reading ability develops?

The research questions were addressed in Chapters 4, 5 and 6. In Chapter 4, the results of the learners' performance on written summaries from mid- and high-level texts on the pre- and post-tests were quantitatively analyzed. Their performance significantly improved for both difficulty levels. For RS1 and RS2, their performance on all five summary categories was also documented. It improved significantly in all five summary categories for high-level texts and on the summary categories of main idea and accuracy for mid-level texts. The analysis in Chapter 5 focused on the change in learners' verbalizations from before instruction to the end of the semester-long studies. The learners wrote verbalizations on (1) the nature of L2 reading; (2) their understanding of Foundation, Organization and Genre; and (3) their use of Foundation, Organization and Genre to guide their thinking and reading. Although each learner's development was unique, they all exhibited marked changes in their respective verbalizations from the outset to the completion of the study. Finally, the analysis for Chapter 6 was focused on the appropriation and internalization of the roles and the change in mediation over time for one particular learner, Claire. Claire's developmental profile was selected as she was placed in the lower scoring of the two small group studies based on her pre-test performance, but was particularly responsive to mediation, which allowed her to exhibit extensive development throughout the study. Using detailed transcriptions of selected excerpts from her interactions with the RT and other learners, the analysis showed that Claire was able to appropriate and internalize the roles and concepts. Consequently, over time she required mediation less often and when it was provided it became increasingly implicit – a clear indication of development. In other words, Claire was able to shift from being co-regulated by the collective and the RT to being self-regulated.

Discussion

Due to the persistent language-literature curricular gap, L2 learners, with implicit L1 reading ability, intermediate L2 proficiency, with little experience reading authentic, full-length texts and no or minimal instruction on how to make meaning with texts, find themselves unprepared for upper-level literature classes, where interpretation and analysis of literary texts is required for the course. Often, learners are not afforded opportunities to read texts in the L2 until they have attained what is assumed to be a 'sufficient' level of L2 proficiency and are expected to make the transition from language to literature courses largely on their own. If reading is assigned, the texts are often adapted or abridged and typically required for homework where learners are more or less on their own. When they face difficulties, they often turn to inserting large sections of text into Google Translate. Therefore, in many current contexts, opportunities for direct and explicit instruction and mediation are limited. While comprehension difficulties experienced by learners center on the main ideas of texts, their ability to detect and interpret supporting details is even more problematic. Because of their challenges and lack of tools, they are often satisfied if they have understood any of the main ideas. Learners too often have a view of language that includes one-to-one correspondences between the L1 and L2 and have difficulty using their L2 proficiency and L1 reading knowledge to aid them in reading texts. They typically are unable to appropriately use bilingual dictionaries or grammatical resources and hence often rely on Google Translate or glossed texts.

In most L2 reading research, which is from a cognitivist (i.e. inside-the-head) perspective, reading is considered an extraction process and generalizations in research are made across variables. By doing this, the particularities that may impact reading development are washed away. Researchers from this perspective investigate the use of cognitive resources not the creation of new resources in the process of reading. Although Bernhardt's (2010) compensatory model has made a significant contribution to L2 reading research, as noted in Chapter 2, it has not given rise to concrete recommendations for L2 reading pedagogy. An L2 literacy or multiliteracies approach, from a social perspective (see Kern, 2000; New London Group, 1996; Paesani *et al.*, 2016) considers reading to be a meaning-making process, a multidimensional relationship between readers, writers, texts, the world, languages and background knowledge, and a tool for thinking that allows learners 'to expand one's understanding of oneself and the world' (Kern, 2000: 39; Roebuck, 1998). Literacy-oriented researchers focus their investigations on the particulars of reading – readers, use of strategies, and contexts (Kern, 2000).

V-SCT, which is in line with a literacy or multiliteracies approach has a different ontology and therefore different epistemology from cognitivist L2 reading research. It is crucial from this point of view to study the developmental process instead of already formed abilities. Because 'consciousness is formed and manifested in activity' (Rubenstein, 1940, as cited in Petrovsky, 1985: 23, 24) it must be studied in motion, in its history. The functional method of double stimulation allows researchers to study, and at the same time promote, the formation of appropriate mediation and the development of higher psychological functions. These internalized cultural and symbolic tools allow people to intentionally control their mental behavior. That is, they are able to use these tools in the ways that they wish. Effective *obuchenie*, the dialectical unity of teaching-learning, which is attuned to learners' ZPD-in-activity, allows researchers-teachers to intervene in the developmental process to help learners to appropriate and internalize culturally constructed artifacts which they then use to mediate (i.e. regulate) their own mental activity. On this view, intermental psychological functioning leads to intramental functioning.

The design of the studies reported on in this book attempted to address past concerns in L2 reading research and pedagogy. C-BLI was adapted and designed to help intermediate learners of French develop the ability to not only read and comprehend, but also to interpret and analyze narrative texts, which in turn should enable them to more smoothly make the transition from language to literature courses in a far more effective and efficient way than has traditionally been the case. A DOLP was created to allow learners to focus on particular roles for the concepts and therefore contribute to the act of reading while benefitting from the role preparation of other members of the collective, until they could each take on the responsibility for the entire process. On this view, each learner in the collective contributed in different ways to the common goal – that of making meaning with texts. The DOLP also allowed learners, individually and as a collective, to be mediated from their current level of development towards independent reading of French texts. The foci of the analysis – performance, verbalizations, appropriation and internalization, and change in mediation over time – are dialectically interdependent and allowed for the product and process of the learners' L2 narrative literacy development to be investigated and promoted. It is important to draw attention to the fact that the participants in RS1 and RS2 were the lowest-performing readers on the pre-test and therefore in all likelihood had a long route to travel to attain functional reading ability in the L2. The learners in RS3 were in a regularly scheduled fourth semester bridge course, running as an 'oral communication and reading' course with the C-BLI and DOLP guiding their literacy development.

Through C-BLI and DOLP, the learners, as collectives, along with mediation from the RT, were able to read authentic French texts for meaning, investigate these texts using Foundation, Organization and Genre, as manifested in improvement in their summary writing. The significant development in the learners' ability to produce adequate summaries for high-level texts, in particular, seems to confirm the effect reported in Oded and Walters (2001) that the creation of a summary correlated more strongly with more difficult texts than for less difficult texts. The summary categories of main idea and accuracy saw greater development across textual difficulty level than other categories suggesting that it was essential for learners to be able to address these areas before focusing on categories that more directly pertained to summary writing than literacy abilities.

Learners' verbalizations for each concept and for how they used these concepts to guide their thinking and reading also dramatically shifted as instruction progressed. Their verbalizations revealed more abstract, systematic, explicit, recontextualizable and complete understandings as well as recognition of the interdependency of Foundation, Organization and Genre. As they gained experience using the three concepts to guide their thinking/reading, some learners remarked that L2 reading had become similar to L1 reading. By the completion of the study, the learners reported a substantial degree of confidence and comfort in reading and analyzing texts, commented that they appreciated reading as an interactive meaning-making process and learned that language involves choices and that the usage of grammar/discourse affects the meaning of a text. They were able to use resources to investigate textual elements, make educated predictions, understand main ideas as well as nuances and appreciate that the concepts could be used for other genres and for texts in other languages. Organization allowed them to understand that stories can be related in different orders for particular effects and to appreciate the intricate nature of how elements of episodes are connected. Genre, for the learners, became a way to investigate an author's language and style choices for particular purposes instead of solely a classification of text types.

The analysis of key excerpts from the instructional sessions in Chapter 6, documented the process of one learner's development as instruction progressed. The learner required less mediation, improved her performance, became more self-regulated, responsive to mediation and more agentive, and appropriated and internalized the conceptual knowledge.

Although the learners significantly improved their L2 narrative literacy ability, their developmental process was not yet complete by the end of the studies as some roles still needed some implicit mediation for some learners, the concepts were not yet fully recontextualizable and the learners were not yet entirely independent readers who were able to produce fully appropriate summaries. However, what was once an arduous, confusing and overwhelming process, which at best yielded limited understanding, became an independent, investigative process that allowed them to deeply comprehend, and confidently interpret and analyze texts. As each learner had different rates of improvement in each area of the study, the RT's mediation was attuned to each of their particular needs as they changed. Development is a revolutionary process, consisting of leaps, twists, backtracking and pauses, that nevertheless continues to move forward, but rarely in a monotonic way. Learners' development of L2 narrative literacy allowed them access to textual content and the ability to interpret and analyze content in a new language. They developed meaning-making resources that allowed them to confidently and independently create different understandings and relationships with the word and the world.

Implications

The findings of these studies suggest that effective L2 literacy pedagogy is achievable at lower levels of language instruction and need not wait until learners reach upper-level courses. Although RS1 and RS2 were small group research studies, RS3, achieving similar results, was part of a regularly scheduled semester course with 21 learners. The C-BLI and DOLP promoted literacy development in both contexts. The findings here suggest that instructors of intermediate bridge courses should consider incorporating C-BLI and DOLP for L2 narrative literacy if they aim to effectively prepare learners to fully participate in upper-level literature courses. Hopefully this pedagogy and other work done from a literacy/ multiliteracy perspective will lead to the full elimination of these bridge courses, helping instructors to revamp their curriculum from beginning to end like the Georgetown University German Department did while making C-BLI and DOLP a part of the process. C-BLI allows learners to develop the conceptual knowledge needed for reading, interpreting and analyzing texts, which in turn contributes to the further development of their conceptual knowledge. Praxis-based *obuchenie*, which incorporates the dialectical relationship between conceptual knowledge and performance in goal-directed practical activities, leads learners' L2 literacy development. A DOLP, with learners working as a collective, can develop intrapsychological functioning and independence. It is necessary for mediation to be continually attuned to individual and collective needs in literacy pedagogy. Through effective literacy C-BLI and DOLP, learners are able to create new resources for thinking, which should, in turn, have an effect on other areas of language learning. Of course, this connection remains to be documented in future research.

In terms of additional implications for pedagogy and L2 teacher education, it is important to note that although all of the learners in the three studies developed, there was individual variation across their developmental trajectories. Claire, who had very little previous L2 reading experience or instruction and was placed in the lower scoring small group study (RS1), nevertheless improved significantly in all areas addressed in the study. As was noted in Chapter 4, similar scores for learners on a pre-test do not predict similar scores for the same learners on the post-test, nor do they take the same path. Therefore, it is important for mediation to remain attuned to the learners' ZPD-in-activity throughout the process. The fact that learners take different paths, even when sharing the same initial scores, pushes us to use dynamic ways to better understand their ZPD-in-activity and to project their future possible development. Finally, as there was more significant development in the main idea and accuracy summary categories for both mid- and high-level texts than in other categories for RS1 and RS2, a possible implication is that learners must attend to these areas before more subtle features of summary writing (i.e. supporting details, synthesis and generalizations) can be addressed.

In terms of implications for L2 literacy research, as this study suggests, significant insights can be gained from investigating the developmental process instead of already formed abilities. In addition, an in-depth analysis of even one learner may provide more insights into the developmental process than generalizations across variables. This study also contributes to and expands on the research using C-BLI in L2 pedagogy, Vygotskian research on second language development and Cole's work using a division-of-labor approach to L1 reading instruction.

The study also has further implications for L2 teacher education, the results suggest that coursework is needed to prepare future teachers to address learners' L2 literacy needs with conceptual knowledge, use collectives to help promote literacy and other development, and promote learners' ability to investigate textual elements using resources and tools that lead to independent reading. Finally, future teachers need to become effective mediators by learning to identify learner-specific needs and the amount and type of mediation that will allow learners to assume maximum responsibility and that will lead them not to merely producing correct answers but importantly will enable them to develop in-depth understanding of the nature of literacy that will result in effective self-regulation.

Limitations

The primary limitations concern the texts and assessments used in the study. The texts may have been too long for practical purposes both for instruction and for the assessments. For the instruction portion of RS1 and RS2, two texts were read and analyzed to completion and the collective had begun to read a third text. For RS3, three texts were read to completion. Given that the learners were not only reading but also analyzing texts using the three concepts, which were novel for the learners, the process took more time than anticipated. If the only literacy instruction in a program were not limited to one semester, this would no longer be an issue. As Organization and Genre were investigated after the first pass through the text (given the developmental needs of the learners), RS1 and RS2 learners had less time to practice using these two concepts under mediation from the researcher-teacher and ultimately to internalize them as they did not finish the third text. Therefore, learners in RS1 and RS2 could have benefitted from more practice with Genre especially, as they each had not had the opportunity to investigate all four of its affiliated concepts by the end of the study. Indeed, when asked at the conclusion of the study for useful suggestions for modifying instruction in the future, several learners responded that they would have liked more time with Genre, as it was the most difficult concept and the one that they were able to investigate the least.

The use of an adaptation of a well-known text (Sleeping Beauty) for the high-level pre-test text for RS1 and RS2 was unintentional and was therefore not used in RS3. It is important to note, however, that the adaptation was significantly different from the original text (either in French or English) and much more difficult in terms of storyline. Nevertheless, inclusion of this text may have compromised the scores on the pre-test to some extent. It is important to keep in mind, however, that if the results of the pre-test were skewed because of learner familiarity with the story narrated in the text, the pre-test scores were likely to have been inflated thus revealing a smaller rather than a larger difference between pre- and post-test performance. Although it cannot be stated with certainty, but since Daisy was the only learner to have identified the text as an adaptation of a French/English text, she may have been the only participant to have recognized elements in the storyline. Finally, there was more variability on the difficulty level ranking for the mid-level pre-test text in RS1 and RS2 than for other texts. Other texts that were also determined to have more variability were not used in the remainder of the studies.

Concerning the assessments, there were three specific areas that may call for modification in the future. Related to the length of the texts, mentioned above, in addition to the pre- and post-tests, a mid-study test had been planned prior to the start of RS1 and RS2. Given the amount of time it took to complete each instructional text, the mid-project assessment was eliminated in order for learners to have more time for the C-BLI, DOLP and mediation. A third data point may have been able to shed more light on Elizabeth and Marie-Claire's respective development, as reflected in their test performance. In addition, a mid-study test could have served as a formative assessment to sharpen the researcher-teacher's understanding of the learners' abilities at the midway point. This mid-study assessment was not used in RS3 either.

Furthermore, both the mid-level and high-level post-tests were almost double in length from the pre-tests, which made it more challenging to directly compare the pre- and post-test results. This may have skewed the results but again, serving to dampen the significance of the results, not inflate them. Due to the length of these tests, the learners' summaries were scored according to whatever portion of the text they indicated that they had read. It would have been preferable for all learners to complete the high-level texts for both pre- and post-tests, which would have allowed for greater precision in the scoring procedure. For RS1 and RS2, the majority of learners failed to complete the high-level pre- or post-test; thus, scoring on the high-level post-tests was the least consistent across learners. Although it was not a perfect solution to score the summaries in this way, given the nature of the scoring rubric, it is difficult to envision a better solution to the problem. In RS3, the majority of learners were able to finish the high-level pre- and post-test texts in the timeframe, making this less of an issue in this study.

The third limitation concerns the use of summaries to assess learners' L2 narrative reading ability. There are other measures that are used in L2 reading research such as recall and multiple-choice questions. Although summaries have advantages and disadvantages as reading/literacy assessment procedures, it was determined that they were the most appropriate of the available options. One of the disadvantages is that there was not a direct link between Organization and Genre and the assessment measure. Moreover, the use of summaries made it more difficult to score if learners did not have time to read the entire text. To my knowledge, thus far, no foolproof assessment for reading/literacy exists.

Future Directions

Any study is but a launching point for future investigations of unresolved questions or questions that spring forth from the process, the data, or the analysis; these studies are no exception. After RS1 and RS2, the research was expanded to a full classroom study in RS3.

Although the performance for the learners in RS1, RS2 and RS3 were analyzed in Chapters 4 and 5, Chapter 6 focused predominantly on details of Claire's development with mediation throughout the C-BLI and DOLP. It would be important and interesting to trace the unique development throughout the process for more of the learners across the three studies.

In terms of the C-BLI portion of the study, there are a number of possible changes needed or future directions to take. As the concept of Organization was specific to narratives, an additional SCOBA could be incorporated to allow Organization to be more recontextualizable across other genres. Also concerning the SCOBAs, the Foundation and Organization concepts may be more effectively presented through a SCOBA that has the roles less in focus and the overall concept more in focus. An updated Foundation SCOBA that could be used in the future was proposed in Chapter 3. Within Organization, it may be helpful to rename two of the elements of the episodes (goal and goal path) to limit confusion. As far as the Genre concept is concerned, in addition to more time for the learners to practice, appropriate and internalize this concept, a more thorough explanation or more emphasis on how field, tenor and mode allow the learners to investigate the context of situation should be included. A dynamic assessment could also be used in addition to, or in replacement of, the static pre- and post-test used in this study. From the results of a dynamic assessment for the pre-test, learners could be grouped by Learning Potential scores (Kozulin & Garb, 2002; Poehner & Lantolf, 2013). It may also be interesting to investigate the nature of each type of collective in terms of learners' development.

For future instantiations of the DOLP, the nature of the collective for more advanced learners should be investigated. In addition, as learners develop their understanding of *passé simple*, for example, it may be more beneficial for the instructor and possibly the collective, to prepare a handout with key details to be used as a collective resource and to which the learners can refer more easily. Related to this idea, it may be more helpful for the collective if the person assigned to the vocabulary role posted (on paper, chalkboard or whiteboard) their selected words and English equivalents as they prepare the role so that the other members of the collective could incorporate them earlier and more easily during their role preparation.

Because literacy involves the dialectic link between reading and writing, future studies could incorporate a more direct writing component in several different ways. Instruction could include the genre of a summary, the nature of the connection between the concepts and summary writing and the categories of the scoring rubric. After scoring the summaries, feedback could be given in a number of ways, but doing so as a dynamic assessment may be especially informative. Summaries could also be compared with the collective or used to identify exemplar components of high-quality summaries. As learners' L2 literacy improves, they may be able to write their summaries in the L2. A writing component could also ask learners to compose their own L2 narratives using what they learned during C-BLI. Finally, results from this type of a study could be used as a diagnostic for future writing or reading/writing instruction.

An important next step includes expanding the C-BLI and DOLP to other courses besides the fourth semester bridge courses and begin to create a curriculum that incorporates literacy from the beginning to the advanced levels using this pedagogy. In the meantime, it is important to know whether this pedagogy used in fourth semester bridge courses is able to close the gap and how learners are prepared for their upper-level literature classes. In RS3, the researcher-teacher asked learners at the end to reimagine the provided SCOBAs. In the future it would be helpful to incorporate this personal SCOBA development throughout the process.

Some work that has already begun on these data but that needs to be finished as well as expanded is looking more deeply into the nature of the dialectical relationship between cognition and emotion throughout the literacy development process. In addition, some work looking specifically at the learners whose L1 was not English and how this affected the C-BLI, DOLP and mediation throughout the process is also underway. In the process of looking more deeply at non-L1 English learners' participation, gestures and other forms of multimodality have been particularly insightful to investigate. The analyses thus far have been quite revealing. While much of the data from RS1 and RS2 are relatively similar, there are some important differences that should continue to be investigated.

Conclusion

These studies expanded Vygotskian C-BLI research into L2 literacy pedagogy, using C-BLI and a DOLP for L2 narrative literacy. As such, it offers insights into L2 reading/literacy research, Vygotskian research on L2 development, and L2 pedagogy, curricular design and teacher education. Although there are limitations and questions that remain for future investigations as these studies served as initial attempts to use C-BLI and DOLP in L2 literacy teaching-learning-research, it will hopefully inspire future investigations of praxis-based teaching-learning-research using C-BLI/DOLP into L2 literacy as well as into other educational domains. I am hopeful that this research will be taken up by researcher-teachers (because all teachers are researchers) in different languages, different contexts and at different levels so that we can gain a better understanding of how to help learners develop their L2 literacy from the beginning to the advanced levels. As a collective proved essential to these research studies, I hope that others will join me in these research-teaching endeavors.

Appendix

Rubric for Scoring of Summaries

	1	2	3	4	5	Score
Main Ideas	Few main ideas		Some main ideas		Includes all of the main ideas	
Supporting Details	Many supporting details or many unnecessary details		Some supporting details and no unnecessary details		No supporting details and no unnecessary details	
Synthesis	Lengthy or wordy and lacks organization		Somewhat condensed Lacks some coherence Some disorganization		Succinct and coherent	
Generalizations	Mostly inappropriate or insufficient or inadequate		Somewhat appropriate and sufficient or adequate		Appropriate and sufficient or adequate	
Accuracy	Many inaccuracies		Some inaccuracies		No inaccuracies	
						Total: $\overline{25}$

References

Abu-Rabia, S. (1996) The influence of culture and attitudes on reading comprehension in SL: The case of Jews learning English and Arabs learning Hebrew. *Reading Psychology* 17 (3), 253–271.
Abu-Rabia, S. (1998a) The learning of Hebrew by Israeli Arab students in Israel. *The Journal of Social Psychology* 138 (3), 331–341.
Abu-Rabia, S. (1998b) Social and cognitive factors influencing the reading comprehension of Arab students learning Hebrew as a second language in Israel. *Journal of Research in Reading* 21 (3), 201–212.
Abu-Rabia, S. (2003) The influence of working memory on reading and creative writing processes in a second language. *Educational Psychology* 23 (2), 209–222.
Adams, M.J. (1994) Modeling the connections between word recognition and reading. In R.B. Ruddell, M.R. Ruddell and H. Singer (eds) *Theoretical Models and Processes of Reading* (4th edn, pp. 830–863). Newark, DE: International Reading Association.
Agar, M. (1994) *Language Shock. Understanding the Culture of Conversation*. New York: Morrow.
Alderson, J.C. (1984) Reading in a foreign language: A reading problem or a language problem? In J.C. Alderson and A.R. Urquhart (eds) *Reading in a Foreign Language* (pp. 1–27). London: Longman.
Alessi, S. and Dwyer, A. (2008) Vocabulary assistance before and during reading. *Reading in a Foreign Language* 20 (2), 246–263.
Allen, H. and Paesani, K. (2010) Exploring the feasibility of a pedagogy of multiliteracies in introductory foreign language courses. *L2 Journal* 2 (1), 119–142.
Anderson, N.J. (2009) ACTIVE Reading: The research base for a pedagogical approach in the reading classroom. In Z. Han and N.J. Anderson (eds) *Second Language Reading Research and Instruction: Crossing the Boundaries* (pp. 117–143). Ann Arbor, MI: The University of Michigan Press.
Appel, G. and Lantolf, J.P. (1994) Speaking as mediation: A study of L1 and L2 text recall tasks. *The Modern Language Journal* 78, 437–452.
Auerbach, E.R. and Paxton, D. (1997) 'It's not the English thing': Bringing reading research into the ESL classroom. *TESOL Quarterly* 31 (2), 237–261.
Baddeley, A. (2010) Working memory. *Current Biology* 20 (4), R136–R140.
Bakhoda, I., Gholamhosseinzade, S. and Shabani, K. (2016) Concept-based instruction (CBI) via synchronous computer-mediated communication (SCMC) context of L2 reading comprehension. Conference Proceedings 3rd International Conference on Research in Science and Technology, Berlin, Germany.
Bengeleil, N.F. and Paribakht, T.S. (2004) L2 reading proficiency and lexical inferencing by university EFL learners. *The Canadian Modern Language Review* 61 (2), 225–249.
Bernhardt, E. (1986) Reading in a foreign language. In B. Wing (ed.) *Listening, Reading, Writing: Analysis and Application* (pp. 93–115). Middlebury, VT: Northeast Conference.
Bernhardt, E.B. (2010) *Understanding Advanced Second-Language Reading*. New York: Routledge.

Bernhardt, E.B. and Kamil, M.L. (1995) Interpreting relationships between L1 and L2 reading: Consolidating the linguistic threshold and the linguistic interdependence hypotheses. *Applied Linguistics* 16 (1), 15–34.
Bhatia, V.K. (1993) *Genre Analysis: Theory, Practice and Applications: Language Use in Professional and Academic Settings.* New York: Longman.
Bossers, B. (1991) On thresholds, ceilings, and short circuits: The relation between L1 reading, L2 reading, and L1 knowledge. *AILA Review* 8, 45–60.
Bourns, S.K., Krueger, C. and Mills, N. (2020) *Perspectives on Teaching Language and Content.* New Haven, CT: Yale University Press.
Brisbois, J.E. (1995) Connections between first- and second-language reading. *Journal of Reading Behavior* 27 (4), 565–584.
Brown, A. and Palincsar, A.-M. (1982) Inducing strategic learning from text by means of informed, self-control training. *Topics in Learning and Learning Disabilities* 2, 1–17.
Bruner, J. (1996) *The Culture of Education.* Cambridge, MA: Harvard University Press.
Buescher, K. (2015) Developing narrative literacy in a second language through concept-based instruction and a division-of-labor pedagogy. PhD thesis, The Pennsylvania State University.
Buescher, K. and Strauss, S. (2015) A cognitive linguistic analysis of French prepositions *à*, *dans*, and *en* and a sociocultural theoretical approach to teaching them. In K. Masuda, C. Arnett and A. Labarca (eds) *Cognitive Linguistics and Sociocultural Theory: Applications to Foreign and Second Language Teaching* (pp. 155–181). Berlin: De Gruyter Mouton.
Buescher, K. and Strauss, S. (2018) Conceptual frameworks and L2 pedagogy: The case of French prepositions. In A. Tyler, L. Ortega, M. Uno and H.I. Park (eds) *Usage-inspired L2 Instruction: Researched Pedagogy* (pp. 95–115). Amsterdam: John Benjamins.
Byrnes, H., Maxim, H.H. and Norris, J.M. (2010) Realizing advanced foreign language writing development in collegiate education: Curricular design, pedagogy, assessment [Monograph]. *The Modern Language Journal* 94, i–235.
Carpenter, P.A. and Just, M.A. (1977) Reading comprehension as eyes see it. *Cognitive Processes in Comprehension*, 109–139.
Carrell, P.L. (1985) Facilitating ESL reading by text structure. *TESOL Quarterly* 19 (4), 727–752.
Carrell, P.L. (1991) Second language reading: Reading ability or language proficiency? *Applied Linguistics* 12 (2), 159–179.
Chan, C.Y.H. (2003) Cultural content and reading proficiency: A comparison of mainland Chinese and Hong Kong learners of English. *Language, Culture and Curriculum* 16 (1), 60–69.
Clapham, C. (2013) The effect of language proficiency and background knowledge on EAP students' reading comprehension. In A.J. Kunnan (ed.) *Validation in Language Assessment* (pp. 155–182). New York: Routledge.
Coady, J. (1979) A psycholinguistic model of the ESL reader. In R. McKay, B. Barkman and R. Jordan (eds) *Reading in a Second Language.* Rowley, MA: Newbury House.
Cohen, J. (1988) *Statistical Power Analysis for the Behavioral Sciences* (2nd edn). Hillsdale, NJ: Lawrence Erlbaum Associates.
Cole, M. (1996) *Cultural Psychology. A Once and Future Discipline.* Cambridge, MA: Harvard University Press.
Cole, M. (2009) The perils of translation: A first step in reconsidering Vygotsky's theory of development in relation to formal education. *Mind, Culture, and Activity: An International Journal* 16, 291–295.
Cole, M. and Engeström, Y. (1993) A cultural-historical approach to distributed cognition. In G. Salomon (ed.) *Distributed Cognitions: Psychological and Educational Considerations* (pp. 1–46). Cambridge: Cambridge University Press.

Cope, B. and Kalantzis, M. (1993) Introduction: How a genre approach to literacy can transform the way writing is taught. In B. Cope and M. Kalantzis (eds) *The Powers of Literacy: A Genre Approach to Teaching Writing* (pp. 1–21). Pittsburgh, PA: University of Pittsburgh Press.

Cope, B. and Kalantzis, M. (2009) 'Multiliteracies': New literacies, New learning. *Pedagogies: An International Journal* 4 (3), 164–195.

Cope, B. and Kalantzis, M. (eds) (2015) *A Pedagogy of Multiliteracies: Learning by Design*. New York: Springer.

Cordero-Ponce, W.L. (2000) Summarization instruction: Effects on foreign language comprehension and summarization of expository texts. *Reading Research and Instruction* 39 (4), 329–350.

de Bot, K., Paribakht, T.S. and Wesche, M.B. (1997) Toward a lexical processing model for the study of second language vocabulary acquisition. *Studies in Second Language Acquisition* 19 (3), 309–329.

DeFina, A. and Georgakopoulou, A. (2012) *Analyzing Narrative: Discourse and Sociolinguistic Perspectives*. Cambridge: Cambridge University Press.

Delye, P. (2006) *Papa long nez*. In P. Delye, C. Gendrin and D. L'Homond (eds) *Tour de France Multicolore des Contes sur le Dos d'un Âne* (pp. 79–87). Yvelines: Rue du Monde.

Dixon-Krauss, L. (1996) Vygotsky's sociocultural perspective on learning and its application to Western literacy instruction. In L. Dixon-Krauss (ed.) *Vygotsky in the Classroom: Mediated Literacy Instruction and Assessment* (pp. 7–24). White Plains, NY: Longman Publishers.

Dumas, P. and Moissard, B. (1980) *La belle au doigt bruyant*. In P. Dumas and B. Moissard *Contes à l'Envers* (pp. 43–52). Paris: l'école des loisirs.

Egan, K. (2002) *Getting it Wrong from the Beginning: Our Progressivist Inheritance from Herbert Spencer, John Dewey, And Jean Piaget*. New Haven, CT: Yale University Press.

Esteve Ruesca, O. (2018) Concept-based instruction in teacher education programs in Spain as illustrated by the SCOBA-mediated Barcelona formative model: Helping teachers to become transformative practitioners. In J.P. Lantolf, M.E. Poehner and M. Swain (eds) *The Routledge Handbook of Sociocultural Theory and Second Language Development* (pp. 487–504). New York: Routledge.

Fazilatfar, A.M., Jabbari, A.A. and Harsij, R. (2017) Concept-based instruction and teaching English tense and aspect to Iranian school learners. *Issues in Language Teaching* 6 (1), 179–145.

Ferreira, M.M. (2005) A concept-based approach to writing instruction: From the abstract to the concrete performance. PhD thesis, The Pennsylvania State University.

Ferreira, M.M. and Lantolf, J.P. (2008) A concept-based approach to teaching writing through genre analysis. In J. Lantolf and M. Poehner (eds) *Sociocultural Theory and the Teaching of Second Languages* (pp. 285–320). London: Equinox.

Fogal, G.G. (2015) Pedagogical stylistics and concept-based instruction: An investigation into the development of voice in the academic writing of Japanese university students of English. PhD thesis, University of Toronto.

Fogal, G. (2017) Developing concept-based instruction, pedagogical content knowledge: Implications for teacher educators and L2 instructors. *Language and Sociocultural Theory* 4 (1), 53–75.

Freire, P. (1985) Reading the world and reading the word: An interview with Paulo Freire. *Language Arts* 62 (1), 15–21.

Friot, B. (2007a) *Archimémé*. In B. Friot (ed.) *Encore des Histoires Pressés* (pp. 133–137). Toulouse: Milan Poche.

Friot, B. (2007b) *Enquête*. In B. Friot (ed.) *Encore des Histoires Pressés* (pp. 15–19). Toulouse: Milan Poche.

Friot, B. (2007c) *Le tableau*. In B. Friot (ed.) *Encore des Histoires Pressés* (pp. 29–34). Toulouse: Milan Poche.

Friot, B. (2007d) *Poubelle*. In B. Friot (ed.) *Encore des histoires pressés* (pp. 53–58). Toulouse: Milan Poche.

Gal'perin, P.Y. (1989a) Mental actions as a basis for the formation of thoughts and images. *Soviet Psychology* 27 (2), 45–64.

Gal'perin, P.Y. (1989b) Organization of mental activity and the effectiveness of learning. *Soviet Psychology* 27 (3), 45–65.

Gal'perin, P.Y. (1992) Stage-by-stage formation as a method of psychological investigation. *Journal of Russian and East European Psychology* 30 (4), 60–80.

Gánem-Gutiérrez, G.A. and Harun, H. (2011) Verbalisation as a mediational tool for understanding tense-aspect marking in English: an application of concept-based instruction. *Language Awareness* 20 (2), 99–119.

García, P. (2012) Verbalizing in the second language classroom: The development of the grammatical concept of aspect. PhD thesis, University of Massachusetts, Amherst.

García, P.N. (2015) Verbalizing in the second language classroom: Exploring the role of agency in the internalization of grammatical categories. In P. Deters, X. Gao, E.R. Miller and G. Vitanova (eds) *Theorizing and Analyzing Agency in Second Language Learning: Interdisciplinary Approaches* (pp. 213–231). Bristol: Multilingual Matters.

García, P.N. (2017) A sociocultural approach to analyzing L2 development in the Spanish L2 classroom. *Vigo International Journal of Applied Linguistics* 14 (14), 99–124.

Gascoigne, C. (2002) Documenting the initial second language reading experience: The readers speak. *Foreign Language Annals* 35 (5), 554–560.

Ghaith, G. (2003) Effects of the learning together model of cooperative learning on English as a foreign language reading achievement, academic self-esteem, and feelings of school alienation. *Bilingual Research Journal* 27 (3), 451–474.

Gisbert, J.M. (2006) *Le Gardien de l'Oubli*. France: Syros.

Goodman, K.S. (1973) *Miscue Analysis: Applications to Reading Instruction*. Washington, DC: National Institute of Education.

Graden, E.C. (1996) How language teachers' beliefs about reading instruction are mediated by their beliefs about students. *Foreign Language Annals* 29 (3), 387–395.

Graesser, A.C., Golding, J.M. and Long, D.L. (1996) Narrative representation and comprehension. In R. Barr, M. Kamil, P. Mosenthal and P.D. Pearson (eds) *Handbook of Research* (vol. II, pp. 171–205). White Plains, NY: Longman.

Gripari, P. (1997a) *Le roman d'amour d'une patate*. In P. Gripari (ed.) *Le Gentil Petit Diable: Et Autres Contes de la Rue Broca* (pp. 30–40). Paris: La Table Ronde.

Gripari, P. (1997b) *Le prince blub et la sirène*. In P. Gripari (ed.) *Le Gentil Petit Diable: Et Autres Contes de la Rue Broca* (pp. 54–74). Paris: La Table Ronde.

Haenen, J. (1996) *Piotr Gal'perin: Psychologist in Vygotsky's Footsteps*. New York: Nova Science Publishers.

Haenen, J. (2000) Gal'perian instruction in the ZPD. *Human Development* 43 (2), 93–98.

Haenen, J. (2001) Outlining the teaching-learning process: Piotr Gal'perin's contribution. *Learning and Instruction* 11, 157–170.

Hall, J.K. (2001) *Methods for Teaching Foreign Languages: Creating a Community of Learners in the Classroom*. Upper Saddle River, NJ: Prentice Hall.

Halliday, M.A.K. and Hasan, R. (1989) *Language, Context, and Text: Aspects of Language in a Social-semiotic Perspective*. Oxford: Oxford University Press.

Han, Z. and D'Angelo, A. (2009) Balancing between comprehension and acquisition: Proposing a dual approach. In Z. Han and N.J. Anderson (eds) *Second Language Reading Research and Instruction: Crossing the Boundaries* (pp. 173–191). Ann Arbor, MI: University of Michigan Press.

Hare, V.C. (1982) Preassessment of topical knowledge: A validation and an extension. *Journal of Reading Behavior* 14 (1), 77–85.

Harun, H. (2013) Individual versus collaborative verbalisation for understanding tense/aspect marking in L2 English: Exploring concept-based instruction for L1 Malay learners. PhD thesis, University of Essex.

Harun, H., Massari, N. and Behak, F.P. (2014) Use of L1 as a mediational tool for understanding tense/aspect marking in English: An application of concept-based instruction. *Procedia-Social and Behavioral Sciences* 134, 134–139.

Harun, H., Abdullah, N., Ab Wahab, N. and Zainuddin, N. (2019) Concept based instruction: Enhancing grammar competence in L2 learners. *RELC Journal* 50 (2), 252–268.

Hasan, R. (1996) Literacy, everyday talk and society. In R. Hasan and G. Williams (eds) *Literacy in Society* (pp. 377–424). New York: Longman.

Hayati, A.M. and Pour-Mohammadi, M. (2005) A comparative study of using bilingual and monolingual dictionaries in reading comprehension of intermediate EFL students. *The Reading Matrix: An International Online Journal* 5 (2), 61–66.

Hedgcock, J.S. and Ferris, D.R. (2009) *Teaching Readers of English: Students, Texts, and Contexts*. New York: Routledge.

Horst, M. (2005) Learning L2 vocabulary through extensive reading: A measurement study. *The Canadian Modern Language Review* 61 (3), 355–382.

Hudson, T. (2007) *Teaching Second Language Reading*. Oxford: Oxford University Press.

Infante, P. (2016) Mediated development: Promoting L2 conceptual development through interpsychological activity. PhD thesis, The Pennsylvania State University.

Ismail, S.A.M.M., Petras, Y.E., Mohamed, A.R. and Eng, L.S. (2015) Compensatory reading among ESL learners: A reading strategy heuristic. *English Language Teaching* 8 (8), 46–55.

Jeon, E.H. and Yamashita, J. (2014) L2 reading comprehension and its correlates: A meta-analysis. *Language Learning* 64 (1), 160–212.

Johns, A.M. (2002) Introduction. In A.M. Johns (ed.) *Genre in the Classroom: Multiple Perspectives* (pp. 3–13). Mahwah, NJ: Lawrence Erlbaum Associates.

Kao, Y.T. (2014) Vygotsky's theory of instruction and assessment: The implications of foreign language education. PhD thesis, The Pennsylvania State University.

Karpov, Y.V. (2003) Vygotsky's doctrine of scientific concepts: Its role for contemporary education. In A. Kozulin, B. Gindis, V.S. Ageyev and S.M. Miller (eds) *Vygotsky's Educational Theory in Cultural Context* (pp. 65–82). Cambridge: Cambridge University Press.

Kendris, C. (1996) *501 French Verbs Fully Conjugated in all the Tenses in a New Easy-to-learn Format Alphabetically Arranged* (4th edn). Hauppauge, NY: Barron's Educational Series, Inc.

Kern, R.G. (2000) *Literacy and Language Teaching*. Oxford: Oxford University Press.

Kern, R. (2003) Literacy as a new organizing principle for foreign language education. In P. Patrikis (ed.) *Reading between the Lines: Perspectives on Foreign Language Literacy* (pp. 40–59). New Haven, CT: Yale University Press.

Keshavarz, M.H., Atai, M.R. and Ahmadi, H. (2007) Content schemata, linguistic simplification, and EFL readers' comprehension and recall. *Reading in a Foreign Language* 19 (1), 19–33.

Kieffer, M.J. and Lesaux, N.K. (2012) Direct and indirect roles of morphological awareness in the English reading comprehension of native English, Spanish, Filipino, and Vietnamese speakers. *Language Learning* 62 (4), 1170–1204.

Kim, J. (2013) Developing conceptual understanding of sarcasm in a second language through concept-based instruction. PhD thesis, The Pennsylvania State University.

Kintsch, W. (1994) Text comprehension, memory, and learning. *American Psychologist* 49, 292–303.

Kintsch, W. and Van Dijk, T.A. (1978) Toward a model of text comprehension and production. *Psychological Review* 85, 363–394.

Koda, K. (2005) *Insights into Second Language Reading: A Cross-linguistic Approach*. Cambridge: Cambridge University Press.

Korthagen, F.A.J. (1999) Linking reflection and technical competence: The logbook as an instrument in teacher education. *European Journal of Teacher Education* 22 (2/3), 191–207.

Kozulin, A. and Garb, E. (2002) Dynamic Assessment of EFL text comprehension of at-risk students. *School Psychology International* 23, 112–127.
Kurtz, L.M. (2017) 'I don't know why. I just make comparisons.': Concept-based instruction to promote development of a second legal languaculture in international LL.M. students. PhD thesis, The Pennsylvania State University.
Lai, W. (2012) Concept-based foreign language pedagogy: Teaching the Chinese temporal system. PhD thesis, The Pennsylvania State University.
Lantolf, J.P. (ed.) (2000) *Sociocultural Theory and Second Language Learning*. Oxford: Oxford University Press.
Lantolf, J.P. (2011) Integrating sociocultural theory and cognitive linguistics in the second language classroom. In E. Hinkel (ed.) *Handbook of Research in Second Language Teaching and Learning* (vol. 2, pp. 303–318). New York: Routledge.
Lantolf, J.P. and Thorne, S.L. (2006) *Sociocultural Theory and the Genesis of Second Language Development*. Oxford: Oxford University Press.
Lantolf, J.P. and Poehner, M.E. (2014) *Sociocultural Theory and the Pedagogical Imperative in L2 Education. Vygotskian Praxis and The Research/Practice Divide*. New York: Routledge.
Lantolf, J.P. and Esteve, O. (2019) Concept-based instruction for concept-based instruction: A model for language teacher education. In M. Sato and S. Loewen (eds) *Evidence-Based Second Language Pedagogy* (pp. 27–51). New York: Routledge.
Lantolf, J.P., Xi, J. and Minakova, V. (2021) Sociocultural theory and concept-based language instruction. *Language Teaching* 54 (3), 327–342.
Lapkin, S., Swain, M. and Knouzi, I. (2008) French as a second language: University students learn the grammatical concept of voice: Study design, materials development, and pilot data. In J.P. Lantolf and M.E. Poehner (ed.) *Sociocultural Theory and the Teaching of Second Languages* (pp. 228–255). London: Equinox.
Laufer, B. and Ravenhorst-Kalovski, G.C. (2010) Lexical threshold revisited: Lexical text coverage, learners' vocabulary size and reading comprehension. *Reading in a Foreign Language* 22 (1), 15–30.
Le Clézio, J.M.G. (1978a) *Celui Qui N'Avait Jamais Vu la Mer*. In J.M.G. Le Clézio (ed.) *Mondo et Autres Histoires* (pp. 167–188). Paris: Gallimard.
Le Clézio, J.M.G. (1978b) *Voyage au Pays des Arbres*. Paris: Éditions Gallimard.
Lee, H. (2012) Concept-based approach to second language teaching and learning: Cognitive linguistics-inspired instruction of English phrasal verbs. PhD thesis, The Pennsylvania State University.
Lee, S.K. (2007) Effects of textual enhancement and topic familiarity on Korean EFL students' reading comprehension and learning of passive form. *Language Learning* 57 (1), 87–118.
Lee, J.W. and Schallert, D.L. (1997) The relative contribution of L2 language proficiency and L1 reading ability to L2 reading performance: A test of the threshold hypothesis in an EFL context. *TESOL Quarterly* 31 (4), 713–739.
Leeser, M.J. (2007) Learner-based factors in L2 reading comprehension and processing grammatical form: Topic familiarity and working memory. *Language Learning* 57 (2), 229–270.
Leow, R.P. (2001) Do learners notice enhanced forms while interacting with the L2?: An online and offline study of the role of written input enhancement in L2 Reading. *Hispania* 84 (3), 496–509.
Leow, R.P., Ego, T., Nuevo, A.M. and Tsai, Y.C. (2003) The roles of textual enhancement and type of linguistic item in adult L2 learners' comprehension and intake. *Applied Language Learning* 13 (2), 1–16.
Mandler, J.M. (1984) *Stories, Scripts, and Scenes: Aspects of Schema Theory*. Hillsdale, NJ: Lawrence Erlbaum Associates.
Martin, J.R. (1984) Language, register and genre. *Children Writing: Reader* 1, 21–30.

Maxim, H.H. (2002) A study into the feasibility and effects of reading extended authentic discourse in the beginning German language classroom. *The Modern Language Journal* 86 (1), 20–35.

Maxim, H.H. (2006) Integrating textual thinking into the introductory college-level foreign language classroom. *The Modern Language Journal* 90 (1), 19–32.

Mbodj, S. (2005a) *Le Champ du Lièvre*. In S. Mbodj (ed.) *Contes d'Afrique* (pp. 6–15). Toulouse: Milan Jeunesse.

Mbodj, S. (2005b) *La Pierre qui Parle*. In S. Mbodj (ed.) *Contes d'Afrique* (pp. 46–53). Toulouse: Milan Jeunesse.

Mbodj, S. (2009) *Le Roi et le Génie du Lac*. In S. Mbodj (ed.) *Contes et Sagesses d'Afrique* (pp. 37–45). Toulouse: Milan Jeunesse.

McNeil, L. (2012) Extending the compensatory model of second language reading. *System* 40 (1), 64–76.

Miller, C.R. (1984) Genre as social action. *Quarterly Journal of Speech* 70 (2), 151–167.

Miller, R. (2011) *Vygotsky in Perspective*. New York: Cambridge University Press.

MLA Ad Hoc Committee on Foreign Languages (2007) Foreign languages and higher education: New structures for a changed world. Retrieved from https://eric.ed.gov/?id=ED500460.

Nation, I. (2006) How large a vocabulary is needed for reading and listening? *Canadian Modern Language Review* 63 (1), 59–82.

Negueruela, E. (2003) Systemic-theoretical instruction and L2 development: A sociocultural approach to teaching-learning and researching L2 learning. PhD thesis, The Pennsylvania State University.

Negueruela, E. (2008) Revolutionary pedagogies: Learning that leads (to) second language development. In J. Lantolf and M. Poehner (eds) *Sociocultural Theory and the Teaching of Second Languages* (pp. 189–227). London: Equinox.

Negueruela, E. and Lantolf, J.P. (2006) Concept-based pedagogy and the acquisition of L2 Spanish. In R. Salaberry and R. Lafford (eds) *The Art of Teaching Spanish: Second Language Acquisition from Research to Praxis* (pp. 79–102). Washington D.C.: Georgetown University Press.

New London Group (1996) A pedagogy of multiliteracies: Designing social futures. *Harvard Educational Review* 66 (1), 60–92.

Oded, B. and Walters, J. (2001) Deeper processing for better EFL reading comprehension. *System* 29 (3), 357–370.

Oh, S.-Y. (2001) Two types of input modification and EFL reading comprehension: Simplification versus elaboration. *TESOL Quarterly* 35 (1), 69–96.

Ohta, A.S. (2017) From SCOBA development to implementation in concept-based instruction: Conceptualizing and teaching Japanese addressee honorifics as expressing modes of self. *Language and Sociocultural Theory* 4 (2), 187–218.

Ollman, B. (2003) *Dance of the Dialectic: Steps in Marx's Method*. Urbana, IL: University of Illinois Press.

Olson, D.R. (1995) Writing and the mind. In J. Wertsch, P. del Río and A. Alvarez (eds) *Sociocultural Studies of Mind* (pp. 95–123). Cambridge: Cambridge University Press.

Paesani, K. (2016) Investigating connections among reading, writing, and language development: A multiliteracies perspective. *Reading in a Foreign Language* 28 (2), 266–289.

Paesani, K.W., Allen, H.W., Dupuy, B., Liskin-Gasparro, J.E. and Lacorte, M.E. (2016) *A Multiliteracies Framework for Collegiate Foreign Language Teaching*. London: Pearson.

Palincsar, A. and Brown, A. (1984) Reciprocal teaching of comprehension-fostering and comprehension-monitoring activities. *Cognition and Instruction* 1, 9–31.

Petrovsky, A.V. (1985) *Studies in Psychology: The Collective and the Individual*. Moscow: Progress Publishers.

Piatek, D. (2006) *L'Enfant et l'Allumeur de Rêves*. Nantes: Le Petit Phare.
Pigada, M. and Schmitt, N. (2006) Vocabulary acquisition from extensive reading: A case study. *Reading in a Foreign Language* 18 (1), 1–28.
Plonsky, L. and Oswald, F.L. (2014) How big is 'big'? Interpreting effect sizes in L2 research. *Language Learning* 64 (4), 878–912.
Poehner, M.E. (2008) *Dynamic Assessment: A Vygotskian Approach to Understanding and Promoting L2 Development*. Berlin: Springer Publishing.
Poehner, M.E. and Lantolf, J.P. (2013) Bringing the ZPD into the equation: Capturing L2 development during computerized dynamic assessment. *Language Teaching Research* 17 (3), 323–342.
Poehner, M.E. and Infante, P. (2017) Mediated development: A Vygotskian approach to transforming second language learner abilities. *TESOL Quarterly* 51 (2), 332–357.
Polizzi, M.-C. (2013) The development of Spanish aspect in the second language classroom: Concept-based pedagogy and dynamic assessment. PhD thesis, University of Massachusetts, Amherst.
Prichard, C. (2008) Evaluating L2 readers' vocabulary strategies and dictionary use. *Reading in a Foreign Language* 20 (2), 216–231.
Reed, D.K., Petscher, Y. and Foorman, B.R. (2016) The contribution of vocabulary knowledge and spelling to the reading comprehension of adolescents who are and are not English language learners. *Reading and Writing* 29 (4), 633–657.
Riley, G.L. (1993) A story structure approach to narrative text comprehension. *The Modern Language Journal* 77 (4), 417–432.
Riley, G.L. and Lee, J.F. (1996) A comparison of recall and summary protocols as measures of second language reading comprehension. *Language Testing* 13, 173–189.
Roebuck, R. (1998) *Reading and Recall in L1 and L2*. Stamford, CT: Ablex Publishing Corporation.
Rommetveit, R. (1974) *On Message Structure: A Framework for the Study of Language and Communication*. London: John Wiley & Sons.
Schmitt, N., Jiang, X. and Grabe, W. (2011) The percentage of words known in a text and reading comprehension. *The Modern Language Journal* 95 (1), 26–43.
Serrano-Lopez, M. and Poehner, M. (2008) Materializing linguistic concepts through 3-D clay modeling: A tool-and-result approach to mediating L2 Spanish development. In J. Lantolf and M. Poehner (eds) *Sociocultural Theory and the Teaching of Second Languages* (pp. 321–346). London: Equinox.
Shih, M. (1992) Beyond comprehension exercises in the ESL academic reading class. *TESOL Quarterly* 26, 289–318.
Shin, J., Dronjic, V. and Park, B. (2019) The interplay between working memory and background knowledge in L2 reading comprehension. *TESOL Quarterly* 53 (2), 320–347.
Stevenson, M., Schoonen, R. and de Glopper, K. (2007) Inhibition or compensation? A multidimensional comparison of reading processes in Dutch and English. *Language Learning* 57 (Supplement 1), 115–154.
Swaffar, J. and Arens, K. (2005) *Remapping the Foreign Language Curriculum: An Approach through Multiple Literacies*. New York: Modern Language Association of America.
Swaffar, J.K., Arens, K.M. and Byrnes, H. (1991) *Reading for Meaning: An Integrated Approach to Language Learning*. Englewood Cliffs, NJ: Prentice Hall.
Swain, M. (2000) The output hypothesis and beyond: mediating acquisition through collaborative dialogue. In J.P. Lantolf (ed.) *Sociocultural Theory and Second Language Learning* (pp. 97–114). Oxford: Oxford University Press.
Swales, J.M. (1990) *Genre Analysis: English in Academic and Research Settings*. Cambridge: Cambridge University Press.
Toomela, A. (2010) Modern mainstream psychology is the best? Noncumulative, historically blind, fragmented, atheoretical. In A. Toomela and J. Valsiner (eds)

Methodological Thinking in Psychology: 60 years Gone Astray? (pp. 1–26). Charlotte, NC: Information Age Publishing, Inc.
Tsai, M.H. (2020) Teaching L2 collocations through concept-based instruction: The effect of L2 proficiency and congruency. *International Journal of Applied Linguistics* 30 (3), 553–575.
van Compernolle, R.A. (2011) Developing second language sociopragmatic knowledge through concept-based instruction: A microgenetic case study. *Journal of Pragmatics* 43 (13), 3267–3283.
van Compernolle, R.A. (2012) Developing sociopragmatic capacity in a second language through concept-based instruction. PhD thesis, The Pennsylvania State University.
van Compernolle, R.A. (2014) *Sociocultural Theory and L2 Instructional Pragmatics*. Bristol: Multilingual Matters.
van Compernolle, R.A. and Henery, A. (2014) Instructed concept appropriation and L2 pragmatic development in the classroom. *Language Learning* 64 (3), 549–578.
van Compernolle, R.A., Gomez-Laich, M.P. and Weber, A. (2016) Teaching L2 Spanish sociopragmatics through concepts: A classroom-based study. *The Modern Language Journal* 100 (1), 341–361.
van Dijk, T.A. and Kintsch, W. (1983) *Strategies of Discourse Comprehension*. New York: Academic Press.
Vygotsky, L.S. (1978) *Mind in Society: The Development of Higher Psychological Processes*. Cambridge, MA: Harvard University Press.
Vygotsky, L.S. (1987) *The Collected Works of L. S. Vygotsky. Volume 1: Problems of General Psychology, including the Volume Thinking and Speech*. In R.W. Rieber and A.S. Carton (eds) New York: Plenum.
Vygotsky, L.S. (1994) The problem of the cultural development of the child. http://www.marxists.org/archive/vygotsky/index.htm.
Vygotsky, L.S. (1997) *The Collected Works of L. S. Vygotsky: Volume 4: The History of the Development of Higher Mental Functions* (ed. R.W. Rieber). New York: Plenum.
Vygotsky, L.S. (2012) *Thought and Language*. Revised and Expanded by A. Kozulin. Cambridge, MA: The MIT Press.
Vygotsky, L.S. and Luria, A.R. (1994) Tool and symbol in child development. See http://www.marxists.org/archive/vygotsky/index.htm.
Walter, D.R. and van Compernolle, R.A. (2017) Teaching German declension as meaning: A concept-based approach. *Innovation in Language Learning and Teaching* 11 (1), 68–85.
Webb, S. and Chang, A.C.S. (2015) How does prior word knowledge affect vocabulary learning progress in an extensive reading program? *Studies in Second Language Acquisition* 37 (4), 651–675.
White, B. (2012) A conceptual approach to the instruction of phrasal verbs. *The Modern Language Journal* 96 (3), 419–438.
Yamashita, J. (2002a) Mutual compensation between L1 reading ability and L2 language proficiency in L2 reading comprehension. *Journal of Research in Reading* 25 (1), 81–95.
Yamashita, J. (2002b) Reading strategies in L1 and L2: Comparison of four groups of readers with different reading ability in L1 and L2. *ITL: Review of Applied Linguistics* 135 (1), 1–35.
Yamashita, J. and Shiotsu, T. (2017) Comprehension and knowledge components that predict L2 reading: A latent-trait approach. *Applied Linguistics* 38 (1), 43–67.
Yàñez-Prieto, M. (2008) On literature and the secret art of (im)possible worlds: Teaching literature through language. PhD thesis, The Pennsylvania State University.
Zhang, X. (2014) The teachability hypothesis and concept-based instruction. Topicalization in Chinese as a second language. PhD thesis, The Pennsylvania State University.

Index

Abu-Rabia 22, 25
Accuracy 57, 59, 62, 76, 77, 82–84, 87, 148, 150, 152, 158
Agar 23, 40
Agentive (agency) 108, 141, 146, 151
Alderson 2, 11, 20
Allen 3, 23
Anderson 21, 26
Appropriation 36, 53, 108–109, 146–148, 150
Authentic texts 1, 3–5, 22–23, 53, 148, 150

Background knowledge 9–10, 12, 25–26, 36, 149
Beginning 41–44, 48, 53, 108, 148
Bernhardt 8–11, 16, 19–23, 25–26, 58, 149
Bottom-up approach 7–10
Bourns 1, 3, 6, 23–24
Brisbois 19–21
Brown 26, 47
Buescher 30–32
Byrnes 1–2, 4, 24–25, 44, 46–47

Carrell 19, 24
Cognitive Linguistics 30
Cognitivist perspective 7–8, 10–12, 14, 22, 27, 149
Cohen 67, 76–78, 81
Cole 9, 15, 17, 26, 35, 37, 47–48, 58, 153
Collaboration 27, 34
Collective 2, 19, 27, 34–35, 47–49, 57, 108–109, 111–112, 116–117, 120, 124, 126, 129, 131, 134, 137–139, 141, 144, 146, 148, 150, 152–153, 155–157
Communicated thinking 33, 35
Compensatory processing model 10–11, 13, 149

Complex Reaction 41–42, 44, 48, 53, 108, 140, 144, 148
Concept-based Language Instruction (C-BLI) 2, 29, 47–48, 53, 61, 74, 83–84, 87, 93, 95, 99, 105, 108, 110, 141, 146, 147, 150, 152–157
Concept(s) 1, 2, 18, 20–21, 24–25, 27, 29–37, 40–51, 53, 55–58, 61, 88–90, 92–109, 111, 115–117, 141, 146–148, 150, 151–153, 155–156
Context of situation 45–46 155
Cope 12–13, 24
Cuisenaire rods 32, 43–44, 48, 57, 97–100, 107, 114–115
Curriculum gap/bridge course 1–3, 5–6, 11–12, 23, 25, 28, 51–52, 61, 113, 147–148, 150, 152, 156

DeFina 24
Development 1–2, 4–7, 14–20, 22–24, 27, 29–37, 41–43, 47, 51–53, 55, 58–59, 66, 71–73, 75, 78, 85–87, 101, 107–109, 141–142, 146–156
Dialectic 13–14, 17, 28, 34, 87, 149–150, 152, 156
Dialogical thinking 33, 35
Dictionary 25, 37–38, 60, 63, 117, 120–122, 124–126, 143–144
Distribution of roles 47, 49–51, 55
Division-of-Labor Pedagogy (DOLP)/ division of labor 2, 18, 29, 34, 36, 47–51, 53, 108, 147, 153

Ending 41–44, 48, 53, 108, 145, 148
Episode 41–43, 48–50, 97, 100–101, 113–115, 140, 144, 151, 155
Epistemology 7–8, 12–14, 16, 34, 149
Everyday concepts 30–31, 101–102, 106
Eye gaze 9, 110–115, 125–126, 131–132, 141, 145

Field 24, 27, 45–48, 53, 102–105, 107–108, 148, 155
First language (L1) 1–5, 7–13, 19–21, 23–24, 26–27, 36–37, 39, 41, 48, 52, 54, 56–57, 60, 63, 81, 84, 88–92, 94–96, 100, 104–107, 112, 148–149, 151, 153, 156
Foundation 36–37, 39–40, 44, 46–50, 53, 55, 58, 61, 88–89, 92–97, 99–100, 105–108, 115–117, 124, 127, 141, 147–148, 150–151, 155

Gal'perin 29, 31–33
Generalizations 57, 59, 62, 76–77, 81–82, 84, 87, 138–139, 152, 158
Genre 3, 7, 19, 22, 24–25, 31, 36–37, 40, 44–51, 53, 55, 58, 88, 92, 95–96, 99, 101–108, 127, 140–141, 147–148, 150–151, 153, 155–156
Gesture/multimodality 56, 110, 141, 156
Goal Path 41–44, 48, 53, 98, 108, 140, 144–145, 148, 155
Graden 23, 27
Grammar/discourse 19, 21, 37, 39–40, 48, 50, 53, 96,108, 112, 117–122, 124, 126–127, 131, 134–137, 142, 147, 151

Haenen 29, 33, 109
Halliday 2, 24, 44–46
Hasan 2, 13, 24, 44–46
High-level text 54–55, 59, 62–66, 69–87, 140, 148, 150, 152–154
Higher psychological/mental functions 15–18, 22, 32–34, 107, 149
Hudson 23–24, 36, 40–42, 57, 106

Imitation 18
Implicit (understanding) 4, 24, 41, 46, 89, 97, 101, 106, 126, 148
Independent raters 52, 54–57, 59, 62, 75, 147
Interactive approaches 7–8, 10
Internalization 16–18, 29, 32–33, 35–36, 44, 53, 107–109, 146–148, 150

Kalantzis 12–13, 24
Kern 11–13, 22–23, 27, 57–58, 149
Kintsch 26, 57
Koda 3, 19–22, 24
Kozulin 59, 73–74, 87, 146, 155

L1 reading knowledge 1–5, 19–20, 36, 149
L2 language knowledge 1, 19–20, 36
L2 narrative literacy 28, 36, 47, 53, 59, 66, 68, 85, 87, 108–109, 117, 146–147, 150–152, 156
Language threshold hypothesis 2–3, 11
Lantolf 2, 12, 14, 16–18, 29–33, 35, 74, 87, 106, 108–109, 146, 155
Laufer 22, 37
Learning Potential Score 59, 73–76, 87, 146, 155
Locus of control 109, 117, 146

Main idea 6, 9, 25–26, 37, 39–40, 48, 53, 57, 59–60, 62, 75–79, 83, 87–89, 91, 93–96, 100, 103, 107–108, 116, 137–139, 147–152, 158
Mandler 24, 41–44, 97, 106
Marx 18, 47, 109
Materializations (materialized) 29, 31–33, 36–37, 39–44, 46, 48, 98, 100, 107
Maxim 12, 23
Mediation (Mediating artifacts/auxiliary stimuli/cultural tool/mediational means) 2, 14–16, 19, 25, 27, 29, 32–33, 35–36, 38, 44, 48, 53, 56–58, 74–75, 87, 89–90, 98–99, 102–103, 108–109, 111–112, 117, 199–122, 124–127, 130–131, 134–156
Mid-level text 64–65, 67–68, 70–71, 74–75, 77–79, 81, 83–87, 112, 148
Mode 24, 27, 45–48, 53, 103–104, 107–108, 148, 155
Multiliteracies 12–13 149, 152

Negueruela-Azarola 15, 30–31, 33
New London Group 12–13, 149

Obuchenie (teaching-learning) 17–18, 20, 28–29, 87, 149, 152
Oded 26, 81, 150
Ontology 7–8, 12, 14, 149
Openness to mediation 74, 146
Organization (role) 36–37, 40–45, 47–51, 53, 55, 58, 88, 92, 95–101, 104–108, 113–115, 140–141, 144, 146–148, 150–151, 153, 155, 158

Paesani 1, 3, 5, 8–9, 12–13, 23, 149
Palincsar 26
Performance 33, 49, 74, 78–79, 81, 107, 109, 141, 146, 148, 150–152, 154–155
Petrovsky 14, 32, 34–35, 47, 108. 149
Plonsky 67, 69, 71, 76, 79, 81–82
Poehner 2, 17, 26, 29–33, 74, 87, 108–109, 146, 155
Practical goal-directed activity 18, 29–30, 32–34, 106, 109, 152
Praxis 2, 34, 152, 157
Prediction (role) 39–40, 48–49, 53, 94, 96, 103, 107, 111–112, 116, 139–140, 144, 148, 151
Prichard 21, 25
Prolept/prolepsis 35, 47–48, 58, 108
Purpose (role) 24, 44–46, 48, 53, 101–104, 107–108, 148, 151

Question-Asking-Reading (QAR) 37, 47

Regulate 17, 19, 108, 117, 146, 148, 150–151
Research studies 1 and 2 (RS1 and RS2) 51–52, 54–57, 59–62, 64–67, 69–86, 88–89, 93, 95, 97–98, 101, 105–106, 109, 146, 148, 150, 152–156
Research study 3 (RS3) 52, 54, 56–57, 59–61, 63–66, 68, 70–73, 75–76, 90, 99–100, 103–106, 150, 152–156
Researcher-teacher (RT) 15, 18–19, 28, 32–33, 35–38, 51, 54–57, 62–63, 89, 93, 101–102, 106, 108, 110–148, 153–154, 156–157
Resources 3–4, 10–12, 15, 26, 34, 38, 56, 59–61, 94, 106, 127, 130–131, 134, 136–137, 149, 151–153, 155
Responsive/responsivity 109, 141–142, 146, 148, 151
Role preparation 48–49, 109–113, 116, 118, 121–122, 124, 126, 127, 131, 134–135, 137, 139–141, 143–146, 150, 156
Role sharing 57, 124, 127
Roles 48–49, 56–57, 93, 109–113, 116–122, 124, 126–127, 131, 134–146, 150, 155–156

Schemas/scripts 9, 21, 23, 25–26, 32, 37, 39, 41, 84, 94, 107
Scientific concepts 29–33, 34, 36, 88

SCOBA 32, 40, 93, 96–97, 101–102, 155–156
Social approach 7, 13
Story grammar 41, 44, 97–98
Strategies 7, 10, 13, 19, 25, 56, 59–61, 91, 149
Strauss 30–31
Summary 26, 37, 39, 53, 55–57, 59, 62–87, 94–95, 105, 138–139, 144, 147–148, 150–152, 154–156, 158
Supporting details 57, 59, 62, 75, 77–80, 84, 87, 90, 139, 149, 152, 158
Survey 56, 59, 62
Swaffar 1, 12, 23, 27
Swain 27, 33
Synthesis 57, 59, 62, 76–77, 79–81, 84, 87, 152, 158
Systemic Functional Linguistics (SFL) 2, 24–25, 27, 30, 44, 47, 58

Tenor 24, 27, 45–48, 53, 102–105, 107–108, 140, 148, 155
Text difficulty 56
Tool/tool for thinking 5–7, 12, 15–17, 19, 35–27, 31–34, 41, 46–48, 75, 84, 90, 93, 98, 106–107, 109, 141, 146, 149, 153
Top-down approach 7–10

van Compernolle 31–32
Verbalization 29, 33, 53, 55–56, 58, 88, 90, 92–98, 100–104, 106–107, 141, 146–148, 150
Vocabulary (lexical) 3, 6, 8, 11, 20–23, 25, 37, 39–40, 47–50, 53, 60–62, 91, 93–96, 106–108, 117, 119–123, 135–137, 143, 147, 155
Vygotskian Sociocultural Theory (V-SCT) 2, 7, 14, 17–18, 22–23, 25, 27–29, 34, 47, 58, 87, 149, 153, 156
Vygotsky 14–18, 23, 27, 29–31, 33–34, 48, 85, 87, 106, 109, 146

Working memory 3–4, 7, 19, 21–22

Yamashita 19, 22

Zone of proximal development in activity (ZPD-in-activity) 17, 25, 36, 47–48, 87, 108, 141, 149, 152

For Product Safety Concerns and Information please contact our EU Authorised Representative:

Easy Access System Europe

Mustamäe tee 50

10621 Tallinn

Estonia

gpsr.requests@easproject.com